GENDER, GOVERNANCE AND ISLAM

Based at the Aga Khan Centre in London, the Aga Khan University Institute for the Study of Muslim Civilisations is a higher education institution with a focus on research, publications, graduate studies and outreach. It promotes scholarship that opens up new perspectives on Muslim heritage, modernity, religion, culture and society. The Institute aims to create opportunities for interaction among academics and other professionals in an effort to deepen the understanding of pressing issues affecting Muslim societies today.

Exploring Muslim Contexts

Series Editor: Farouk Topan

This series seeks to address salient and urgent issues faced by Muslim societies as they evolve in a rapidly globalising world. It brings together the scholarship of leading specialists from various academic fields, representing a wide range of theoretical and practical perspectives.

Development Models in Muslim Contexts: Chinese, 'Islamic' and Neo-liberal Alternatives
Edited by Robert Springborg

The Challenge of Pluralism: Paradigms from Muslim Contexts
Edited by Abdou Filali-Ansary and Sikeena Karmali Ahmed

Cosmopolitanisms in Muslim Contexts: Perspectives from the Past
Edited by Derryl MacLean and Sikeena Karmali Ahmed

Ethnographies of Islam: Ritual Performances and Everyday Practices
Edited by Badouin Dupret, Thomas Pierret, Paulo Pinto and Kathryn Spellman Poots

Genealogy and Knowledge in Muslim Societies: Understanding the Past
Edited by Sarah Bowen Savant and Helena de Felipe

Contemporary Islamic Law in Indonesia: Sharia and Legal Pluralism
Arskal Salim

Shaping Global Islamic Discourses: The Role of al-Azhar, al-Madina and al-Mustafa
Edited by Masooda Bano and Keiko Sakurai

Gender, Governance and Islam
Edited by Deniz Kandiyoti, Nadje Al-Ali and Kathryn Spellman Poots

edinburghuniversitypress.com/series/ecmc

Gender, Governance and Islam

Edited by Deniz Kandiyoti, Nadje Al-Ali
and Kathryn Spellman Poots

EDINBURGH
University Press

IN ASSOCIATION WITH

THE AGA KHAN UNIVERSITY
(International) in the United Kingdom
Institute for the Study of Muslim Civilisations

We publish academic books and journals in our selected subject areas across the humanities and social sciences, combining cutting-edge scholarship with high editorial and production values to produce academic works of lasting importance. For more information visit our website: edinburghuniversitypress.com

The opinions expressed in this volume are those of the authors and do not necessarily reflect those of the Aga Khan University, Institute for the Study of Muslim Civilisations.

© editorial matter and organisation, Deniz Kandiyoti, Nadje Al-Ali and Kathryn Spellman Poots, 2019, 2021
© the chapters their several authors, 2019, 2021

Edinburgh University Press Ltd
The Tun – Holyrood Road
12 (2f) Jackson's Entry
Edinburgh EH8 8PJ

First published in hardback by Edinburgh University Press 2019

Typeset in Goudy Oldstyle by
Servis Filmsetting, Stockport, Cheshire

A CIP record for this book is available from the British Library

ISBN 978 1 4744 5542 8 (hardback)
ISBN 978 1 4744 5543 5 (paperback)
ISBN 978 1 4744 5545 9 (webready PDF)
ISBN 978 1 4744 5544 2 (epub)

The right of the contributors to be identified as authors of this work has been asserted in accordance with the Copyright, Designs and Patents Act 1988 and the Copyright and Related Rights Regulations 2003 (SI No. 2498).

Contents

Preface   vii

1. Introduction – Beyond Women, Islam and the State: Situating the Politics of Gender in a New Century   1
   Deniz Kandiyoti, Nadje Al-Ali and Kathryn Spellman Poots
2. Protest, Resistance and Shifting Gender Orders in Egypt: Crossing Red Lines?   18
   Heba El Kholy and Nadia Taher
3. Manufacturing Consent in Iran: from Moral Subjects to (Un)Healthy Citizens   40
   Nazanin Shahrokni
4. Saudi Women: between Family, Religion and State   62
   Madawi Al-Rasheed
5. Against All Odds: the Resilience and Fragility of Women's Gender Activism in Turkey   80
   Deniz Kandiyoti
6. Discrete Moves and Parallel Tracks: Gender Politics in Post-2001 Afghanistan   101
   Torunn Wimpelmann
7. Palestine: Gender in an Imagined Fragmented Sovereignty   120
   Islah Jad
8. Iraq: Gendering Violence, Sectarianisms and Authoritarianism   145
   Nadje Al-Ali

Contents

9. Defiance not Subservience: New Directions in the Pakistani Women's Movement 165
   Afiya Shehrbano Zia
10. Muslim Diasporas in Transition: Islam, Gender and New Regimes of Governance 186
    Kathryn Spellman Poots

    Epilogue – Locating Gender in Contentious Politics 215
    Deniz Kandiyoti

About the Contributors 219
Index 222

Preface

Over the past decades, Deniz Kandiyoti's *Women, Islam and the State* (1991) has been a fixture in syllabi for courses taught globally on women and gender in the Middle East, as well as reading lists and bibliographies of undergraduate and postgraduate students writing essays and dissertations. At the time it was published, over a quarter of a century ago, the edited volume provided the most systematic and in-depth empirically grounded challenge to essentialist approaches to women in the Middle East that frequently reified culture and religion.

Both of us were amongst the many generations of students who were profoundly inspired by and learnt greatly from *Women, Islam and the State*, as well as Deniz's other interventions. In fact, five of the contributors, Nadje, Kathryn, Heba, Islah and Torunn had all been students of Deniz in the 1990s and 2000s. What has made Deniz's work so unique and precious over the years is the combination of intellectual breadth – in an almost renaissance-type manner – with an incredible depth. Her original research always links the analysis of relevant macro structures with the specificities of concrete historical and ethnographic contexts. Looking back on a career that has been rich in variety in terms of regional focus and substantive research, the guiding intellectual passion of Deniz's work has consistently been to achieve a better understanding of gender as a social relation and of the dynamics of gender inequality and hierarchies. The corpus of scholarship she developed in seeking answers to these questions – from post-Soviet Uzbekistan and post-9/11 Afghanistan to the back streets of Istanbul where she worked on transsexuals – was always animated by the same passion.

No doubt, Deniz's feminist approach and methods are firmly based in political economy, but she defies dichotomous thinking, as she has also been interested in the discursive realms of gendered processes and phenomena, and through her

Preface

work has contributed greatly to cultural studies as well. Yet, unlike some other contemporary feminist scholars, Deniz's analysis never indulged in postmodern nihilism or relativism. It is always grounded, rooted in and linked to concrete material conditions. She employed intersectional theory, long before it became a buzzword and an established mode of analysis in gender studies.

While studying under Deniz in the 1990s, we also greatly benefited from her input, along with the wider group of dynamic scholars' contributions, at the Middle East Studies Group, a forum first pioneered by Sami Zubaida, Talal Asad and Roger Owen in the 1970s. The regular meetings, twice a year in London and once in Oxford, as well as events at our respective home institutions, the Institute for the Study of Muslim Civilisations at the Aga Khan University (AKU-ISMC) and the Centre for Gender Studies at SOAS, University of London, became regular settings for discussion and debate. The lively parties at Sami Zubaida's house and lunches in the Bloomsbury neighbourhood in London that followed many of these meetings provided the perfect settings for our exchanges and discussion to slowly develop into this new book project.

Deniz pushed the project forward by synthesising our thoughts and discussions into a concept paper. This provided the intellectual grounding for a two-day workshop convened under the umbrella of the Governance Programme at AKU-ISMC in February 2017, entitled: 'Gender and Governance in Muslim Contexts'. We launched the workshop with a public event that examined the underlying concepts of *Women, Islam and the State* and probed into the question 'Is gender a governance issue?', the title of Deniz's keynote address. The plenary session generated a very lively discussion on global transformations over the past twenty-five years and the ways in which gender ideologies became entangled with systems of governance.

Over the following two days, the workshop participants anchored and informed the discussions with their rich empirical research on gender politics in Egypt, Tunisia, Iraq, Turkey, Iran, Palestine, Kurdistan, Pakistan, Afghanistan and the Muslim Diaspora. Several contributors to the book partcipated in the workshop. In addition, we warmly thank Shahrzad Mojab and Naila Kabeer, whose insightful comments helped to raise important issues for debate. We would also like to thank AKU-ISMC for generously hosting the workshop and for supporting us through the publication process with, respectively, AKU-ISMC Publications and Edinburgh University Press. We are particularly grateful to Charlotte Whiting, who has been a joy to work with from start to finish.

Our final and greatest thanks go to Deniz Kandiyoti. Over the years she has been a constant source of knowledge, strength and inspiration. Far more than a mentor, she is a dearly loved and cherished friend.

Nadje Al-Ali and Kathryn Spellman Poots
10 November 2018

Chapter 1

Introduction – Beyond Women, Islam and the State: Situating the Politics of Gender in a New Century

Deniz Kandiyoti, Nadje Al-Ali and Kathryn Spellman Poots

The generational span that separates the publication of *Women, Islam and the State* (Kandiyoti, 1991) (*WIS* hereafter) from our new volume has radically transformed the universe of action and meaning surrounding the key terms of its title. *WIS* was the product of an era pre-dating the momentous re-articulations between states and societies ushered in by global neo-liberal transformations and by the geopolitical convulsions that followed armed interventions in Afghanistan and Iraq in the aftermath of the 11 September 2001 (9/11 hereafter) attacks on the US. Popular uprisings in the Middle East and North Africa led to the overthrow of long-established authoritarian ruling regimes in Egypt and Tunisia, while some formerly unitary states, such as Iraq, Libya, Yemen and Syria, were fragmented as a result of a succession of armed interventions and civil wars. Meanwhile, the ongoing struggles for self-determination of stateless peoples like Palestinians and Kurds showed no signs of resolution. Although we continue to operate in a world organised around nation states, and despite the fact that diverse histories of decolonisation and nation-building continue to cast a long shadow over the present, the parameters that informed *WIS* have been comprehensively reconfigured.

Our new title, *Gender, Governance and Islam*, tells its own story. How did the question of women's status and rights – which were once the hallmarks of post-colonial nationalisms – evolve into new and contested understandings of gender that now permeate apparatuses of governance at the global, national, and sub-national levels? How does the politics of gender get embroiled in struggles over identity and legitimacy? What types of collaboration and resistance do these struggles elicit? What effects do they have on gender activism and modes of organisation at the local level? In what ways is Islam deployed and redefined in this new governance landscape as an idiom of rule and legitimacy? And, indeed, how did Islam (the only term of the *WIS* title that seems deceptively unchanged) accrue new and shifting political meanings in the era of the War on Terror and of rapidly shifting policies vis-à-vis Muslim diasporas and migrants in the West?

These are some of the key questions that our Introduction aims to address as we weave through the contributions to this volume. These represent diverse contexts and clusters of concerns. The cases of Afghanistan and Iraq, which were the settings of military interventions in the aftermath of the 9/11 attacks, occupy one end of a spectrum characterised by more direct interventions by global governance institutions and fragmented societies that are in the grip of ongoing conflict. The same applies to Palestine, which continues to be under Israeli occupation. Pakistan, which found itself in the eye of the storm, both during the war against the Soviets in Afghanistan and the ensuing civil war that saw the rise of the Taliban, was propelled into becoming a frontline ally of the US during the so-called War on Terror. The military regime under General Musharraf found it expedient to burnish its liberal credentials by combining anti-extremism and development discourse with the enhancement of women's rights. In all these instances, donor-led projects, government action and local initiatives on gender equality and women's rights were actively shaped by their highly charged and volatile geopolitical contexts.

Other countries also experienced major upheavals. Between 2011 and 2014, Egypt witnessed popular uprisings followed by the overthrow of Mubarak's long-lived authoritarian regime, a brief period of Muslim Brotherhood rule and the takeover by the army under General el-Sisi. These ruptures led to competing appropriations of Islam and contradictory attempts to challenge, re-inscribe and consolidate a gender order based on masculine privilege. Turkey underwent regime change from parliamentary democracy to an executive presidency, sealed by elections in June 2018. The new regime abolished the checks and balances inherent in the principle of separation of powers, concentrating all decision-making in the person of the president. Authoritarian consolidation took place against a background of rising nationalism, militarism, mounting conflict with the Kurds and a systematic project of social engineering to establish 'New Turkey' as a Sunni Muslim hegemon. Gender relations and the family became explicit policy targets as the ruling regime consolidated its power.

Saudi Arabia and Iran also underwent significant transformations despite a nominal continuity in their regimes. Founded on the marriage between the House of Saud and the Wahhabi clergy, the Saudi state under dynastic rule veered between state-led religious nationalism and truncated cosmopolitan modernity, using women and gender as symbolic referents of both. Despite timid overtures at expanding women's visibility in society, especially after the unfavourable scrutiny the kingdom received in the aftermath of 9/11 as a promoter of fundamentalism, depriving women of basic rights remains a reflection of how much the state fears the language of rights per se in an authoritarian and undemocratic context. Likewise, the focus on the Islamic Republic of Iran as a theocratic state conceals the transformations that its diverse mechanisms of rule have undergone. In the case of gender segregation, the Islamic Republic's mode of governance shifted from reliance on the application of prohibitive punitive measures, which proved largely ineffective and created adverse consequences, to the development of more productive measures that are responsive to bottom-up pressures from women by designing new spaces and addressing their needs on the government's own terms in order to contain their demands and achieve a compliant citizenry through consent.

In what follows, we chart the shifts in academic discourse and in global development practice that had an impact on redefining and locating gender as both an object of policy and a terrain for activism. We also acknowledge the role of transnational and geopolitical influences in establishing new frames of thought and action around the politics of Islam and their effects in shaping the terrain of gender relations and women's rights. We show, moreover, that ultimately internal struggles over control, identity and legitimacy (albeit in the context of global entanglements) play a decisive role in setting the parameters of the politics of gender.

From Women to Gender: Changing Canons, Global Governance and Gender Regimes

The terms of reference of feminist theory have shifted comprehensively since the 1980s. Discomfort with the category of 'women' became increasingly manifest as the universalist pretensions of feminisms emanating from predominantly white, Western and middle-class contexts were called into question by Third World and post-colonial feminists (Lazreg 1988; Minh-ha 1989; Mohanty 1988, 1991; Narayan 1997). The experiences of women under colonial rule, of women of colour and of working-class women suggested that gender cannot be separated from forms of oppression based on race, class, caste, ethnicity or religion, and that these axes of differentiation and domination are, as theories of intersectionality argue, mutually constitutive of each other (Crenshaw 1989 for the US; Anthias and Yuval-Davis 1983, 1992; Brah 1996 in the UK).

Meanwhile, feminist appropriations of post-structuralism had unsettled categories such as the state, oppression, patriarchy and, indeed, sexual difference itself (Barrett and Phillips 1992; Bartky 1988; Connell 1987; Fraser 1997; Scott 1988; Pringle and Watson 1992). Calling into question the binaries behind the original conception of gender (as the social construction of sexual difference) brought the issue of sexualities and body politics to the fore, cumulating into the now broad field of Queer theory and studies (Berlant and Warner 1995; Butler 1990; Namaste 1996; Sedgwick 1990) at a point in time when new forms of claim-making were being articulated by LGBTQ constituencies in the North. The remit of the field now encompassed the study of men and masculinities, not only in relation to the subordination of women, but to other institutionalised forms of power and domination (Connell 1987, 1995; Carrigan et al. 1985; Cockburn 1991; Cornwall et al. 2016). The study of masculinities in relation to systems of rule as well as in the context of war, conflict and the militarisation of societies contributed to the emergence of a growing feminist IR scholarship (Cockburn 2001; Enloe 1990, 2000; Peterson 1992; Tickner 1992). As new forms of mobilisation around gender proliferated, a more varied range of platforms and actors populated the field.

The changing canons of academia coincided with new developments in the policy arena which fed into each other in a critical dialogue. The lobbying activities of transnational women's advocates and the policies of the United Nations (UN) eventually led to the articulation of a comprehensive international regime for women's rights.

The first UN World Conference on Women in Mexico City in 1975 presented women as a disadvantaged group whose exclusion detracted from the process of development itself. By the third UN Conference on Women in Nairobi in 1985 there was a belated acknowledgement that the systemic problems created by global North–South inequalities positioned impoverished Third World women as the principal losers of development. However, any redistributive impulses between North and South would be swept away by the global turn to neoliberalism. Movements for gender justice and social justice increasingly drifted apart while powerful global players and religious movements with conservative gender agendas (such as the Vatican, diverse Evangelical denominations, and various Islamic constituencies) took up platforms for social justice. Arguably, the discursive gap between North and South had widened, and vocabularies and priorities had become more divergent in the 2000s than they were in the 1970s. This was to have profound consequences: especially in societies where top-down modernisation agendas were implemented by authoritarian regimes, it marked out women's rights as the alleged preoccupation of a privileged elite. Ironically, while critiques of second-wave feminism in the North fed into a backlash against what was presented by some as a tyrannical regime of feminist puritanism (Halley 2006), in countries of the South, feminism was interpreted (and castigated) as libertarianism and licentiousness when it wasn't denounced outright, as we shall see below, as the handmaiden of imperialism.

The fourth World Conference on Women held in Beijing in 1995 represented the coming of age of the 'gender agenda'[1] and its official incorporation into development policy through gender mainstreaming and the establishment of national monitoring apparatuses in the bureaucracies of member states. This led to the 'technocratisation' of gender issues[2] and the creation of new 'gender literate' cadres capable of transmitting and implementing the objectives set out in successive platforms for action and standard setting instruments such as Convention on the Elimination of All Forms of Discrimination Against Women (CEDAW). This development signalled the advent of what we might broadly define as 'donor-driven gender activism' as distinct from local women's movements with much older histories, generally operating within more contextually grounded idioms (Kandiyoti 1996). The relations and tensions between women's movements, state apparatuses monitoring standards of gender equality and donor-funded NGOs became the object of heated controversies (Alvarez 1990).

For instance, a critique emanating from critical legal theory suggested that feminist norms and values gained institutional traction, most notably in the development of international criminal law aimed at prosecuting sexual violence. The term 'governance feminism' came to signify a reliance on state-centred forms of power and the promotion of a politics of respectability and political correctness that criminalises and marginalises certain practices and subjectivities (Halley et al. 2018; Amar 2011a, 2011b). This turned the discussion of patriarchy on its head by arguing that the enforcement of women's rights had itself become an oppressive governance practice and an adjunct of security states. Translated into Middle Eastern, North African or South Asian contexts, this implied that women's movements and sexual rights platforms making references to international standard setting instruments as a bargaining chip in their negotiations with their governments were mere conveyors of an oppressive neo-liberal order. These global blueprints were assumed to be disseminated in the South by donor-funded women's NGOs which are either co-opted by governments, guided by external agendas or both.

Although we recognise that gender-based activism encompasses a broad field, including anti-sexual harassment initiatives that now involve men as well as growing LGBTQ mobilisation and organising, particularly in Lebanon, Turkey, Palestine and in diaspora contexts, the contributors to this volume principally focus on women's movements and civil society initiatives. This reflects both the fact that women's rights remain central to wider contestations about governance and the nature of the polity and that women's and sexual rights platforms continue to be marginalised or kept under severe threat in the countries under study.

The debate on the 'NGOisation' of women's rights organisations is not unique to the Middle East and North Africa, but became widespread as a consequence of Western governments' failed efforts to 'democratise' authoritarian states in the South through the promotion of civil society. At a time when economic liberalisation and structural adjustment measures, imposed by the International Monetary Fund (IMF), severely limited states' ability to provide welfare services, civil society organisations, including women's NGOs, increasingly stepped in to fill the gaps and deliver 'development'. Yet, in many instances NGOs contributed to the emergence of new elites, often remote from grassroots' needs and initiatives that competed fiercely with each other for available resources and outside recognition.

There is, however, no singular logic informing donor action. The case of Pakistan (Chapter 9) clearly shows that donor-assisted, faith-based projects have empowered and legitimised actors with little interest in gender equality, while local women's NGOs have multiplied and diversified their calls for equal rights. Likewise, in Afghanistan (Chapter 6) women's NGOs and parliamentarians have tried to make the most of the spaces opened up by (donor-backed) new legislation on violence against women while other donors have favoured and backed alternative dispute resolution (ADR) mechanisms as part of their counter-insurgency measures, empowering local patriarchal formations that entrench gender inequalities in the process. In the Egyptian context, even at the height of Western donors' intense support for civil society initiatives, women's NGOs were positioned differently towards funding organisations and their agenda, and pursued a range of politics and aims (Al-Ali 2000). The more recent uprisings and ongoing political contestations in Egypt (Chapter 2) and Iraq (Chapter 8) show that feminist activists have been at the forefront of challenging corruption and authoritarianism, sometimes rejecting NGOs as an organisational form, but not inevitably so. At a point in time when donor funding for civil society is drying up and numerous governments are clamping down on civil society initiatives, young activists seem less encumbered with concerns about the professionalisation of feminist politics than previous generations, although there are clearly diverse attitudes and positions among them in the region. While in some contexts, such as Iraq, feminists across a secular and religious continuum have embraced NGOs; in other contexts, like Turkey, Egypt and Lebanon, especially young feminists explore alternative forms of mobilisation.

Underlying many of these debates and critiques was the assumption of a purportedly immutable hegemonic liberal order. Yet, whatever its limitations, the assumed liberalism of 'the West' is being put to the test by the wave of illiberal right-wing populisms sweeping North America and Europe. Reinstating rigid gender (and racial) hierarchies lies at the heart of these right-wing conservatisms. At the UN, a group of states, led by Egypt, proposed a resolution on the 'protection of the family' in an attempt to reverse hard-won rights and gains over the decades. Such is the momentum of these platforms that the UN failed to pass a resolution for a fifth World Conference on Women, wary of the consequences of reopening international agreements on women's rights. In many countries in the global South and in Europe, right-wing movements have been up in arms against so-called 'gender ideology' and have targeted gender studies programmes and scholars (Corrêa, Paternotte and Kuhar 2018). Yet, as challenging as the global conjuncture might be, it is ultimately at the national and local levels that struggles for political control and legitimacy determine the room for manoeuvre of different actors. We shall first consider the ways in which these struggles are embedded in major shifts in the politics of Islam.

Islam: Geopolitical Conjunctures, Transnational Networks and Diasporas

For over a decade, our conceptual horizons on questions relating to Islam and women's rights have been dominated (and to a large extent constricted) by the consequences of military interventions by Western powers following the 9/11 events, the ensuing War on Terror and the continuing moral anxieties triggered by new waves of terrorism and immigration in the West. The growing volume of critiques of feminism-as-imperialism (Abu-Lughod 2013; Toor 2012; Kumar 2012) marked a revival of earlier debates on the colonial entanglements of feminism – a theme that featured centrally in WIS. Indeed, one of the central contentions of WIS was that the place of Islam in relation to women's status and rights could only become intelligible in the context of diverse paths of post-dynastic and post-colonial nation-building and the patterns of modern state consolidation they gave rise to.

WIS predated the growing momentum of more radical indictments of political liberalism, secularism and the modern state as Western impositions and oppressive modes of governmentality (Enayat 2017), which followed Talal Asad's critique of Western secularism interpreted as a unique configuration of post-reformation Christianity and as part of the apparatus of the cultural hegemony of the West (Asad 2003). In this perspective, Islam and its 'discursive tradition' stood in the place of 'non-Enlightenment societies' and critiques of secular modernity inevitably led to a search for the 'non-Enlightenment' subject. This approach inspired the late Saba Mahmood's work on pious women in *da'wa* groups in Egypt (Mahmood 2005) and led to her contention that their cultivation of virtue points to a different register of selfhood and agency than that predicated by feminist theory with its alleged liberal roots.

The recuperation of agency through pietistic Islam also needs to be set in the context of 'securitisation' policies that prompted Western interventions in the search for so-called 'moderate' Islam (Mahmood 2006). This rendered, for some, all calls for Islamic reform potentially suspect and inadvertently led to the stigmatisation of secular-leaning Muslims and Islamic feminists. Moreover, top-down strategies to fund and mobilise 'moderate' forms of Islam (such as state-sponsored Sufism), perceived as imperialistic and offensive by quietist Salafis and others, helped, in conjunction with numerous other influences, to fuel the growth of transnational and pan-Islamic movements (Aidi 2014; Corbett 2016).

Indeed, one of the major developments since the publication of WIS has been the proliferation of transnational Islamic networks and their campaigns to seek adherents among marginalised and disaffected Muslims. The policies devised to deal with Muslim diasporas in the West have, in turn, reflected a defensive reaction to the reach of these movements into the heartlands of Western liberal democracies, fuelling further 'securitisation' and surveillance measures vis-à-vis Muslim communities. These measures and counter-measures have created their own noxious dynamic.

Moreover, the geopolitical dimensions of a growing defensiveness around Islam must also be fully taken into account. Wars and violence in Afghanistan, Palestine, Bosnia and Chechnya strengthened global Muslim solidarity and stimulated a shared perception that Islam was under attack and needed to be defended (Li 2016; Maira 2016). Taking advantage of crises of governmentality across the MENA region, pervasive anti-Western sentiment and the steep rise of Islamophobia in the West, various Islamic movements have deployed Islam as an idiom of legitimate rule in the Muslim world and in diasporic communities abroad. They have been adept at mastering the tools of globalisation, including the use of the Internet and social media to disseminate Islamic doctrines, ideologies and symbols, particularly among the younger generations.

Behind this unitary facade of solidarity, the landscape of transnational Islam in fact originates from varied roots, alignments and ideologies that stem from different histories and political contexts (Zubaida 2016). These influences include the 1979 Iranian Revolution and the 'Shia revival' (Nasr 2008; Louer 2007), the effects of international missions exporting Salafi teachings through mosques and schools backed by Saudi Arabia and other Gulf states (Pall 2018; Meijer 2009) and new forms of grass-roots Islamic mobilisation in the face of failing nationalist and developmental projects in the Middle East and South Asia (Kepel 2004; Mandaville 2007). Whereas mainstream parties like the Muslim Brotherhood in Egypt, Ennahda in Tunisia and the Justice and Development Party (AKP) in Turkey attempted to operate within the parameters of the modern nation state, so-called 'purist' Salafists, mostly non-violent and quietist in political orientation, aimed to transcend national polities and strictly emulate the early traditions of the Prophet. In contrast, 'active' militant movements, including the Taliban, al-Qaida and IS, have used violence and terror to establish Islamic rule in regions under their control in accordance to their literal interpretations of Islamic law (Lacroix 2011; Pall 2013).

INTRODUCTION

These tensions and divergences around Islamic politics are reflected in all the case studies in this volume. As we spell out more fully in our discussion of governance and legitimacy below, Egypt, Afghanistan and Pakistan provide rich examples of shifting alliances and realignments among key competing Islamic players and their respective governments. Gender relations and ideologies have become a central stake in these struggles. Likewise, in Palestine, Islamic politics is inseparable from the reality of continuing Israeli occupation, the noxious international policies that have resulted in the split between the Palestinian authority and Hamas, and the fact that donor-funded gender platforms have often left activists on the ground with impossible choices. In Turkey, behind a facade of nominally secular laws and apparent compliance with international conventions, systematic changes in institutional design such as the significant expansion of the mandate of the Directorate of Religious Affairs, the marginalisation of autonomous civil society actors and the consolidation of government-backed women's organisations pushing a conservative agenda have transformed the landscape of rights activism. In Iran, where there is a marked tendency in scholarship to put everything down to Islamic governance, changes around gender segregation rules reflect very worldly concerns, such as stemming the uncontrollable tide of global influences in leisure and consumption and meeting the expectations of an active female citizenry. Paradoxically, it is here that we see a progression from Islamic justifications for gender segregation to references to public health and women's wellbeing in the provision of women-only parks for leisure and exercise. The fact that the provision of women's needs (for outdoor exercise, in this case) is couched in the language of public health rather than with reference to Islamic injunctions is revealing in itself.

A final major departure since *WIS* concerns the sharpening of regional hegemonic struggles among players such as Saudi Arabia (and other US-backed monarchies), Iran, Turkey and their local proxies, heightening and congealing sectarian conflicts among Sunnis, Shia, Alawites and other communal minorities in Iraq, Syria, Lebanon and the Gulf states, against a background of US–Russian rivalry in the region. These alignments have shaped internal politics across the region and diasporic communities alike. Women and sexual minorities have been at the sharp end of these conflicts. A case in point is Chapter 8 on Iraq, which shows that contestations around gender norms and legislation have been central to sectarian tensions and political struggles following the invasion in 2003. Indeed, our various case studies show that both diverse interpretations of Islam and liberal human rights frameworks are used as malleable resources and bargaining tools by parties, groups and social movements vying for representation, advantage and ultimately political control.

DENIZ KANDIYOTI, NADJE AL-ALI, KATHRYN SPELLMAN POOTS

GOVERNANCE AND LEGITIMACY: COLLUSION, COMPROMISE AND RESISTANCE

The academic debate on women's rights is, as we have seen in the discussions above, disproportionately dominated by issues of global governance and imperialism. What often gets overlooked is that the most proximate drivers of the politics of gender in concrete societal settings inevitably reflect the complex interactions of state, non-state and popular actors locked in power struggles and contestations over the direction of their polity.

Heba El Kholy and Nadia Taher analyse the ways in which the politics of gender has become central to ruptures and contestations during the turbulent post-Mubarak period in Egypt. The massive protests of 2011, which initially appeared to unite women and men across class, religion as well as urban–rural divides, have contributed to the emergence of new femininities and masculinities that have challenged not only prevailing gender norms but also the increasingly authoritarian state, first under the Muslim Brotherhood and then under el-Sisi. In the attempt to establish legitimacy and gain control, President el-Sisi, Al-Azhar and even the Salafists have been competing over their respective interpretations of Islam in their bargaining over women's rights. The chapter on Egypt illustrates most poignantly the way that the backlash against a popular resistance to state authoritarianism took the form of a politics of 'masculinist restoration'.[3]

While the Egyptian government has increasingly used coercion, stressing the centrality of 'the family' and notions of 'real' manhood and womanhood to gain legitimacy amongst the majority of the population, the Iranian state had to find creative ways to address dissent and generate consent. Nazanin Shahrokni looks at the example of women-only parks as an entry point for a discussion of changing state practices and policies of gender segregation in the Islamic Republic of Iran. Both local forms of resistance, such as the campaigns and demands of Iranian women's rights activists, as well as global and transnational trends, such as access to globalised media and trends, have forced the regime to devise new forms of control and governance. The advantages of consent over coercion are evident in a country where women have remained active and vocal.

Global and internal pressures also coincide in relation to Saudi Arabia's paradoxical politics of gender. Madawi Al-Rasheed's contribution provides ample evidence that Saudi women have been resisting male guardianship and the existing gender regime, either by fleeing the country or by protesting. In the context of gaining new legitimacy globally, but also seeking a modernised form of governance, the Saudi king has been championing new freedoms for women, such as lifting the driving ban, while simultaneously persecuting and imprisoning local women's rights activists. Saudi Arabia is an example par excellence of a state fearing the language of rights as an existential threat to its authoritarian character. Moreover, the state's specific form of sectarian nationalism, combining Wahhabism, Sunni militancy and anti-Shia sentiments, has contributed to the privileging of a militarised Sunni sectarian masculinity.

The instrumentalisation of gender platforms is also clearly evident in Turkey. Here, the government has played the 'gender equality' card when it suited its purposes in the process of meeting EU accession criteria, or signing up to international standard setting instruments while simultaneously pursuing a gradual Islamisation or, as Deniz Kandiyoti argues, a masculinist restoration agenda attempting to claw back men's lost privileges under secular laws with reference to Islamic justifications. In this process, women's rights platforms were instrumentalised in dealings with international governance actors (UN, EU, bilateral and multilateral donors). Nonetheless, a lively network of NGOs, including some with explicitly feminist agendas (across the spectrum of secular, Muslim or Kurdish NGOs) flourished in the 1990s and early 2000s. The government, on the other hand, increasingly allocated administrative and financial resources as well as a network of government approved NGOs (or GONGOs) to re-educating women to fit an Islamic mould. The top-down social engineering policies of the state have marginalised secular women's movements, exerted a demobilising effect on Islamic women's NGOs and had a crippling effect on Kurdish women's civil society initiatives. Yet, as Kandiyoti argues in this volume, a politics of masculinist restoration that requires systematic indoctrination, greater surveillance and higher levels of intrusion into citizens' private lives may paradoxically bring personal liberties and gender issues closer to the heart of democratic struggles, giving rise to new cross-gender alliances.

In the cases of Afghanistan, Palestine and Iraq, countries exposed to prolonged war, conflict and violence, a mixed picture has emerged as internal conflicts sharpened and global actors pursuing a range of priorities in the domain of gender (such as including women in peace-building and combating gender-based violence) interacted with local women's organisations.

Torunn Wimpelmann argues that in Afghanistan, both local and external visions of women's roles and entitlements have been multiple and contradictory. The government under former President Karzai engaged in a balancing act, paying lip service to the demands of donors while placating powerful internal Islamist constituencies. As a result, laws on women's rights were enacted by decree rather than through due political process. Meanwhile, international donor involvement has itself been inconsistent with donors supporting women's rights platforms at the same time as pushing for alternative dispute resolution, reinforcing highly patriarchal mechanisms for counter-insurgency purposes. Despite these contradictions, women's rights advocacy has proven to be unexpectedly resilient and has been invigorated under the government of President Ghani.

The importance of engaging in careful local, national and regional analysis has also become apparent in the Iraqi context where the interplay of different local, regional and international actors, in a context characterised by violence and authoritarian governance, has become one of the major drivers of the politics of gender. Nadje Al-Ali's chapter shows how, in the context of a failed state and continuous conflict, or rather multi-conflicts, gender norms and relations have been used as bargaining chips by both state and non-state actors. The chapter reveals that the institutionalisation of sectarianism in Iraq has not only been gendered, but has contributed to state fragmentation, a shift towards competing conservative gender regimes and an increase in different forms of gender-based violence. Despite these multiple challenges, Iraqi women's rights mobilisation has not only attempted to challenge the shrinking of political and social spaces for women, but also the different forms of violence they have been exposed to, as well as being at the forefront of the struggle against sectarianism and political authoritarianism.

The bargaining over women's rights issues by sectarian constituencies in Iraq resonates with the various ways Islamist women linked to Hamas in Palestine instrumentalised women's rights discourse to gain political legitimacy within the Palestinian polity. Islah Jad's chapter highlights the contradictions that arise when the goals of national resistance to Israeli occupation and combatting patriarchy are put at loggerheads with one another as a result of the perverse effects of governance and aid models imposed by the international community, which eventually precipitated the split of the Palestinian polity between the West Bank (Fatah) and Gaza (Hamas). Jad argues that in a situation of imagined sovereignty in a still-occupied territory, gender agendas are driven by global governance actors and conflicting donor interests in a manner that marginalises women's roles in national resistance. We see the donor-dependent Palestinian Authority in the West Bank buying into women's empowerment packages promoted by international funders while the Gaza administration both adopts and tries to subvert them.

The impact of donor-driven agendas, particularly 'donor-driven Islam', is also apparent in Afiya Shehrbano Zia's chapter on Pakistan. Yet, Zia highlights the significance of national and local agendas and contestations. Her chapter traces the interplay and tensions between religious politics, the War on Terror, women's rights campaigns, and contemporary sexual politics that have contributed towards the emergence of a more confident, if risky, form of feminist resistance in contemporary Pakistan. Questions of gender identity and sexual autonomy have emerged as sites of contestation about the politics of gender and governance. After decades of Islamisation policies under previous governments, we have seen an instrumental adoption of women's rights platforms by the Musharraf regime, clearly looking for antidotes to radical Islam after 9/11. In the post-Musharraf era, the adoption of gender-sensitive development policies and the creation of a nation-wide infrastructure for their implementation, reveals a continued commitment to break with the Islamisation policies of the past. Yet, everything remains in the balance with a new incumbent after the 2018 elections who appears to be driven by populism and is receptive to Islamisation measures that could imperil the gains achieved.

The various chapters in this volume highlight the complex interplay of local, regional and international actors and governance structures. They also point to the emergence and development of significant transnational spheres of political mobilisation and economic entanglement. Indeed, Kathryn Spellman Poots demonstrates in Chapter 10 that the boundaries between local, regional and transnational levels have become totally porous and illusory in an age where the politics of Muslim diasporas in the West feed into, collide with and often import conflicts in migrants' home countries. She argues, furthermore, that gender roles, gender relations and sexual politics have become key ingredients in the making of a so-called 'Muslim Diaspora'. Her chapter shows how culturalised notions of 'good Muslim'/'bad Muslim' have been instrumentalised by both new regimes of governance in the West and by Islamist groups to control women's bodies and bolster dominant gender ideologies. With the simultaneous rise of Islamophobia, Muslim fundamentalisms and right-wing xenophobic populist movements, the chapter contends that women's rights advocates and activists face new challenges in navigating the best avenues to realise their agendas both locally and transnationally.

We hope to have demonstrated that the politics of gender is invariably mediated by systems of governance and processes of political contestation that may deploy Islam in very different ways in response to shifting dynamics at subnational, national and transnational levels. The cases covered by our volume illustrate the diverse ways in which the issue of women's rights and gender identities become caught up in a political maelstrom, buffeted between contested global standards and the dictates of various state and non-state actors who use gender as a battleground of identity or as a litmus test of Islamic authenticity. However, the lazy expedient of exporting 'patriarchy' to the 'non-West', however defined, now seems more outlandish than ever. The authoritarian populist wave currently sweeping the politics of the Americas, Asia and Europe has made it amply clear that the polarising potential of debates about gender is greater and more widespread than ever. As enforcing gender hierarchies and upholding male entitlement emerge as core components of this rising wave, it has never been clearer that the politics of gender is at the frontlines of democratic struggles everywhere.

Notes

1. The shift from women to gender in the field of development followed a critique of the limitations of 'women-targeted' projects, giving way to gender as a relational construct taking into account relations between genders and generations.
2. For a critique of how these developments may have stymied the transformative potential of feminist interventions, see Cornwall (2016).
3. Kandiyoti (2013) coined this term in relation to the wave of gender-based violence in the aftermath of the Arab uprisings. Masculinist restoration comes into play at a point when patriarchy is challenged and no longer fully secure, when notions of female subordination are no longer securely hegemonic and when authorities require higher levels of coercion and the deployment of more varied ideological state apparatuses to ensure the reproduction of the status quo.

Bibliography

Abu-Lughod, Lila (2013), *Do Muslim Women Need Saving?*, Cambridge, MA: Harvard University Press.

Aidi, Hisham (2014), *Rebel Music: Race, Empire, and the New Muslim Youth Culture*, New York: Pantheon.

Al-Ali, Nadje (2000), *Secularism, Gender and the State in the Middle East: the Egyptian Women's Movement*, Cambridge and New York: Cambridge University Press.

Alvarez, Sonia (1990), *Engendering Democracy in Brazil: Women's Movements in Transition Politics*, Princeton: Princeton University Press.

Amar, Paul (2011a), 'Turning the gendered politics of the security state inside out? Charging the police with sexual harassment in Egypt', *International Feminist Journal of Politics*, 13: 3, pp. 299–328. Published online on 12 August 2011, <https://doi.org/10.1080/14616742.2011.587364> (last accessed 1 November 2018).

—— (2011b), 'Middle East masculinity studies: discourses of "men in crisis", industries of gender in revolution', *Journal of Middle East Women's Studies*, 7: 3, pp. 36–70, <https://doi.org/10.2979/jmiddeastwomstud.7.3.36> (last accessed 1 November 2018).

Anthias, Floya and Nira Yuval-Davis (1983), 'Contextualizing feminism: gender, ethnic and class divisions', *Feminist Review*, 15, pp. 62–75.

—— (1992), *Racialized Boundaries: Race, Nation, Gender, Colour and Class and the Anti-Racist Struggle*, London: Routledge.

Asad, Talal (2003), *Formations of the Secular, Christianity, Islam, Modernity*, Series: Cultural Memory in the Present, Stanford: Stanford University Press.

Barrett, Michèle and Anne Phillips (eds) (1992), *Destabilizing Theory*, Cambridge: Polity Press.

Bartky, Sandra L. (1988), 'Foucault, femininity, and the modernization of patriarchal power', in I. Diamond and L. Quinby (eds), *Feminism and Foucault: Reflections on Resistance*, Boston, MA: Northeastern University Press, pp. 61–86.

Berlant, Lauren and Michael Warner (1995), 'What does queer theory teach us about X?' *PMLA*, 110, pp. 343–9.

Brah, Avtar (1996), *Cartographies of Diaspora*, London: Routledge.
Brah, Avtar and Ann Phoenix (2004), 'Ain't I a woman? Revisiting intersectionality', *Journal of International Women's Studies*, 5: 3, pp. 75–86.
Butler, Judith (1990), *Gender Trouble: Feminism and the Subversion of Identity*, New York: Routledge.
Carrigan, Tim, Robert Connell and John Lee (1985), 'Toward a new sociology of masculinity', *Theory and Society*, 14, pp. 551–604.
Cockburn, Cynthia (1991), *In the Way of Women: Men's Resistance to Sex Equality in Organizations*, London: Macmillan.
—— (2001), 'The gendered dynamics of armed conflict and political violence', in C. O. N. Moser and F. Clark (eds), *Victims, Perpetrators or Actors? Gender, Armed Conflict and Political Violence*, London: Zed Books, pp. 13–29.
—— (2007), *From Where We Stand: War, Women's Activism & Feminist Analysis*, London: Zed Books.
Collins, Patricia Hill (1990), *Black Feminist Thought: Knowledge, Consciousness, and the Politics of Empowerment*, Boston: Unwin Hyman.
—— (1999), 'Moving beyond gender: intersectionality and scientific knowledge', in M. M. Ferree, J. Lorber and B. B. Hess (eds), *Revisioning Gender*, Thousand Oaks, CA: Sage, pp. 261–84.
Connell, Raewyn W. (1987), *Gender and Power*, Cambridge: Polity Press.
—— (1995), *Masculinities*, Sydney: Polity Press.
Corbett, Rosemary (2016), *Making Moderate Islam: Sufism, Service, and the 'Ground Zero Mosque' Controversy*, Stanford: Stanford University Press.
Cornwall, Andrea (2016), 'Women's empowerment: what works?', *Journal of International Development*, 28, pp. 342–59.
Cornwall, Andrea, Frank Karioris and Nancy Lindisfarne (eds) (2016), *Masculinities under Neo-Liberalism*, London: Zed Books.
Corrêa, Sonia, David Paternotte and Roman Kuhar (2018), 'The globalisation of anti-gender campaigns: transnational anti-gender movements in Europe and Latin America create unlikely alliances', *International Politics and Society*, 31 May, <https://www.ips-journal.eu/topics/human-rights/article/show/the-globalisation-of-anti-gender-campaigns-2761/> (last accessed 1 November 2018).
Crenshaw, Kimberlé Williams (1989), 'Demarginalizing the intersection of race and sex: a black feminist critique of antidiscrimination doctrine, feminist theory and antiracist politics', *University of Chicago Legal Forum*, pp. 139–67.
—— (1991), 'Mapping the margins: intersectionality, identity politics, and violence against women of color', *Stanford Law Review*, 43: 6, pp. 1241–99.
Enayat, Hadi (2017), *Islam and Secularism in Post-Colonial Thought*, Cham, Switzerland: Springer.
Enloe, Cynthia (1990), *Bananas, Beaches and Bases: Making Feminist Sense of International Politics*, Berkeley: University of California Press.
—— (2000) *Maneuvers: the International Politics of Militarizing Women's Lives*, Berkeley and London: University of California Press.
—— (2004), *The Curious Feminist: Searching for Women in a New Age of Empire*, Berkeley: University of California Press.
Fraser, Nancy (1997), 'Equality, difference and democracy: recent feminist debates in

the United States', in J. Dean (ed.) *Feminism and the New Democracy: Resisting the Political*, London: Sage, pp. 98–110.

Halley, Janet (2006), *Split Decisions: How and Why to Take a Break from Feminism*, Princeton: Princeton University Press.

Halley, Janet, Prabha Kotiswaran, Rachel Rebouché and Hila Shamir (2018), *Governance Feminism: an Introduction*, Minneapolis: University of Minnesota Press.

Hodzic, Saida (2014), 'Feminist bastards: toward a post-humanist critique of NGOization', in V. Bernal and I. Grewal (eds), *Theorizing NGOs: States, Feminisms, and Neoliberalism*, Durham, NC: Duke University Press, pp. 221–47.

Jad, Islah (2004), 'The NGO-isation of Arab women's movements', *IDS Bulletin*, 35, pp. 34–42.

—— (2007), 'NGOs: between buzzwords and social movements', *Development in Practice*, 17: 4–5, pp. 622–9.

Kandiyoti, Deniz (ed.) (1991), *Women, Islam and the State*, London: Macmillan.

—— (1996) 'Contemporary feminist scholarship and Middle East studies', in D. Kandiyoti (ed.), *Gendering the Middle East*, London: I. B. Tauris, pp. 1–28.

—— (2013), 'Fear and Fury: Women and post-revolutionary violence' *Open Democracy*, 10 January, <http://www.opendemocracy.net/5050/deniz-kandiyoti/fear-and-fury-women-and-post-revolutionary-violence> (last accessed 1 November 2018).

Kepel, Gilles (2004), *The War for Muslim Minds*, Cambridge, MA: Harvard University Press.

Kumar, Deepa (2012), *Islamophobia and the Politics of Empire*, Chicago: Haymarket Books.

Lacroix, Stephane (2011), *Awakening Islam: the Politics of Religious Dissent in Contemporary Saudi Arabia*, Cambridge, MA: Harvard University Press.

Lazreg, Marnia (1988), Feminism and difference: the perils of writing as a woman on women in Algeria', *Feminist Studies*, 14: 1 (Spring), pp. 81–107.

Li, Darryl (2016), 'Jihad in a world of sovereigns: law, violence, and Islam in the Bosnia crisis', *Law and Social Inquiry*, 41: 2, pp. 371–401.

Louer, Laurence (2007), *Transnational Shia Politics: Religious and Political Networks in the Gulf*, New York: Columbia University Press.

Mahmood, Saba (2005), *Politics of Piety: the Islamic Revival and the Feminist Subject* Princeton: Princeton University Press.

—— (2006), 'Secularism, hermeneutics, and empire: the politics of Islamic reformation', *Public Culture*, 18: 2, pp. 323–47.

Maira, Sunaina Marr (2016), *The 9/11 Generation: Youth, Rights, and Solidarity in the War on Terror*, New York: New York University Press.

Mandaville, Peter (2007), *Globalization and the Politics of Religious Knowledge: Pluralizing Authority in the Muslim World*, Fairfax, VA: George Mason University.

Meijer, Roel (2009), *Global Salafism: Islam's New Religious Movement*, Oxford: Oxford University Press.

Minh-ha, Trinh (1989), *Woman, Native, Other: Writing Postcoloniality and Feminism*, Bloomington, IN: Indiana University Press.

Mohanty, Chandra (1988), 'Under Western eyes: feminist scholarship and colonial discourses', *Feminist Review*, 30 (Autumn), pp. 61–88.

—— (1991), *Third World Women and the Politics of Feminism*, Bloomington, IN: Indiana University Press.

Namaste, Ki (1996), 'The politics of inside/out: queer theory, poststructuralism, and a sociological approach to sexuality', in S. Seidman (ed.), *Queer Theory/Sociology*, Cambridge, MA: Blackwell, pp. 194–212.

Narayan, Uma (1997), *Dislocating Cultures: Identities, Traditions and Third World Feminism*, New York and London: Routledge.

Nasr, Vali (2008), 'The Sunni-Shia Divide and the Future of Islam', *Being*, 20 November, <https://onbeing.org/programs/vali-nasr-sunni-shia-divide-future-islam/> (last accessed 1 November 2018).

Pall, Zoltan (2013), *Lebanese Salafis between the Gulf and Europe: Development, Fractionalization and Transnational Networks of Salafism in Lebanon*, Amsterdam: Amsterdam University Press.

—— (2018), *Salafism in Lebanon: Local and Transnational Movements*, Cambridge: Cambridge University Press.

Peterson, Spike (ed.) (1992), *Gendered States: Feminist (Re)Visions of International Relations Theory*, Boulder, CO: Lynne Rienner Publishers.

Pringle, Rosemary and Sophie Watson (1992), '"Women's interests" and the poststructuralist state', in M. Barrett and A. Phillips (eds), *Destabilizing Theory*, Cambridge: Polity Press, pp. 53–73.

Roy, Srila (2015), 'The Indian women's movement: within and beyond NGOization', *Journal of South Asian Development*, 10: 1, pp. 96–117.

Scott, Joan (1988), 'Deconstructing equality-versus-difference: or, the uses of poststructuralist theory for feminism', in *Feminist Studies*, 14: 1 (Spring), pp. 32–50.

Sedgwick, Eve K. (1990), *Epistemology of the Closet*, Berkeley: University of California Press.

Steans, Jill (2006), *Gender and International Relations: Issues, Debates and Further Directions*, Cambridge: Polity Press.

Tickner, J. Ann (1992), *Gender in International Relations: Feminist Perspectives on Achieving Global Security*, New York: Columbia University Press.

Toor, Saadia (2012), 'Imperialist feminism redux', *Dialectical Anthropology*, 36: 3–4, pp. 147–60.

Zubaida, Sami (2016), 'Islamic reformation?' *Open Democracy*, January, <https://www.opendemocracy.net/north-africa-west-asia/sami-zubaida/islamic-reformation> (last accessed 1 November 2016).

CHAPTER 2

Protest, Resistance and Shifting Gender Orders in Egypt: Crossing Red Lines?

HEBA EL KHOLY AND NADIA TAHER

INTRODUCTION

Between 2011 and 2014, Egypt saw the ousting of an authoritarian ruler in power for over thirty years, the holding of three referenda, the drafting of two constitutions (in 2012 and 2014), two interim authorities, two presidential elections (in 2012 and 2014) and unprecedented levels of public violence. This period of turmoil, which involved major ruptures in governance and competing appropriations of Islam, was rich in contradictory attempts to unsettle, challenge, reinscribe and consolidate a gender order based on masculine privilege. In this chapter, we aim to analyse the ways in which the politics of gender in post-Mubarak governance between 2011 and 2017 became intrinsic to attempts to establish legitimacy, national identity and social control.

As a point of entry to our discussion, we have selected two 'episodes' for detailed analysis. The first took place in 2011 at the height of the uprisings that resulted in the overthrow of the Mubarak regime. It focuses on a pivotal public protest against the unprecedented levels of sexualised gender-based violence that occurred in public spaces. The second took place in 2017, on the sixth anniversary of the 25 January protests, and ushered in an unparalleled public controversy between President Abel Fatah el-Sisi and the Sheikh of Al-Azhar, Ahmed al-Tayeb, triggered by the president's proposal to ban men's right to verbally divorce their wives (*talaq shafawi*). Analysed together, these episodes shed light on some key paradoxes and bargaining processes and highlight both continuities and discontinuities in gender discourse and practice in Egypt.

We argue that the massive protests which began in 2011 and included numerous women crossing class, religion, age and rural–urban divides resulted in (and made visible) new expressions of gender identities, some of which challenged male privilege. Part of the backlash against this insurrection and the return to authoritarian rule took the form of a politics of 'masculinist restoration' (Kandiyoti 2013, 2014)[1] whereby existing gender hierarchies and the privileges they entail were renegotiated and largely reimposed. As our episodes will demonstrate, once Mubarak was overthrown, public and institutional reactions to the protestors centred on re-establishing the status quo. State sponsored piety and a 'chauvinistic' nationalism focused on security, combined with an 'othering' process that stigmatises all dissenters, were intertwined in the establishment of new 'patriarchal bargains' (Kandiyoti 1988) in the domain of governance. Restoring the 'ideal' Egyptian family became a litmus test of success. The chapter concludes by exploring whether the more egalitarian, inclusive and democratic impulses on display during the protests – and the new masculinities and femininities they expressed – could give us pointers for transformations in both gender relations and the polity.

Ruptures and Shifting Alliances in Post-Mubarak Egypt

To contextualise our key episodes, this section highlights the events leading to decisive ruptures in governance involving alliances and realignments between the military and key competing Islamic players (the Muslim Brotherhood and its Freedom and Justice Party, the Salafi movement[2] and its al-Nour Party and Al-Azhar).[3]

Starting on 25 January 2011 (National Police Day),[4] the first eighteen days of the 'revolution' were hailed as a celebration of diversity, with a unity of purpose across gender, generation and faiths. The main demands were 'bread, freedom and social justice' and 'down with Mubarak'. As an emergency measure the police withdrew and the army stepped in to oversee security.

Mubarak's ousting on 11 February 2011 was met with celebrations all over Egypt. Power was transferred to the Supreme Council of the Armed Forces (SCAF) that pledged to support a legitimate civilian government (Batty 2011). A short-lived alliance was formed between the military and the Muslim Brotherhood (MB hereafter) paving the way to the presidential elections that followed. During this time (by mid-2011) most of the women and men who led the 'revolution' were excluded from all formal political processes. Liberal and leftist political parties were fragmented and marginalised. Leading up to the first referendum to decide whether a new constitution should precede parliamentary elections or not, the campaign launched by the MB calling for parliamentary elections first (counting on a majority that would sway the constitutional process in their favour) was framed in divisive religious rhetoric: 'say yes to the Muslim identity of Egypt', 'say yes to Islam' (Ibrahim 2015).

The first presidential election after Mubarak was won by the first elected civilian president, Mohamed Morsi (with 51.7 per cent of the vote in June 2012). A year later, Morsi was ousted on 30 July following street protests against the MB regime. New alliances between the military and other Islamic forces, including Al-Azhar and the Salafi movement came to the fore. Indeed, it is important to recall that when Marshal Abdel Fattah el-Sisi, who was then minister of defence and head of SCAF, announced the overthrow of President Morsi, two of the key figures standing beside him were the Sheikh of Al-Azhar and the head of the Salafi al-Nour Party. SCAF then appointed Adly Mansour, chief justice of the Constitutional Court, as interim president. El-Sisi, who was running the interim regime de facto, won a landslide victory in the presidential election of May 2014.

One of the most surprising elements of the post-2011 period was not the victory of the MB and its Justice and Freedom Party, which was in some ways predictable, but rather the highly visible and rapid ascent of the Salafi movement and its al-Nour Party into political power (with 24.3 per cent of the seats), making it the second largest party after the MB (with 47.2 per cent of seats) in the 2012 parliament (Brown 2011; Lacroix 2016). Indeed, after the ousting of the MB and the fall of Morsi, the alliance between the regime and the Salafi party continued.

The effects of these alignments were manifest in the drafting of two post-Mubarak constitutions, in 2012 and in 2014. The 2012 Constitution, drafted by a committee dominated by Islamists, and seen by many as 'an Islamist' constitution, scrapped the existing constitutional guarantee on gender equality.

The 2014 Constitution reinstated an article and clauses in support of gender equality. The fifty-member Constitutional Committee included members from the so-called 'secular' forces as well as Salafis, representatives from Al-Azhar, the Church and the military. There were only five women on the committee. Nonetheless, feminists formed a strong lobby to safeguard gender equality in this constitution. Article 11 committed the state to equality in all rights between women and men, 'in accordance with the provision of the Constitution' (The Egyptian Constitution 2014). While not explicit, this refers to article 2, stating that sharia is the principal source of legislation. A member of the committee described how 'bitter struggles' around the wording led to this compromise. Article 11 also committed to protect women against all forms of violence, a direct outcome of decades of lobbying, which reached a new scale in the context of post-2011 activism (Elsadda 2015). Article 7 also gave additional authority to the Al-Azhar,[5] designating it as the sole institution with authority over Islamic religious matters, giving it greater control over its own affairs and assigning it a separate and increased budget. These expanded powers and autonomy have, as discussed below, puts Al-Azhar's role in society and the politics of gender in the spotlight (El Masry 2013).

Between 2011 and 2014, the protests – and their repression – continued. Under SCAF rule, the 'revolutionaries' resumed demonstrations, fearing that 'their revolution will die' (McGreal and Borger 2011). In response, the military police displayed unprecedented brutality and sexualised violence (Fadl 2011). Protest chants changed from '*al-guesh wel shaab eed wahda*' (the army and people are one hand) in the early days, to '*yaskot hokm al-askar*' (down with military rule).

Opposition to President Morsi's rule quickly grew and there were large demonstrations demanding his resignation. His ousting with the direct intervention of the army led to further polarisation between those who supported this move and those who saw it as a signal of the resumption of military rule. The second governance 'transition' (ending in May 2014) under Adly Mansour, was marked by more violence and arrests. Two pro-Morsi sit-ins in greater Cairo around Rabaa al-Adawiya mosque and al-Nahda, were crushed by security forces, killing 800 to 1,200 demonstrators in Rabaa alone – one of the world's largest killings of demonstrators on a single day in recent history (Human Rights Watch 2014).

Al-Azhar publicly announced its opposition to the bloodshed, creating a crack in its alliance with the regime (*Egypt Independent* 2017a). The mass killings also generated sharp divisions in the country, within institutions, political entities and movements, and even within families. This included the women's movement (Al-Ali 2014). Some supported the violence, others were conspicuous by their silence and some expressed outrage, mostly through social media.

The MB was declared as a terrorist organisation in December 2013 (*Ahram Gate* 2013) and protests continued with large pro-Morsi demonstrations, and in parallel smaller protests against the military trial of civilians and the 2014 Protest Law. This ushered in another wave of thousands of arrests and the banning of activist and human rights groups for conspiring with foreign 'agents' against the state. According to estimates, there have been 41,000 political detainees since el-Sisi took over (*Egyptian Streets* 2014), hundreds of forcibly disappeared and extrajudicial killings (Amnesty International 2016). The regime also used religion, taking its fight to the mosques, with the minister of Islamic endowments decreeing in 2016 that protesting on the anniversary of 25 January 'contravenes sharia law' (Trager 2016).

Despite the constitutional ban on religious parties, the Salafi al-Nour Party remains represented in parliament.[6] Its representatives have, like the majority of other MPs, opposed attempts to reform regressive legislation, such as those related to blasphemy and inciting debauchery. In fact, in 2016 and 2017 there has been an increase in the number of arrests and prison sentences under these laws. The 2016 parliament, dominated by supporters of President el-Sisi, has also proposed changes signalling further ultra-conservative trends, such as outlawing homosexuality for the first time in Egypt (EIPR 2017).

Mobilising the public against the MB, President el-Sisi called on 'all honourable Egyptians to go onto the streets and ask (him) for *tafweed* (authorisation) to fight what we know is coming – terrorism' (Helmy 2017). The essence of the regime is captured in a poster depicting a military man with the caption 'a hand that builds and a hand that fights terrorism' (Afifi 2017). The coupling of security with economic development also signals the army's increasing role in Egypt's economy, particularly through big construction projects. The increased attacks on the military, churches, Christian communities and tourists, and the sharp hike in prices, however, undermined the promise of security and a dignified livelihood, posing challenges to the legitimacy of the regime.

Some have argued that the increasing repression and heightened attempts at social control are signals that the regime knows it has to govern a significantly transformed citizenry (Bayat 2015), whose 'revolutionary spirit' remains resilient (Hamzawy 2017). It also appears that women's powerful presence in the protests, and their visibility in political opposition and activism, were particularly unsettling to those who fear signs of change in the gender order. As the analysis of two episodes below will show, these developments posed a challenge to the 'masculine' state, to the 'ideal' Egyptian family and to male privilege in society at large.

The Daughters of Egypt Are a Red Line: Women's Demonstration against Sexual Violence

'*Banat Masr Khat Ahmar*' ('The daughters of Egypt are a red line!'), '*Banat Masr Matet'arash*' ('The daughters/girls of Egypt are not to be stripped!') (Hafiz 2011). These were the main slogans of a large women's demonstration held on 20 December 2011 in Cairo and other cities in Egypt. The demonstrations were a direct response to increasingly violent and targeted attacks on women.

The first stark attack (on 9 March 2011) targeted thirty-five women arrested at an overnight sit-in at Tahrir Square in Cairo. Stood in line, unmarried women were asked to identify themselves, and seventeen of them were forced to undergo a 'virginity test' by a military doctor.[7] Initially denying this incident, the military later admitted it and argued that it was a procedure 'to avoid future allegations of rape by female protesters' (Shams El-Din 2012). Justifications followed with comments such as 'these women who were detained were not like your daughters or mine' (Amin 2011), alluding to them as 'loose women'. Samira Ibrahim, one of the women who went through this ordeal, took SCAF to court (Abdel Kouddous 2012) and became one of the main icons of the 'revolution', with her image appearing on posters and in graffiti.

Other serious and widely publicised incidents occurred during a sit-in around the cabinet building from 16 to 19 December 2011, where women were viciously beaten and verbally abused by military police using sexualised language. On 17 December, a young woman in an *abaya*,[8] whom the media dubbed the 'blue bra woman', was caught on camera being dragged along the street by military officers, and an officer stamping on her torso, with her blue bra exposed.[9]

Shortly afterwards – and for the first time – a written apology was issued by SCAF under the title 'Egypt's Great Women' (Maher 2011). This did not appease women or diminish their resolve, and the massive 20 December demonstrations took place with no interference from police or military. 'Egyptian women can no longer be intimidated or humiliated', said one demonstrator (*Al-Masry al-Youm* 2011). Posters read 'Egypt was stripped', and slogans demanded the end of military rule. As women of different ages, classes and political persuasions marched down the streets, they were accompanied by male sympathisers forming a human chain along the pavements to ward off possible attacks. Some men were chanting *'al-regala fen al-settat ahom'* ('Where are the men? Here are the women') (Hafiz 2011).

At the same time, an 'unholy' alliance between the MB, Salafis and the majority of liberal and leftist political parties and pro regime media was evident in the almost total silence about the December attacks. Some voices were raised blaming the women themselves – questioning their presence and behaviour in public spaces – and the men 'who allowed them to be in the protests'. Some even asked why the 'blue bra' woman was on the street, and why her attire could so easily come undone.

Although demonstrations were often a daily occurrence at the time, the 20 December demonstration stood out as not only a declaration of the integrity of women's bodies as 'a red line', but also as one of the first public condemnations of the military and the legitimacy of its rule. It was a turning point where demands for women's rights were intertwined with demands for political change.[10]

This demonstration also highlighted a new configuration of masculinities. During earlier protests, some male revolutionaries, while respecting their female counterparts, saw themselves as their protectors in the 'traditional' sense of *shahama* and *gadaana* (gallantry, vigour and manliness). However, another more 'egalitarian' stance became increasingly evident, with some of the men present acting in solidarity with women. Some analysts at the time argued that '[i]t is fairly undeniable that a new masculine imagination is coming out at a grassroots level', and that '[t]he old order of masculinity in Egypt is slowly but surely crumbling, and a new order – one that demands equality and rejects hierarchy – is emergent . . .' (Gardner 2011).

Controlling women, controlling protests?

Following the 'daughters of Egypt are a red line' demonstration, assaults against female and some male protestors became increasingly sexualised, targeted and violent. This occurred in the midst of continuing generalised violence.[11] Subsequent incidents of sexualised violence peaked at different moments. With women unsafe on the streets, all three regimes (SCAF, Morsi and el-Sisi) in effect established their control by creating a sense of urgency to 'reinstate police protection and social respectability', using women's public behaviour as the marker (Amar 2011: 300). Blaming women protesters was the norm. Islamist party members in the Shoura Council[12] argued that protests are male spaces, not a place for women (FIDH et al. 2014: 25). Some went as far as claiming that most women who go to protests are divorced – and perhaps 'they want to be raped'. By contrast, the MB, stressed that 'their' women were never harassed in Brotherhood-led demonstration (FIDH et al. 2014: 26). There seems to be no independent research on this claim.

Sexual assaults culminated in shocking gang rapes of women, unprecedented in Egypt on this scale. The first documented cases occurred on 23 November 2012 (FIDH et al. 2014: 15), followed by a series of incidents during the elections won by Morsi (16–17 June 2012). One of the women attacked described what became a pattern in future assaults: 'groups of dozens of men seemed to appear from nowhere . . . It didn't seem normal . . . It didn't seem like the day-to-day harassment that women get, it seemed organized' (El Baramawy 2013). Activists were often, but not exclusively, targeted. Around 233 cases of rape or attempted rape (Mohei 2014), often using fingers and sharp instruments, occurred between 2012 and 2014.

There is no consensus on who the perpetrators were. Gang rapes were attributed by some to plain-clothes police and/or *baltagia* (hired thugs), and by others to members of the MB. Some saw the attacks as a strategy to damage the revolutionary movement and re-establish the status quo. Dina Wahba said: 'For me, this is part of the counterrevolution: SCAF, the military, remnants of the old regime, interested parties, people who have a vested interest in returning to the old system' (Wahba 2012).

The inherent paradoxes and fluidity of men's responses and the masculinities these embodied were revealed in the reactions to violence against women during the protests. In a response to the assaults, NGOs, women and human rights groups formed 'vigilante' groups to document the incidents and to act as 'bodyguards'. Initially the role of female 'bodyguards' was to alert the men to come to the rescue. Gradually, however, the notion of the male as the 'rescuer' was challenged, and both women and men rushed to the help of assaulted women. Vigilantes and male protestors who tried to rescue women were also criticised as unmanly – as traitors to their 'male brethren'. Some were subjected to sexualised violence themselves (Tadros 2016).

Emergence of 'new' identities: a threat to hegemonic masculinity?

The protests saw new articulations of gender identities among women and men, challenging not only the regime but also starting to question existing gender hierarchies. Sherine Hafez suggests that 'Notions of masculinity . . . have observably shifted the terms of the patriarchal bargain between genders and ages and between the state and its people' (Hafez 2012: 39), resulting in a new consciousness among men and women. Deniz Kandiyoti talks of a new generation of youth 'who are fully alert to the intimate relations between authoritarian rule and forms of oppression based on gender' (Kandiyoti 2014).

These new expressions of masculinity constituted a threat to both hegemonic masculinity and to the regime. In an attempt at 'othering' male dissenters, they were labelled by the regime and their supporters as *mokhanasseen* (she-males), *noshataa*, *mosakafeen* and *hokookeyeen* (activists, intellectuals and human rights advocates). These terms continue to be written and enunciated in effeminate tones in an attempt to degrade and undermine them. A journalist in 2016 described them as

> those men who grow their hair, put it up in pony tails and wear women skinny jeans . . . No wonder they are anti-military! It is because the military is the factory of men. Where is the Azhar on this? Egypt is squeezed between two polar opposites, them and the religious extremists, both of whom are against the military. (El-Hawary 2016)

Significantly, it is Al-Azhar's version of Islam that is specifically invoked to undermine both 'religious extremists' and 'activists'.

The rise of 'insurgent femininities' was also seen as a threat. As Bahaa Ezzelarab points out, 'the state does not want to see a woman who dares to raise her voice against the government in the street' (Ezzelarab 2014). There was a concerted effort by the regime and its media to portray women protestors as loud and wild, with loose morals (sleeping in tents with men in Tahrir). This was juxtaposed with images of women voting for President el-Sisi and celebrating the return to respectability, and to 'passive and demure models of conservative behaviour' (Zaki-Chakravarti 2014), a woman who turns to 'the strong man' who will protect her and Egypt.

'Protection' was not what 'insurgent' women were demanding. Rather, as illustrated in the December 2011 demonstration and what followed, women demanded the right to safe public spaces. These demands follow on the work of women's and human rights organisations who have lobbied for new legislation on sexual harassment and rape for many years (FIDH et al. 2014). It was only under interim President Mansour that a law defining and prohibiting sexual harassment (in May 2014) was approved for the first time (FIDH et al. 2014). Women's rights campaigners argued that the law does not go far enough (McRobie 2014). Joined by a new generation of activists of both sexes, and with the support of a larger constituency, they are continuing their pressure to amend the law. One of their concerns is that the current law only applies to civilian perpetrators, not members of the state apparatus, including the police and the military (McRobie 2014). It is not clear if the proposed legislation and amendments will be accepted, given the recent clampdown on women's human rights/ legal NGOs and activists for working on legal amendments that specifically holds state institutions to account.

In this context, it is not surprising that the president's only call for new legislation related to women's rights in 2017 – which he designated as the 'Year of the Woman' – was to annul undocumented verbal divorce, a proposed law that does not fundamentally challenge the regime or the existing gender order. As the episode below shows, it appears to be more about restoring 'traditional' roles of men and women in the 'ideal' family, and a case of instrumentalising gender issues to further the goals of establishing legitimacy, national identity and control.

'You Tire me Your Eminence:' the President's Call to Annul 'Verbal Divorce'

Exactly six years after the protests of 25 January 2011, President el-Sisi made a speech at the Police Academy to mark Police Day. Amidst the military and national symbols typical of such an event, he expressed alarm at the high rates of divorce in Egypt.[13] Concerned about 'the unity of the Egyptian family', the president proposed to annul verbal divorce – *talaq shafawi* – a practice whereby husbands can divorce their wives just by saying 'I divorce you',[14] without necessarily registering the divorce. He said: 'We need a law to deal with divorce issues before the *"maazoun"* [a government cleric who administers marriage and divorce), so that people will have the time to consider their decision' (F. Farid 2017), so as to prevent 'inappropriate behaviour' (Hendawi 2017). Smiling, the president turned to the Grand Sheikh of Al-Azhar, al-Tayeb, sitting in the front row, and said half-jokingly: 'You tire me, your eminence' (Shams El-Din 2017; Shahine 2013). This was a reference to the possibility that Al-Azhar might want to block such a move, in the context of a long-standing struggle between the state and the clerical establishment, which escalated post-2011 (Magued 2015).

Immediately after the president's call, the head of Dar al-Ifta,[15] and members of parliament expressed their support for the proposal. The Religious Committee in parliament announced it would start drafting a law and that it would be fully in line with sharia.

However, on 12 February 2017, in an act of unprecedented public defiance, the Council of Senior Scholars of Al-Azhar, the highest authority on Islamic matters, convened by al-Tayeb, issued a statement refusing the president's proposal. The statement maintained that verbal divorce was valid and established by Islamic law. The only concession made was to consider imposing a penalty on a husband if divorce is not registered within a specific period. The statement added: 'People do not need divorce legislation to be changed; rather they are in need of measures that would ensure a decent livelihood.' Al-Azhar thus affirmed its legitimacy as the ultimate voice on religious matters.[16] Trampling upon Al-Azhar's territory was also 'a red line'.[17]

This brief episode betrayed a lurking tension between two key governance institutions – a struggle over legitimacy and national identity, with gender politics coming to the fore as a key marker and litmus test. The president's comments acknowledged that he needed the sheikh's approval while insinuating that Al-Azhar was obstructing attempts at 'modernisation'. Tensions have escalated since the president's call in 2015 for 'a religious revolution' to renew religious discourse – on which Al-Azhar is seen as dragging its feet (Mourad and Bayoumy 2015). The roots of the tension are historical and more structural. While publicly supporting the ousting of Morsi, Al-Azhar was also vocal in claiming it was a choice of the lesser of two evils and that it did not condone the violence (Abdallah 2017).

This controversy between Egypt's top political institution and its supreme religious institution – watched live by millions of Egyptians – spilled into a polarised debate exposing how politics, religion and gender are intimately intertwined (English al Arabiya 2017).[18] Some saw el-Sisi's proposal as a victory for 'the Egyptian family', welcoming it as a move by a president who supports women. Others were critical of raising a rule of law issue at a ceremony showcasing police and military strength. Discussions pitted not only the Al-Azhar and the presidency against each other, but also the law and Islamic jurisprudence (F. Farid 2017; Brown and Ghanem 2017).

Mainstream media eventually coalesced on attacks on Al-Azhar, accusing it of obstructing reforms to fight terrorism and of harbouring extremists, pointing, among other things, to its refusal in 2015 to label *daesh* (or Islamic State – IS) fighters as 'infidels'. Some interpreted the attacks as a strategy to shift responsibility away from the regime's inability to ensure security without resorting to violence. The severity of the attacks on Al-Azhar may have also been fanned by external influence given the imam's declaration at an international conference in 2016 that 'Salafis are not Sunnis', causing a major uproar among the pro-government clerics in Saudi Arabia (Dehlvi 2016),[19] a key Egyptian ally. There were calls for al-Tayeb to resign (Elbaz 2017; Saleh 2017).

'Tahya Masr' ('long live Egypt'):[20] nationalism, masculinity and state-sponsored piety

This episode highlights the crucial link between nationalism, piety and masculinities in the post Mubarak era – an era where nationalism is ever more closely tied to both a 'security' and a 'morality' discourse. This connection has precedents as President Sadat, concerned about the rise of Islamist groups in the 1970s, flaunted his piety to legitimise his rule and projected himself as the *rab al-eela al-Masreya* (father of the Egyptian family). It was under his rule that 'morality' began to take centre stage within nationalist discourse, with his promulgation of *qanoun himayat al-qiyam min al-eib* (the law of shame) (Dyer 2014).

The nationalist fervour and 'pious masculinity' displayed by President el-Sisi, however, is evoked more specifically in relation to 'counter terrorism' – terrorism being used by the regime interchangeably with the banned Muslim Brotherhood.[21] The regime seems to struggle to paradoxically reassert a national identity that both downplays religion (both Islam and Christianity) as a source of identity, yet projects a form of Islamic piety – a 'holier than thou' approach, in competition with the MB, the Salafis and even Al-Azhar.[22]

In its nationalistic drive, an appeal to women – as mothers and wives – an important electoral constituency, was evident early on under el-Sisi's rule and as part of the 'Tahya Masr' campaign. In his first televised speech, the president called on women to 'help him' by saving on electricity and food (el-Sisi 2014). The use of 'patriotic manhood and exalted motherhood as icons of nationalist ideology' is a trend also captured in earlier studies on Egypt (Hatem 1992).

In its quest to foster 'national loyalty' and counter 'terrorism', the government's targeting of women was also taken to the mosques, this time in collaboration, not in competition, with Al-Azhar. The Ministry of Religious Endowment's first ever state-led campaign to train women preachers was launched in 2017, whereby candidates undergo four years of religious training by either the Ministry or Al-Azhar, after which they are given a licence to preach. This campaign, which aims to give licences to 2,000 female preachers by the end of 2018, is an attempt to 'win hearts and minds' using women as mothers and wives. It is also a way to regulate the widespread grassroots movement of women preachers and women's religious classes in mosques which began in the 1980s (F. Farid 2017). On its side, Al-Azhar has recently launched a new campaign in schools and universities linking religion and nationalism by promoting the message: 'love of nation is part of faith' (Associated Press 2015).

By choosing the Police Day celebration to make his proposal, the president sent a clear signal about who is in control. The speech was nationalistic and security-focused, paying tribute to the bravery and achievements of the police, stressing national pride, the preservation of national institutions and collaboration between the police and the military. This 'toughness', however, was tempered with a 'tender'[23] message, a tribute to the role of women in the police force, and a call to 'take care of Egyptian women' (*khahlo balkom menhom*), and to 'respect them and treat them well in the street' (el-Sisi 2017).

The proposal to annul verbal divorce also affirmed the president's image as the 'protector' of women and the family. The National Council for Women (NCW) issued a statement supporting the proposal. It is 'a new victory for women and the best proof that the president is keen . . . on keeping up with the renewed religious discourse'. . . 'Sharia calls for the unity and stability of families . . . [the proposal] would give couples a chance to reconsider a decision possibly made in a moment of anger' (El Shalakany 2017). However, marking a shift in the alliance between some women's groups and the regime, the chair of the Arab Women Organization, an inter-governmental organisation affiliated with the Arab League,[24] instead supported Al-Azhar and its role.

Abolishing verbal divorce is perceived by some in a favourable light as it could enhance women's negotiating power in marriage, making *ourfi* (customary) marriage less popular[25] (Mandour 2017). The proposal, however, is grounded in the image of a married woman within a 'traditional' family, reinforces negative views of divorced (or unmarried) women and comes at the expense of women's personal rights and freedoms. This view is in line with the 'moral rescue' and 'protecting the family' clauses mandated in the 2014 Constitution[26] – despite the clauses on gender equality in this constitution.

Underlying this public disagreement between the religious establishment and the political regime about who is the final arbiter on matters pertaining to marriage and the family, there seems to be a tacit agreement on the 'appropriate' roles of women and men, centred on their complementarity in the 'ideal family'. Abolishing verbal divorce, as stated astutely by Sahar Mandour,

> does not threaten the role of the state or entrenched norms of patriarchal masculinity; it neither radically protects nor radically confronts. It neither threatens divorce laws nor aspires to equality . . . At the centre of the Egyptian year of woman is the relationship between two men who share similar ideas about masculinity and women's roles. (Mandour 2017)

'Toghian al-sitat' ('tyranny of women'): the politics of masculinist restoration unfolds

The high divorce rates which alarmed the president were blamed by some, including the Grand Mufti, on *khulu* (Egypt Independent 2017b). *Khulu* is a practice sanctioned in 2002 whereby a woman is granted the right to initiate divorce herself as long as she renounces all her financial rights (Sonneveld 2004). Prior to *khulu*, it was extremely difficult for a woman to initiate a divorce and it became one of the most controversial clauses in the new Personal Status Law of 2000.[27] It was seen by many as a direct attack on the established gender order provoking widespread discussion in the People's Assembly and among religious scholars and the public at large (Sonneveld 2014). Many lawyers scoffed at it with one stating: 'What kind of a man would agree to marry a woman who got divorced by means of *khulu*?' (Tadros 2002). The law was repealed shortly afterwards. In 2002, however, the High Constitutional Court declared *khulu* constitutional, marking a major victory for women's groups.[28]

Although *khulu* cases represent a tiny proportion of all divorces – partly because some judges obstruct the implementation process and lawyers often refuse to take it up – the law apparently still terrifies many men. Some see it as 'a sword hanging over men's head' (Madkour 2009). So much so, that in direct response to *khulu*, the first ever men's rights organisation in Egypt, the Organization for Divorced Men, was set up in 2009 with a mandate to protect men from *toghian al-sitat* (the tyranny of women) (Madkour 2009).

The perceived damage to masculine prerogatives of this miniscule right granted to women has stimulated and accelerated the 'politics of masculinist restoration' in the post-2011 period. In 2012, under President Morsi, a few months before the parliament was dissolved, *khulu* (and the entire Personal Status Law which was relabelled Suzanne Mubarak's law in an attempt to discredit it) was challenged in the People's Assembly.[29] The National Council of Women and civil society lobbied strongly and the Supreme Constitutional Court subsequently confirmed (once again), that *khulu* is constitutional (Egypt Independent 2012).

Public debates around divorce have taken place largely in the framework of a 'restoration' discourse, 'restoring morality' and 'restoring the family', revealing how divorced women are still widely seen as a 'threat' to society. In 2016, a male led campaign, 'Enough Divorce in Egypt' was launched by a group of psychiatrists and preachers from Al-Azhar, to address the increase in divorce rates because of the 'moral and mental repercussions on Egyptians' (Egypt Independent 2016). In 2018, a call to establish a 'Men's Council', to counter 'oppression against men', made headlines. 'The National Council (for men) will aim to support men harmed by the Personal Status Laws issued during the last twenty years and passed with the support of the National Council for Women', argued Attorney Hajjaj. The Personal Status Laws, he added, especially the *Khulu* Law, is biased and has totally 'destroyed Egyptian families' (Hajjaj, quoted in Hosny 2018).

This bargaining around the ideal family is taking place among competing Islamic players – represented by the MB, al-Nour Party, Dar al-Ifta and the regime – and increasingly by Al-Azhar, armed with its new constitutional powers, on the one hand, and by feminist civil society groups, and for the first time 'men's rights' groups, on the other. The alliance between Al-Azhar and the ruling regime remains fragile, and Al-Azhar has struck new 'bargains' with key allies, including some women's groups.[30] How these bargaining processes unfold will continue to shape the future of the country and the official construction of masculinities and femininities – and will continue to be shaped by them.

Crossing Red Lines? Continuities and Discontinuities

We have argued in this chapter that attempts to re-establish key governance functions of legitimacy, national identity and social control following a challenge to the regime also ushered in a new reactive politics of 'masculinist restoration'. This included new strategies and discourses for 'restoring' hegemonic masculinities, 'authentic' views of what it means to be a man or a woman, and 'protecting' the family.

The episodes analysed in this chapter provided two snapshots of how these complex and paradoxical processes unfolded following the ousting of Mubarak with a view to capturing both continuities and discontinuities in the post-2011 gender orders. The first episode illustrates how the brutal response to sustained protests by women and men seeking political and societal transformation set the stage for new expressions of gender identity: insubordinate femininities and insurgent masculinities challenging both authoritarianism and patriarchy. This has prompted a wave of 'masculinist restoration' and renewed assertion of male prerogatives. According to Mustafa Abdalla, there was 'a backlash on women's rights and the emergence of a kind of masculinity that considers women as its opponents ... masculine identities were being negotiated and articulated in a religious discourse that sought more power for men over women' (Abdalla 2014: 68–9). Other attempts at masculinist restoration became manifest in the politicisation of sexual assaults and everyday harassment as a means of intimidation. A focus on blaming women for their behaviour and appearance in public spaces threw a veil of impunity over a mix of policing and moralisation, which united very different actors in state and society.

The second episode occasioned by the debates over verbal divorce (*talaq shafawi*), shows how power struggles and the shifting alliances between women's groups and power centres, both religious and political, may lead to the instrumentalisation of gender politics. To establish their legitimacy as the guardians of 'moderate Islam', the el-Sisi regime and Al-Azhar have projected themselves as the rescuers of 'traditional masculinity', vying, in effect, to 'save' the nation through 'saving' the family. Underlying the unprecedented public disagreement between these power centres was an implicit agreement on the definition of masculinity. Despite apparent divergences, these were in fact the product of competition over whose authority would prevail in matters pertaining to gender. Both the government and Al-Azhar cultivated alliances with women's organisations to consolidate their legitimacy, posing as champions of women's rights.

The episode also exposes how, over the past decade, men have been organising in a formal manner to protect perceived threats to their gender interests from the 'tyranny of women'. This societal trend to 'restore masculinity' continued and intensified after 2011 with the 'No to Divorce' campaign in 2016, and an even more vocal call by some men (and women) in 2018 to set up a 'Men's Council' (to mirror the existing Women's Council) to support 'oppressed' men (Hosny 2018).

As these episodes demonstrate, nurturing a compliant citizenry is central to establishing regime legitimacy and retaining social control, including the maintenance of male prerogatives. Henceforth, anyone who opposes the regime could be considered as a traitor and excluded both from the nation and from definitions of what it means to be a 'real' Egyptian women or man, setting in motion an 'othering' process that exacerbates societal divisions.

An important shift that occurred, however, is that the debate on gender politics has become more 'indigenised' post-2011 and feminists have become more 'organic' (see El Kholy 2002). Gender issues are no longer seen as linked to donor agency agendas or confined to conference room discussions. They are now more firmly grounded in Egyptian realities and history, with some 'local reframings of sexuality, police governance and class struggle' (Amar 2011: 321).

With the crackdown on civil society and opposition groups that followed street protests, mobilised activist networks find new and creative outlets in social media participating in fluid networks of 'cyberactivism' (Radsch 2016). Concerns about their potential influence are reflected in the closure or blocking of numerous outlets (al-Marsad 2017).[31]

The challenges posed during the years of protest subverting patriarchal governance and the gender order were countered by state-sponsored piety, a security focused nationalism and an 'othering' process that stigmatises all dissenters. At the societal level, they were also countered by an increasing trend of men more proactively standing up for their gender interests, including by setting up formal men's groups. Despite this official and societal backlash, some Egyptians, who have been personally and politically changed through their experiences, have maintained their resolve to keep the demands of the 'revolution' alive and treat it as an unfinished project (Bayat 2015). Although only time can tell whether new forms of consciousness, including new expressions of gender identity, will find political expression in Egypt, it has become clearer than ever before that gender is a governance issue which cannot be separated from aspirations for a more just and inclusive democratic society.

Notes

1. '"Masculinist restoration"... is a sociopolitical process which comes into play at the point when patriarchy-as-usual is no longer fully secure, and requires higher levels of coercion and the deployment of more varied ideological state apparatuses to ensure its reproduction' (Kandiyoti 2013). Kandiyoti further describes that a 'reliance on a new politics of masculinist restoration – a politics that requires systematic indoctrination (Islamic, nationalistic or mixtures of both), greater surveillance and higher levels of intrusion in citizens' lives – becomes essential to the maintenance and reproduction of patriarchy' (Kandiyoti 2014).
2. Salafism is an Islamic movement that aims to restore Islamic piety and practice as was perceived to exist during the time of the Prophet Muhammad and his early followers, the *salaf* (forefathers) (multiple references).
3. Al-Azhar is one of the most prestigious religious institutions of the Sunni world and is the highest clerical authority in Egypt. Al-Azhar University, the world's oldest educational institution, was founded in 972 (see Zeghal (1999)).
4. The demonstration started on Police Day to mark opposition to police practice of oppression and brutality.
5. It was in the 1970s and 1980s, with the rise of Islamic militants (a trend which was initially tolerated by Sadat in an attempt to counter communist and leftist movements), that Al-Azhar began to be posited as the 'moderate' Islam, '*al-wasati*', and was given leeway to engage in cultural and media censorship. The institution was used by the Mubarak regime to discredit militant Islamists.
6. By opening the door to Christians to join the party, al-Nour Party was able to get around constitutional limits to religious parties.
7. They were all working class women in their twenties and early thirties.
8. An *abaya* is a long robe, usually black in colour, worn over the clothing and covering the whole body.
9. Multiple sources.
10. For more detail, see Badran (2011).
11. The death toll of civilian men and women reached around 900 in 2011, see McGreal and Borger (2011).
12. The 'Consultative Council', the upper parliamentary chamber, has limited legislative powers but was the only elected entity when the parliament was dissolved under Morsi.
13. According to the Central Agency for Public Mobilization and Statistics, there was a rise of 10.6 per cent in divorce rates in 2014/15.
14. Verbally stating you are divorced once is enough to make the divorce religiously binding. Saying it three times makes the divorce *baaen* (irrevocable).
15. Dar al-Ifta is part of the executive branch and is a separate institution from Al-Azhar.
16. The same call to annul verbal divorce was rejected by Al-Azhar in 2016. The question arises thus if the president proposed this as a strategic move in his power struggle with the Grand Imam.
17. It is interesting that the notion of 'red line' originally used to describe women during the protests was appropriated by Al-Azhar in this context, see Al Sherbini (2017).
18. According to a poll by the Egyptian Center for Public Opinion Research (Baseera)

in April 2017, 63 per cent of Egyptians support the proposal, 16 per cent did not and 21 per cent were undecided.
19. Also see conference coverage (Kumail12 2016).
20. 'Tahya Masr' (long live Egypt) is a campaign launched by el-Sisi to collect donations from Egyptians to fund development projects.
21. Although 'revolutionaries' and human rights supporters are also 'othered' and portrayed as internal enemies, trying to 'divide and destroy the state', they are not seen as dangerous as the MB.
22. During his historic visit to the 2016 Coptic mass, President el-Sisi stressed the importance that the world sees Egyptians as 'Egyptians' in terms of identity, not as 'Muslims' or Copts (Associated Press 2015).
23. The 'tough and tender' masculinity was coined by Duncanson (2015).
24. The head of the Arab Women's Organization is Mervat al-Talawy, the former Head of the NCW
25. One of the few and most vocal organisations on the value of abolishing verbal divorce during this controversy was the Centre for Egyptian Women's Legal Assistance.
26. For example, article 10. For further analysis, see Badran (2016: 115).
27. The law became known as the *Khulu* Law, although the amendments to the law were broader, indicating how sensitive the *khulu* clause in particular was. For a description of how fierce the debates were against *khulu* in parliament in 2000, see Moussa (no date).
28. This was a vibrant period for the women's movement in Egypt (see Al-Ali 2000).
29. The reference is to Suzanne Mubarak, the former first lady, who set up and chaired the NCW and was seen to have played a key role in pushing for reforms in the Personal Status Law.
30. The most prominent organisation siding with the regime was the NCW, but there were others, such as the Association for the Development and Enhancement of Women. The most prominent one siding with Al-Azhar was the Arab Women Organization, linked to the Arab League and set up by Arab First Ladies in 2002.
31. Al-Marsad is one of a number of sources with estimates.

Bibliography

Note: all Internet links last accessed 13–15 June 2018

Abdalla, Mustafa (2014), 'Masculinity on shifting grounds: emasculation and the rise of the Islamist politcal scene in post-Mubarak Egypt', in H. Rizzo (ed), *Masculinities in Egypt and the Arab World*, Cairo Papers, AUC, 33: 1, pp. 68–9.

Abdallah, Belal (2017), 'Al-Azhar and Sisi's regime: structural roots of disagreement', *Atlantic Ocean*, 7 April, <http://www.atlanticcouncil.org/blogs/menasource/al-azhar-and-sisi-s-regime-structural-roots-of-disagreement>.

Abdel Kouddous, Sharif (2012), 'No justice no peace', *Egypt Independent*, 17 March, <http://www.egyptindependent.com/no-justice-no-peace/>.

Afifi, Gameel (2017), 'The Egyptian army: one hand builds the nation and the other fights terrorism, *Al Ahram*, 22 May (Arabic), <https://bit.ly/2S1pYXL>.

Ahram Gate (2013), 'Declaration of the MB as a terrorist organisation', 25 December (Arabic), <http://gate.ahram.org.eg/News/435113.aspx%3E>.
Al-Ali, Nadje (2000), *Secularism, Gender and the State in the Middle East: the Egyptian Women's Movement*, Cambridge: Cambridge Middle East Studies.
—— (2014), 'Open space: reflections on (counter) revolutionary spaces in Egypt' *Feminist Review*, 106: 1, pp. 122–8.
Amar, Paul (2011), 'Turning the gendered politics of the security state inside out?', *International Feminist Journal of Politics*, 13: 3, pp. 299–328.
Amin, Shahira (2011), 'Egyptian general admits "virginity checks" conducted on protesters', *CNN*, May 31, <http://edition.cnn.com/2011/WORLD/meast/05/31/egypt.virginity.tests/index.html>.
Amnesty International (2016), 'Egypt: hundreds disappeared and tortured amid wave of brutal repression', 13 July, <https://www.amnesty.org/en/latest/news/2016/07/egypt-hundreds-disappeared-and-tortured-amid-wave-of-brutal-repression/>.
Associated Press (2015), 'From Egypt's leader, an ambitious call for reform in Islam', *Mail Online*, 8 January <http://www.dailymail.co.uk/wires/ap/article-2901511/From-Egypts-leader-ambitious-call-reform-Islam.html>.
Badran, Margot (2011), 'Egypt's revolution and the new feminism', *SSRC*, 3 March, <https://tif.ssrc.org/2011/03/03/egypts-revolution-and-the-new-feminism/>.
—— (2016), 'Creative Disobedience: Feminism, Islam, and Revolution in Egypt', in F. Sadiqi (ed.), *Women's Movements in Post-'Arab Spring' North Africa*, New York: Palgrave Macmillan.
El Baramawy, Yasmine (2013), 'Gang rape testament', *Facebook*, 13 July (Arabic), <https://www.facebook.com/y.baramawy/posts/10151748239756948>.
Batty, David (2011), 'Egypt the day after Mubarak quits', *The Guardian*, 12 February, <https://www.theguardian.com/world/blog/2011/feb/12/egypt-day-after-mubarak-quits>.
Bayat, Asef (2015), 'Revolution and despair', *Mada Masr*, 25 January, <https://www.madamasr.com/en/2015/01/25/opinion/u/revolution-and-despair/>.
Brown, J. Nathan (2011), 'Post-revolutionary Al-Azhar', *Middle East, Carnegie Endowment for International Peace*, September, <https://carnegieendowment.org/files/al_azhar.pdf>.
Brown, J. Nathan and Mariam Ghanem (2017), 'Divorce Egyptian style: why is a marriage question dividing Abdel-Fattah al-Sisi and Sheikh Ahmad al-Tayyib?' *Carnegie Middle East Centre*, 15 February, <http://carnegie-mec.org/diwan/68001>.
Dehlvi, Ghulam Rasool (2016), 'Islamic conference in Chechnya: why Sunnis are disassociating themselves form Salafists', *Firstpost*, 9 September, <https://bit.ly/2m7w8mZ>.
Duncanson, Claire (2015), 'Hegemonic masculinity and the possibility of change in gender relations', *Men and Masculinities*, 18: 2, pp. 231–48.
Dyer, Emily (2014), 'Egypt shame: why violence against women has soared after Mubarak', *Foreign Affairs*, 27 January, <https://www.foreignaffairs.com/articles/egypt/2014-01-27/egypts-shame>.
Egypt Independent (2012), 'Parliament rejects proposal to cancel women's right to divorce', 8 April, <http://www.egyptindependent.com/hold-al-azhar-refuses-mps-proposal-cancel-khula-law/>.
—— (2016), 'Psychiatrist launches campaign to reduce divorce rate', 9 March,

<http://www.egyptindependent.com/psychiatrist-launches-campaign-reduce-divorce-rate/>.

—— (2017a), 'Rift escalates, becomes public Between Sisi, Al-Azhar', 26 January, <http://www.egyptindependent.com/rift-escalates-becomes-public-between-sisi-al-azhar/>.

—— (2017b), 'Grand Mufti attributes Egypt's high divorce rate to Khula Law', 3 February, <http://www.egyptindependent.com/grand-mufti-attributes-egypt-s-high-divorce-rate-khula-law/>.

Egypt's Constitution of 2014 <https://www.constituteproject.org/constitution/Egypt_2014.pdf>.

Egyptian Initiative for Personal Rights (EIPR) (2017), 'EIPR condemns the ongoing crackdown targeting LGBTQI individuals', press release, 4 October, <https://eipr.org/en/press/2017/10/egyptian-state-wages-unprecedented-arrest-campaign-against-individuals-based-their>.

Egyptian Streets (2014), '41,000 Egyptians arrested since Morsi's ouster says NGO', 25 May, <https://egyptianstreets.com/2014/05/25/41000-egyptians-arrested-since-morsis-ouster-says-ngo/>.

Elbaz, Mohammed (2017), 'Why does Sheikh Al-Azhar not resign?' 25 January (Arabic), <http:/www.dostor.org/1294343>.

Elsadda, Hoda (2015), 'Feminists negotiating power in Egypt', *Open Democracy*, 5 January, <https://www.opendemocracy.net/5050/hoda-elsadda/article-11-feminists-negotiating-power-in-egypt>.

English Al Arabiya (2017), 'Poll on verbal divorce', 13 March, <https://english.alarabiya.net/en/News/middle-east/2017/03/13/Poll-63-percent-of-Egyptians-against-verbal-divorce.html>.

Ezzelarab, Bahaa (2014), Sexual violence led by the law, *Mada Masr*, 13 May (Arabic), <https://bit.ly/2KMu8iH>.

Fadl, Belal (2011), *Akher Kalam ONTV* (talk show), 20 December (Arabic), <https://www.youtube.com/watch?v=yZV5mjgJQBI>.

Farid, Farid (2017), 'Muslim women preachers enlisted in Egypt's fight against extremism', *The Sydney Morning Herald*, 20 April, <https://bit.ly/2JaadUZ>.

Farid, Sonia (2017), '"I hereby divorce you!" Egypt's verbal divorce phenomenon surges', *Al Arabiya English*, 29 January, <https://bit.ly/2L30ZM2>.

FIHD, Nazra for Feminist Studies, New Woman Foundation and the Uprising of Women in the Arab World, Cairo (2014), 'Egypt: keeping women out: sexual violence against women in the public sphere', <https://www.fidh.org/IMG/pdf/egypt_women_final_english.pdf>.

Gardner, Annie Rebekah (2011), 'The role of masculinity in the Egyptian uprising', *The Canonball Blog*, 10 February, <https://thecanonball.wordpress.com/2011/02/10/the-role-of-masculinity-in-the-egyptian-uprising/>.

Hafez, Sherine (2012), 'No longer a bargain: women, masculinity, and the Egyptian uprising', *American Ethnologist, Journal of the American Ethnological Society*, 28 February, <https://doi.org/10.1111/j.1548-1425.2011.01344.x>.

Hafiz, Jihan (2011), 'Outraged Egyptian women say "We Have No Fear"', *YouTube* (Arabic with English subtitles), <https://www.youtube.com/watch?v=ExvobNSzzVE>.

Hamzawy, Amr (2017), 'Egypt's resilience and evolving social activism', *Carnegie*

Endowment for International Peace, 5 April, <http://carnegieendowment.org/2017/04/05/egypt-s-resilient-and-evolving-social-activism-pub-68578>.

Hatem, Mervat F. (1992), 'Economic and political liberation in Egypt and the demise of state feminism', *International Journal of Middle East Studies*, 24: 2, pp. 231–51.

El Hawary, Dandrawy (2016), 'Activist revolution changing the image of masculinity in Egypt: make-up and long hair', *Al-Youm al-Sabei*, September (Arabic), <https://bit.ly/2m3Pt8i>.

Helmy, Y. (2017), 'What after the *tafweed*?' *Yanairgate*, 14 July (Arabic), <http://yanairgate.net/?p=105354>.

Hendawi, Hamza (2017), 'Egypt's el-Sissi says he is alarmed by high divorce rates', *Associated Press*, 14 January <https://bit.ly/2L4gW4J>.

Hosny, Hagar (2018), 'Egyptian men's rights activist sees oppression in female empowerment', *Al-Monitor*, 26 February, <https://bit.ly/2J8b6O8>.

Human Rights Watch, (2014), 'All according to plan: the Rab'a massacre and mass killings of protesters in Egypt', 12 August, <https://bit.ly/1NaCcCS>.

Ibrahim, Mahmoud (2015), 'The fourth anniversary of the "ballot invasion"', *Dotmsr.com*, 19 March (Arabic). <https://bit.ly/2NEx3aT>.

Kandiyoti, Deniz (1988), 'Bargaining with patriarchy', *Gender and Society*, 2: 3, special issue to honour Jessie Bernard, September, pp. 274–90, <https://bit.ly/2KNqRPW>.

—— (2013), 'Fear and fury: women and post-revolutionary violence', *Open Democracy*, 10 January, <https://www.opendemocracy.net/5050/deniz-kandiyoti/fear-and-fury-women-and-post-revolutionary-violence>.

—— (2014), 'Contesting patriarchy-as-governance: lessons from youth-led activism', *Open Democracy*, 7 March, <https://www.opendemocracy.net/5050/deniz-kandiyoti/contesting-patriarchy-as-governance-lessons-from-youth-led-activism>.

El Kholy, Heba (2002), *Defiance and Compliance, Negotiating Gender in Low-Income Cairo*, London: Berghahn Books.

Kumail12 (2016), 'Al-Azhar dean: Wahhabi/Salafi are not Sunnis', *YouTube*, 7 September, <https://www.youtube.com/watch?v=Gc1LhnzDHRw>.

Lacroix, Stephane (2016), 'Egypt's pragmatic Salafis: the Politics of Hizb al-Nour', *Carnegie Endowment for International Peace*, November, <http://ceip.org/2f8QpEr>.

McGreal, Chris and Julian Borger (2011), 'Tahrir Square protesters defy army to keep Egypt's revolution alive', *The Guardian*, 13 February, <https://www.theguardian.com/world/2011/feb/13/tahrir-square-protesters-egypt-revolution>.

McRobie, Heather (2014), 'The common factor: sexual violence and the Egyptian state, 2011–2014', *Open Democracy*, 6 October, <https://bit.ly/1BM2mCN>.

Madkour, Mona (2009), 'Egypt men slam giving women right to divorce', *Al Arabiya New*, 9 December, <https://www.alarabiya.net/articles/2009/12/09/93654.html>.

Magued, Amany (2015), 'Al-Azhar: authority and legitimacy', *Al-Ahram Weekly*, 1275, 17–30 December, <http://weekly.ahram.org.eg/News/15037.aspx>.

Maher, Hatem (2011), 'Egyptian army issues apology after woman stripped', *Ahram Online*, 20 December, <https://bit.ly/2L1bgbF>.

Mandour, Sahar (2017), 'Verbal divorce: a man-to-man fight in the "year of women"', *Mada Masr*, 14 March, translated from Arabic by Asma Naguib, <https://bit.ly/2Lo4iqw>.

Marsad (2017), 'Egypt blocks 405 websites', 29 August (Arabic), <https://bit.ly/2KZohTn>.

Al-Masry al-Youm (2011), 'Thousands of women marching in protest against army violations', 20 December (Arabic), <http://www.almasryalyoum.com/news/details/135459>.

El Masry, Sahar (2013), 'Al-Azhar of post-revolutionary Egypt', *Daily News Egypt*, 20 March, <https://dailynewsegypt.com/2013/03/20/al-azhar-of-post-revolutionary-egypt/>.

Mohei, Mostapha (2014), 'The state and sexual violence', *Mada Masr*, 16 June (Arabic), <https://bit.ly/2L3u6Pq>.

Mourad, Mahmoud and Yara Bayoumy (2015), 'Special report: Egypt deploys scholars to teach moderate Islam, but skepticism abounds', *Reuters*, 31 May, <https://reut.rs/2NDHQ5i>.

Moussa, Jasmine (n.d.), 'The reform of *shari'a*-derived divorce legislation in Egypt: international standards and the cultural debate', <https://www.nottingham.ac.uk/hrlc/documents/publications/hrlcommentary2005/divorcelegislationegypt.pdf >.

Nagel, Joane (1998), 'Masculinity and nationalism: gender and sexuality in the making of nations, *Ethnic and Racial Studies*, 21: 2, pp. 242–69. Published online on 2 December 2010, <https://www.tandfonline.com/doi/abs/10.1080/014198798330007>.

Radsch, Courtney C. (2016), *Cyberactivism and Citizens Journalism in Egypt: Digital Dissidents and Political Change*, New York: Palgrave Macmillan.

Saleh, Heba (2017), 'Sunni clerics in Sisi sights after ISIS targets Christians, *Financial Times*, 16 May, <https://www.ft.com/content/0d96c2d4-3623-11e7-bce4-9023f8c0fd2e>.

Shahine, Gihan (2013), 'Risks to Al-Azhar?', *Al-Ahram Weekly*, 1157, 18–24 July <http://weekly.ahram.org.eg/News/3403.aspx>.

El Shalakany, Sarah (2017) 'Sisi call to annul verbal divorce sparks controversy', *Al-Monitor*, 20 February (translated from Arabic by Sahar Ghoussoub), <https://www.al-monitor.com/pulse/originals/2017/02/egypt-sisi-call-law-annul-verbal-divorce.html>.

Shams El-Din, Mai (2012), 'Activists testify in virginity tests case, verdicts expected March 11', *Daily News Egypt*, 26 February, <https://dailynewsegypt.com/2012/02/26/activists-testify-in-virginity-tests-case-verdict-expected-march-11/>.

Shams El-Din, Mai (2017), 'The cleric and the president: Egypt's critical power struggle', *Mada Masr*, 12 March <https://www.madamasr.com/en/2017/03/12/feature/politics/the-cleric-and-the-president-egypts-critical-power-struggle/>.

Al Sherbini, Ramadan (2017), 'Egyptian lawmakers reject attacks on Al Azhar', *Gulf News*, 11 May, <http://gulfnews.com/news/mena/egypt/egyptian-lawmakers-reject-attacks-on-al-azhar-1.2025895>.

El-Sisi Inauguration Speech (2014), *Rotana Masreya*, 8 June (Arabic), <https://www.youtube.com/watch?v=vK8Rh_8FTrU>.

Sonneveld, Nadia (2004), 'The implementation of the "Khul' Law" in Egyptian courts: some preliminary results', *Recht Van de Islam*, 21, pp. 21–35.

Tadros, Mariz (2002), 'The third option', *Al-Ahram weekly*, 610, 31 October – 6 November, <https://bit.ly/2MXNWMs>.

Tadros, Mariz (2016), 'Challenging reified masculinities: men as survivors of politically motivated sexual assaults in Egypt', *Journal of Middle East Women Studies*, 12: 3, November, pp. 323–42.

El-Tayeb, Ahmed (2013), 'Statement by Al-Azhar Grand Imam', *YouTube*, 14 August (Arabic), <https://www.youtube.com/watch?v=sKEAxbZKLug>.

Trager, Eric (2016), 'Sisi's fracturing regime, *Foreign Policy*, 22 January, <http://foreignpolicy.com/2016/01/22/sisis-fracturing-regime/>.

Wahba, Nadine (quoted in Sarah A. Topol) (2012), 'Sexual assault as political tool: men attacking women at Tahrir Square', *The Daily Beast*, 6 October, <https://www.thedailybeast.com/sexual-assault-as-political-tool-men-attacking-women-at-tahrir-square>.

Zaki-Chakravarti, Leila, (2014), 'From strongman to superman: Sisi the saviour of Egypt', *Open Democracy*, 28 April, <https://www.opendemocracy.net/5050/leila-zaki-chakravarti/from-strongman-to-superman-sisi-saviour-of-egypt>.

Zeghal, Malika (1999), 'Religion and politics in Egypt: the ulema of Al-Azhar, radical Islam and the state (1952–1994)', *International Journal of Middle East Studies*, 31: 3, August, pp. 371–99. Published online at <http//www.jstpr.org/stable/176217>.

Chapter 3

Manufacturing Consent in Iran: from Moral Subjects to (Un)Healthy Citizens[1]

Nazanin Shahrokni

In the Abbas Abad hills in north-east Tehran is the Mothers' Paradise, one of the city's 2,135 parks and the first of its five women-only parks. Founded in 2007, the Mothers' Paradise spreads over an area of about thirty-seven acres. Women are not banned from attending mixed parks, but their presence in these parks – like in all other public spaces – is conditional upon their donning the veil. In the Mothers' Paradise, in the absence of men, women are allowed to take off their veils and wear the clothing of their choice.[2] The park is equipped with fitness machines, a daycare centre, a playground, a three-mile bike trail, a library, a health centre, picnic areas and chess tables. An all-female staff of more than seventy employees runs the park. Female guards hired by the Iranian police department maintain security inside the park, and two male guards monitor the entrance to ensure that no man can enter the park or harass women outside the entrance.

In their public statements and media interviews, city and government officials alleged that the state provided parks to women out of a concern for women's health problems that arose from lack of fresh air and exercise. Yet in the 1980s, immediately after the Iranian revolution, women's outdoor exercise was seen as a problem – unnecessary, even un-Islamic, and thus prohibited. This chapter explores how the Iranian state came to see women-only parks as a solution to women's health problems. Today, the Iranian state not only coordinates women's group exercises in mixed parks, but also provides women with a green space of their own: one women-only park in each district of Tehran.

This chapter focuses on a single arena – the women-only parks – as a useful point of entry for a discussion of changing state practices and policies of gender segregation in the Islamic Republic of Iran. It examines what shifts in the politics of gender segregation can tell us about modes of state governance. I dispel the comfortably accepted assumption about the decisive role that Islam plays in the formation of the Iranian state's policies. I also move beyond the view of Iranian state power as essentially a system of top-down coercive projects and policies and flesh out the more productive side of its power – that is, the state's ability to produce new subjects, spaces, discourses and practices. I contend that analyses that reduce gender segregation to its Islamic (and therefore, ideological) dimensions tell us little about actual shifts in the Islamic Republic's modes of governance.

The literature on gender and Islam, often, decontextualises gender-segregated spaces, decoding them as though they have a fixed religious meaning separable from the full range of social relations, discourses and practices.[3] I approach these spaces not as bounded and static entities but as the producers and products of social meanings and processes (Massey 1994). It is often in the intersection of the political struggles over the interpretation of Islam (Mir-Hosseini 1999) and the state's negotiation of a distinct set of problems within a broad set of priorities that the true story of gender segregated spaces lies. I treat the creation of the Mothers' Paradise as an archive of the formation of the Islamic state that reveals the state's move toward developing its governmental arm. The Mothers' Paradise signifies the end point of a process in which the Iranian state, through dealing with the question of women's leisure and exercise activities in the parks, has moved away from governance through the application of prohibitive measures, that is the disabling of its undesired behaviours and practices through coercion, towards the use of productive ones, that is the enabling of its desired behaviours and practices through consent. The state still attempts to demarcate space and control women's bodily movements, but in this more productive mode, it does so by directing activity within defined spaces, rather than instating a blanket prohibition, and by using a discourse that permeates both the state and society and that justifies gender segregation as a response to publicly acknowledge health problems and not merely as a requirement for an Islamic order.

Understanding State Power in Iran

Despite the geopolitical importance of Iran and the mounting global concern over the state's practices at both the domestic and international levels, the Iranian state and its diverse mechanisms of rule have largely been neglected in mainstream sociology. Studies of state formation in Iran largely focus on the state's religious dimension or on its (trans)formation as a theocratic state (Arjomand 1988, 2009; Banuazizi 1994; Chehabi 1991; Moaddel 1986). Ali Banuazizi (1994), for example, shows how, by mobilising Islam as a source of legitimacy, the state has ironically contributed to the delegitimisation of clerics, who, as the bastions of religion, have come to be blamed for the failures of the Islamic state. Similarly, H. E. Chehabi (1991) points out that by drawing on Islam as the main source of its legitimacy, the Iranian state has created a legitimation crisis. By insisting on a narrow focus on Islam, these studies miss the possibility that the state may draw on multiple sources for its legitimacy. Additionally, most studies of the Iranian state focus on the state's negative, prohibitive and repressive power. These studies characterise the state as an Islamist state that thrives on its anti-American and anti-West rhetoric (Kraus 2010; Saghafi 2005), a patriarchal state that discriminates against women (Moallem 2001, 2005; Tohidi 2007), or an authoritarian state that curtails human rights (Miller 1996; Osanloo 2009). In most of these studies, the resilience of the Islamic Republic of Iran is attributed to its application of force, coercion and repression. This emphasis on repression raises questions as to why and how the state has survived. After all, 'power would be a fragile thing if its only function were to repress, if it worked only through the mode of censorship, exclusion, blockage and repression, in the manner of a great Superego, exercising itself only in a negative way' (Foucault 1980: 59). Overstating Iran's repressive power leads to the neglect of the various ways in which the state enables its desired effects, rather than (or alongside) disabling its undesired effects. Some exceptions aside (Harris 2017; Keshavarzian 2005; Najmabadi 2013), the Iranian state's productive power is rarely discussed.

Heeding Steinmetz's insights (1999), I move away from the conceptualisation of the formation of the Islamic Republic as an event that took place on 1 April 1979, and instead view it as a constant process whose ultimate product is contingent upon broader temporal and societal configurations (such as economy, politics and culture) occurring at both the domestic and international levels.[4] Steinmetz characterises states as constantly transforming entities that are 'shot through with circuits of meaning that cut across the state–society frontier' (Steinmetz 1999: 12). Instead of treating the state as a power that is separate from society and stands above and beyond it, as is the case with (neo-) Marxist and (neo-)Weberian approaches (Block 1987; Evans 1995; Evans et al. 1985; Jessop 1990), I take insights from the Foucauldian framework with its emphasis on governmentality, which is the exercise of power at a distance and through (not on) individuals (Barry et al. 1993; Dean 1999; Ferguson and Gupta 2002; Miller and Rose 1990; Mitchell 2005; Ong 2006). Governmentality is about the state's ability to rationalise its power, to articulate certain problems and offer certain strategies for solving those problems to further the wellbeing of its population (Lemke 2001).

The state, I argue, should not be conceived of in negative terms as something that represses, excludes, refuses, prohibits, disables and denies – in short as an exclusively coercive entity. The state maintains its dominance not just through coercion exercised by its repressive apparatuses, but also through manufacturing consent, that is its ability to secure the active consent of those over whom it rules (Carnoy 1986). In fact, what makes state power more effective is its ability to produce spaces, ideas, concepts and categories, and to reward and enable its desired subjects. The state as such turns into a force that runs through the whole social body and not as a force that stands above or separate from the society (Foucault 1991; 1995b).

Additionally, I argue that modern state power – including that of the Islamic Republic of Iran – cannot be studied as a singularity detached from the global and transnational context within which it is embedded. Following John Meyer (1999), I treat state power as 'devolving from a global (political) culture'. 'Culture,' Meyer argues, 'is less a set of values and norms, and more a set of cognitive models defining the nature, purpose, resources, technologies, controls and sovereignty of the proper nation-states' (Meyer 1999: 123). National elites around the world increasingly adopt 'world ideologies' (what I refer to as Western liberal discourses), a practice that leads to an increasing similarity among the 'categories of social problems' that various states 'recognize as warranting intervention' (Steinmetz 1999: 31).

Thus, the Iranian state officials presented the women-only parks, not merely as a site of Islamic governance, but as a solution to globally recognised health problems. To put a Gramscian slant on this conceptual framework, I suggest that Islamic discourse has finally become hegemonic to the extent that even initially proscribed spaces and activities for Iranian women are now made available within the parameters of Islamic regulation (that is, the segregation of space) but with reference to a universal public good, namely health. It is, therefore, a successful method of containing demands by decreeing their parameters (on pain of irrelevance, or worse, insubordination by totally ignoring demands.) The Mothers' Paradise represents multiple layers of historically shifting factors that have helped the Iranian state with manufacturing consent among its (female) citizens. By situating the Mothers' Paradise in the broader sociopolitical context within which it was produced, I peel back these layers and reveal the processes that have enabled the production of this park.[5]

Women's Outdoor Exercise: from Problem to Solution

Upon its establishment in 1979, the Islamic Republic of Iran sought to establish an Islamic public order through the 'moral purification' of public spaces (Najmabadi 1999). As the capital of the Islamic Republic of Iran, Tehran was to be transformed into an 'Islamic city'.[6] And since Islam is understood to value modesty, the free mixing of unrelated men and women was discouraged. Consequently, schools and university classrooms, public transportation and beaches were segregated along gender lines. The new state implemented gender segregation as one of the defining principles of an Islamic city,[7] and created a set of architectural and spatial imperatives to divide places along the gender lines, marking them with visual screens: walls, fences, curtains and signs that read 'for women only' or 'for men only'. During the 1980s, the state's regulation of gendered bodies appeared in the form of domination and prohibition, a power that stood above and outside its citizens.

However, the state's policies of prohibition were often contested and never complete. As I will show in detail in this chapter, this form of regulation was not entirely effective. It fell short of reaching into the obscure corners of everyday life, leaving room for resistant acts to ferment – acts that in their daily repetition transformed the very rules they were transgressing (Bayat 2010). In the decades that followed, the masculinised public space of the earlier post-revolutionary years gave way to a more feminised one, as women became increasingly mobile and frequented public spaces of the city as workers, students and consumers. This was accompanied by the development of a feminist consciousness among the youth, especially women, which shaped many of their demands and activities (Kurzman 2008). Faced with a new generation of women who had become vocal about their rights and laid claims to various city spaces, the state was prompted to accommodate these new conditions and backtrack to a more inclusive agenda.

In historically locating the state's regulation of women's outdoor exercises and its production of women-only parks, this chapter highlights the gradual expansion of women's access to the city which has been accompanied by their discursive transformation as subjects of Islamic morality ('sisters'), to rights-bearing citizens in need of the state's protective and welfare services. The deepening of gender segregation practices, then, signifies a gradual expansion – and not contraction – of women's access to the city. In what follows I zoom in on the Mothers' Paradise, as an illustrative case of gender segregation in Tehran, to chart shifts in Iranian state power and its move from prohibitive to productive forms of power, set against the background of internal political struggles, on the one hand, and pressure from the circulation of globalised norms and commodities, on the other.

Women's exercise as a problem of Islamic morality

During the 1979 revolution and the early 1980s, while the Islamic Republic consolidated its political rule at home and fought a territorial war on the international front, moral corruption was viewed as 'the lynch-pin of imperialist designs'. Within such a framework, women were simultaneously subjects and symbols of Islamic morality; their bodies were both onstage, and stages on which various politics and ideologies played out. Protecting women's chastity meant upholding the Islamic identity of the city and, by extension, the state. There were conflicts among the revolutionaries as to how drastic the gender segregation measures should be. Nevertheless, 'even as the Iran–Iraq war raged, prominent conservative figures took the line that the struggle over moral issues should not take a back seat' (Khatam 2009). In fact, in April 1979, Ayatollah Khomeini ordered the Revolutionary Council to create a morality bureau that would uproot corrupt pre-revolutionary cultural habits and prosecute cases of 'prohibited activities'. The morality police rigidly enforced 'Islamic' codes of behaviour in the streets, workplace and parks of Iranian cities (Khatam 2009).

Under such circumstances, leisure sports came to be considered unnecessary and un-Islamic. Former Tehran governor Hassan Ghafourifard recalled in a 1986 interview that 'in such an atmosphere, when I was the governor, I remember someone called and asked me if playing volleyball was *haram* [religiously forbidden]'. Sports were considered *haram* or at best a form of boisterous carousing' (*Zan e Rooz* 1986). Women's sports and leisure-time activities especially were seen as morally decadent and therefore were considered unnecessary and prohibited. The regime's main concern with regard to women was to craft pious mothers; the question of women's leisure and/or physical exercise was addressed in a prohibitive way, by determining where women could not go and what they could not do. The dominant view was that in an Islamic public order, the home should be valorised as the woman's place, unless the 'common good' required women to step out to show their support for the new regime. Shahla Habibi, Iran's presidential adviser of women's affairs in the 1990s, recalled in her interview with me how difficult it was to get officials, such as Ghafourifard, to support women's sports and make them less taboo by speaking publicly about them.

Issues from that period of *Zan e Rooz* magazine, founded in 1964 and one of the oldest women's weeklies in Iran, provide a window to the atmosphere of public parks in those days. Its reports suggest that under such circumstances women's outdoor exercise in the parks had turned into a stressful activity. Their daily exercise was, therefore, often carried out under the suspicious gaze of male guards and the morality police, who would monitor their activities to make sure that no rule was breached and that their moves were in accordance with the Islamic codes and not provocative. During this time, the state's regulation of gendered bodies appeared in the form of domination and prohibition, a power that stood above and outside its citizens. The new state relied on a 'politics of masculinist restoration', which as Kandiyoti (2014) states, is a politics that 'requires systematic [Islamic] indoctrination, greater surveillance and higher levels of intrusion in citizens' lives'.

In the same interview, Ghafourifard suggests that new social restrictions had made it necessary for the state to build indoor exercise and sports facilities for women:

> In general three tasks should be carried out before women are able to exercise: (1) erase the negative image of women's sports which has been inherited from the previous regime, (2) avoid extremist [fundamentalist] behaviour, (3) provide women with necessary sports facilities.

But women could not wait until these three conditions were fulfilled, and, as the national budget was spent mostly on the war with Iraq (1980–8), there was little indication that these tasks would be completed any time soon. Thus, in the 1980s, despite frequent warnings and interruptions by the guards, those women who were enthusiastic about outdoor group exercise, although still few in number, would go to the parks to silently and secretly perform their morning exercises. This 'quiet encroachment' (Bayat 2010) by individual women is evidence of the futility of prohibitive measures. In fact, as Khatam (2009) points out, as time went by 'it was clear that the morality police had lost its power to intimidate'.

By the 1990s, Tehran's landscape began to look different. Women were gradually being included in public spaces – albeit spaces that were segregated – as shifts in social, political and economic imperatives slowly but surely drove women into the spaces of work, education and consumption, demonstrating the failure of 'the ideology of domesticity' promoted by the Islamic Republic (Moghadam 1988). Several factors contributed to this shift. Ironically, their mobility outside the home, and across the city, was partially enabled by the initial gender segregation plans in the 1980s.[8] In the meantime, 'the populist considerations of the Islamic state, the religious ideal of charity, the Iran–Iraq war,[9] and the US-led economic sanctions led to the emergence of a welfare state' that provided state-funded social services in different areas, including, but not limited to, health and education. All these services induced changes in the size, structure and social functions of the family (Ladier-Fouladi 2002). The fertility rate decreased, the age of first marriage increased, and, following the successful state-funded family-planning programme, the annual population growth rate declined from 3.4 per cent in 1986 to 1.5 per cent (Hoodfar and Assadpour 2000). These demographic shifts further facilitated women's entrance into the public spaces of the city. Additionally, the growth in the rate of divorce and the lagging number of new marriages left many women in charge of their own lives, further necessitating their entrance into the city. Thus, during the 1990s, the gradual weakening of women's ties to the domestic sphere, along with the expansion of spaces of education, work, leisure and consumption, brought women out of their homes and into schools, jobs, shopping malls and parks.

Long before these developments, one of the male members of the Iranian parliament had expressed his concerns about the 'threat' of women's work, and had stated: 'In Islamic society woman's upkeep is the responsibility of her husband and she should not have to work ... If this changes, everything will change; there will be no submission by women' (Paidar 2007: 323). By the 1990s, to the deputy's dismay, 'everything [had] changed'. It had become clear to state officials that prohibition as a strategy of governance was unsuccessful. The Islamic Republic had run up against all sorts of resistance in the matter of gender, not least because there was a lively women's movement both among Islamists and the more secular oriented. The paradox of revolutionary mobilisation is that it unwittingly creates the very conditions that stimulate expectations for more participatory citizenship that up the stakes in the race to manufacture consent.

Women's exercise as a solution to 'Western cultural invasion'

In the 1990s, with the termination of the eight-year war with Iraq, the reconstruction era began, under the presidency of Hashemi Rafsanjani (Karshenas and Pesaran 1995). With the appointment[10] in 1990 of Gholamhossein Karbaschi as the mayor of Tehran, the city embarked on a path to growth and development (Adelkhah 2000). The new mayor of Tehran was well aware of the fact that, with the diminishing of revolutionary zeal in the post-war reconstruction era, the new middle class was moving away from 'the republic of piety' (Moruzzi and Sadeghi 2006); something other than the revolution and war monuments was needed for the citizenry to develop a sense of belonging to the city.

Thus, through the municipality's efforts, both the appearance of the city and its relationship to its inhabitants were transformed. The cult of citizenship and 'the right to the city' were promoted. 'Our City, Our Home!' was a slogan used by the mayor to generate a sense of belonging to, respect for and entitlement to the city. Tension was escalating over how to maintain the ethical order. This was mainly due to the conflicts within and between different state apparatuses, which, as many have pointed out, have existed since the inception of the new regime (Arjomand 2009; Keshavarzian 2005; Takeyh 2006). Said Amir Arjomand (2009) points specifically to the emergence of hardliner and reformist factions as a result of revolutionary power struggles in the post-Khomeini era.[11] Therefore, while the conservative faction of the state continued to push for the adoption of prohibitive measures, the municipality, with the backing of Rafsanjani as the president, leaned towards the application of productive measures by opening up the urban space to different sectors of society, including women, who had become a major force in the society. As Alex Shams (2015) notes: 'Between 1989 and 1995 alone, for example, the number of parks leaped from 184 to 680, and the level of green space available on per capita level jumped from two square meters to eleven, despite a rapidly growing population.'

During the early 1990s, the state faced several dilemmas. While local governments were preoccupied with the citizens' attachment to the city, the central government was planning a turn towards a free market economy. Following World Bank-inspired structural adjustment policies, Rafsanjani's goal was to renew the country's ties with the world and develop an economy that was well integrated into the global economy. Advocating a free market economy might have been helpful in temporarily saving Iran from a post-war economic crisis; nevertheless, like many other state projects and policies, it produced undesired effects as well. Opening the domestic market to consumer imports as part of the liberalisation of the economy (and as a salve to a war-deprived population) also brought unintended consequences along the lines of what Ayatollah Khamenei, the leader of the Islamic Republic, labelled 'cultural invasion'. Western (cultural) products had 'invaded' the domestic market through widespread informal and black-market networks. These 'alarming' social developments generated a sense of urgency among some state officials to advocate for the expansion of public spaces and spheres. Some realised that the state could no longer rely merely on prohibition and the banning of Western cultural products (as the new technologies had made it difficult and costly to monitor each and all individuals); these officials advocated that, instead, the state should produce alternative (cultural) products and spaces.

It was at this time that the idea of women-only parks first came into being. In 1993, the Presidential Centre of Women's Affairs and Participation, led by Shahla Habibi, pushed Tehran Municipality to convert the seventy-five-acre Taleghani Park into a women-only park so that 'women could exercise in open air with their gym clothes and without the veil' (*Zan e Rooz* 1993). The municipality's rationale for providing alternative spaces of leisure and exercise was the importance of directing attention away from the infiltrating Western cultural goods and preventing the consumption patterns associated with such goods. 'Since the Western countries do everything in their capacity to corrupt [our] youth,' said Shahla Habibi in an interview with *Zan e Rooz* (1993), 'the lack of healthy sports and entertainment facilities could have dangerous implications for our youth and teenagers.' Here emerges a discourse that refers to exercise and sports not as a problem but as a solution to the problems associated with the 'Western cultural invasion'. The importance of physical exercise for women's health is only introduced as an afterthought. In the same interview, Habibi refers to the opening of women-only parks and similar acts as a necessity; she highlights the implications of such acts for the mental and physical health of the population and invites women to show their support for such projects by attending the park and using its facilities.

But as Habibi explained in my 2009 interview with her, the project initially suffered from poor advertising and a lack of cooperation from other state organisations. The municipality did not fully convert the park into a women-only park; instead it implemented the necessary security measures to reserve the park exclusively for women only on Saturdays,[12] Mondays and Wednesdays from 6 a.m. to 4 p.m. The project was a failure, not just because other state institutions did not cooperate, but also because, despite Habibi's call, women showed little interest in using the space. Jane Fonda Workout videos had just found their way into the houses of the well-to-do families, and aerobics and physical exercise had not yet become popular. Thus, Taleghani Park was deserted on women-only days. Soon the empty space was reclaimed by men, leaving the park as an example of the state's failed attempt to create a women-only park in the early 1990s.

Nevertheless, during the same period, Habibi had also expressed hope that the parks of all districts in Tehran would allocate a specific space for women's sports and exercise activities, and this call created a chain of activities in district municipalities. As a result, district municipalities became equipped with women's sports offices, which were mostly responsible for organising and coordinating women's morning and group exercises, now conducted under the supervision of female instructors in public parks, where women, still observing their *hijab*, could do aerobics and stretching exercises – something unimaginable a decade earlier. This is important, as it paved the way for women's increased ability to claim their own space of authority in the years that followed.[13] This, and similar developments in the years that followed, marked the engagement of women in what Kandiyoti (1988) has labelled as patriarchal bargain,

> A set of strategies to demand protection, maximise security, and optimise life options in exchange for submissiveness and propriety, and without challenging the boundaries set by the system.

Consequently, women's morning exercises and competitions in public parks were no longer policed by the state, but rather organised by it. As the state started to (re)shape the public space to accommodate women's presence, it simultaneously increased its grip over previously unregulated spaces of everyday life. The state in this way exercised a more effective form of power that was focused more on regulation than prohibition and was more concerned with the enabling of desired practices than with the disabling of undesired ones. The story of the gradual (re)opening of the space for women, therefore, is the story of the gradual (re)orientation of state power.

Women's exercise as a solution to health problems

With the election of Mohammad Khatami, the reformist candidate, in the 1996 presidential elections, the reform era (1996–2004) began. This period was characterised by the state's move toward political liberalisation, as opposed to the economic liberalisation of the previous era (Behdad 2001; Boroujerdi 2004). Khatami was less interested in economic policy, but since that was still controlled by other factions, economic liberalisation continued. In this era, two decades after the establishment of the Islamic Republic of Iran, the problems related to and/or caused by the earlier state projects and national trends started to surface.

A post-revolution population spike, which peaked in the 1980s, meant that there was an enormous baby-boom generation growing up, whose families expected to be provided with opportunities for health and education. At the same time, the global commercialisation of Western leisure products and practices had put Iran in a disadvantageous position vis-à-vis the West in what was termed the 'cultural war'. The loosening attachment to the revolutionary and religious ideals and values thus turned into one of the greatest concerns of the state. Official governmental reports, such as a 2009 report published by the High Council of Iranian Youth, listed factors responsible for the expansion of 'morally corrupt networks': unemployment; the 'marriage crisis' (the increasing age of marriage for both men and women, caused at least in part by the increasing expense of beginning a new household); and the lack of cultural, sports and entertainment spaces and facilities.

After two decades of unsuccessful attempts to reinforce bans on Western (cultural) products, different factions within the state acknowledged the need for the provision of alternative spaces, even if in the name of 'cultural defence'. They unanimously agreed on what the problem was: a lack of conviviality, entertainment and sports facilities (*Salam* 1999). Different policy-making institutions and organisations with different political affiliations passed bills or designed proposals demanding the allocation of sufficient funds and resources for the organisation and facilitation of leisure-time activities for both women and youths. Within this atmosphere, the idea of women-only parks was revived.

On 17 May 2004, *Ettelaat*, one of Tehran's leading daily newspapers, published a news story questioning the postponement of the construction of women-only parks and pointed to a report published in 2000 by the 'social and cultural experts' at the Education and Training Organisation of Tehran (ETO), which contained information about schoolgirls' poor health conditions. The report suggested that due to their lack of access to sports facilities and thus their lack of physical activity, schoolgirls were suffering from various bone and joint diseases. This, the report suggested, was partially the outcome of the state's earlier project of urban development and partially caused by women's obligation to veil and cover their bodies in public.[14] The report also suggested that the covering, which is required by law, had caused a lack of exposure to sunlight, which in turn caused hair loss (see also *Iran* 2001). The same news story quoted Masoomeh Taghi, the adviser to the director of the ETO, describing 'women's access to natural and green spaces in big cities' as their 'natural right'. One of the main recommendations listed in the report and the news piece was that the city facilitate the expansion of space for schoolgirls' sports by creating women-only parks. While in the earlier decades women's exercise was formulated as an antidote to the 'Western cultural invasion' – with considerations for women's health only as an afterthought – in this report, the health aspect is brought to the fore and women-only parks are presented as a solution to public health problems.

The 2002 bill permitting the municipality to pursue the creation of women-only parks reads:

> With respect to mothers'[15] constructive position, their role in the growth of society, their emotional and educational centrality within the family, and their effective role in the process of human cultivation and reduction of social pathologies, and with the aim of boosting their mental and physical capabilities, directing their leisure time, and providing them with appropriate opportunities for healthy entertainments in Tehran, the municipality is obliged to provide and allocate proper spaces in the existing parks. Furthermore, it will design and establish exclusive spaces in Tehran to be called 'Mothers' Parks'. (Tehran City Council 2002)

Turning the bill into a national policy, the Ministry of Interior sent a directive to all of the provincial governors asking them 'to consult with the women's affairs offices and municipalities to locate a space of at least 107,000 square feet, which could be immediately purchased and transformed into a cultural and entertainment hub for women' (*Iran* 2007). Despite the support from the government, the bill was not acted upon. In 2003, Mahmoud Ahmadinejad, then the newly appointed conservative mayor of Tehran, retrieved the bill from the archives. He demanded that the Tehran Parks and Green Space Organisation locate the ideal spots across Tehran and convert them, whether partially or in their entirety, to women-only parks. Four parks from among the 2,135 existing parks were chosen.

Meanwhile, Mayor Ahmadinejad tried to push for the construction of the first women-only park in Tehran. But his attempts failed partly because of the political opposition he received from the Presidential Centre for Women's Affairs and Participation, headed by the reformist Zahra Shojaee, who allegedly blocked the budget allocated for the creation of such parks (*Iran* 2007). At this point, the state was totally fragmented. The administration and the parliament were in the hands of the reformist faction while the Tehran City Council and Tehran Municipality were in the hands of the conservatives. Thus, although the push for the creation of women-only parks had originally come in 2002 from the reformist-led Ministry of Interior, the Presidential Centre for Women's Affairs and Participation obstructed the municipality's formation of these parks, due to the reformists' political rivalry with the conservatives in Tehran's municipal government and their competing visions about women's provisions.[16] In her 2009 interview with me, Fereshteh Alimohammadi, the city expert who had prepared the final proposal for the Tehran City Council, claimed that the tensions had nothing to do with the parks per se but were about 'who delivers, who gets the credit for such provision'. By this time, both factions within the state had realised that their legitimacy and popularity depended on how well they provided for the population.

In 2005, Ahmadinejad became Iran's president and Mohammad Baqir Qalibaf, another conservative, replaced Ahmadinejad as mayor of Tehran. Upon assuming the mayorship, Qalibaf announced that he would not launch new projects because he would instead finish what his predecessor had left unfinished; among these projects was the creation of women-only parks. With a conservative heading the municipality and a conservative now in the presidential office, there was no political opposition to the project. Thus, in 2007, the Mothers' Paradise, Iran's first women-only park, was opened in the north-east of Tehran and, in 2008, the Women's Paradise was opened in the south-east of the city. The three other women-only parks were constructed in subsequent years.

Reaffirming the 2002 bill, these parks were designed to fulfil women's need for exercise and leisure. That the officials made the effort to formulate the construction of women-only parks, not in terms of the requirements of an Islamic morality but in terms of women's need for exercise, is not surprising if we take into account that according to 'data from two values surveys conducted by researchers from the University of Tehran, Iran' in 2000 and 2005, 'the stress on the Islamic identity of the nation [by the Iranian government]' has begot 'oppositional responses from Iranians' (Moaddel 2010: 535). Moaddel argues that among the Iranian population there is a shift toward 'social individualism, liberal democracy, [and] gender equality', and also an increasing demand on the state to 'take more responsibility for meeting citizens' needs' (Moaddel 2010: 535, 542).[17] Under such circumstances, to maintain its legitimacy, the Islamic Republic of Iran has had to develop a governmental arm that provides for its citizens. In response to the patriarchal bargain, the state relied on what a colleague and I have labelled 'patriarchal accommodation', policies and practices that adapted to and accommodated new forms of female mobility and presence, yet formally enshrined gender differences associated with male dominance (Andrews and Shahrokni 2014). Gender segregation as a system of urban governance remains intact.

Furthermore, women-only parks provided an opportunity for the Iranian state to reconstruct its image in the international arena by presenting itself as a provider and protector – rather than a violator – of women's rights. Ahmadinejad's coming to power as president heightened animosity from the US and its allies, but the construction of women-only parks in 2007 earned the praise not only of the clerics in Qom, but also of the *Agence France-Presse* (2008) reporter, for example, who was amused to see Iranian women in 'spaghetti strap vests and lycra shorts'. Later Qalibaf was acknowledged and awarded for his efforts as the mayor of Tehran by both the City Mayor Foundation and the Washington-based International Institute for Transportation and Development Policy.

Manufacturing Consent

Women's outdoor exercise in public parks, once characterised as unnecessary and un-Islamic, is now encouraged and promoted by the state. The language used in the officials' interviews and reports on women-only parks highlights the shift in the state's attitude towards women's leisure-time activities and exercise. Women are now recognised as both mothers of the nation (with needs) and citizens (with rights), whose health is in danger and who therefore must be 'served' by the state. 'As citizens, they have paid their dues during the revolution and the war,' wrote 175 ministers of parliament in a letter, stating that it is now the state's obligation to serve them (*Resalat* 2006). In various interviews with the press, Rasool Khadem, the head of the Social and Cultural Commission of the City Council of Tehran; Mohammad-Ali, the legal adviser to the commission; and Soheila Jelodarzadeh, MP, all emphasise that women as citizens have the right to freely and comfortably exercise in public – a right that, as they all say, had long been forgotten. Emphasising the responsibilities of the state toward its citizens, Zahra Moshir, the head of the Women's Office of Tehran Municipality, points to the results of a survey of Tehrani women that was conducted in 2006: 'The survey showed that access to sports and entertainment hubs was ranked first among women's requests of the municipality. Thus, we decided to seriously pursue the project of constructing women-only parks' (*Resalat* 2006). Mokhtari, the head of the Parks and Green Space Organisation of Tehran Municipality, says: 'If, because of our religious and moral beliefs, we impose specific codes of conduct on women, then we have to provide them with a space where they can enjoy the green space peacefully and securely' (*Javan* 2003).

The Mothers' Paradise, the first park of its kind in Tehran, now hosts more than 1,000 women per day (*Abrar* 2008). Although as early as the late 1980s some state officials had expressed concerns over the lack of exercise space for women and its negative impact on their mental and physical health, the first attempt to establish a women-only park in 1993 failed partly because women, as the potential users of this space, did not see the merits of the project and showed no interest in using a women-only park. The success of this new emphasis on the discourse of 'women's health' and its appeal to women can only be understood in the context of the global focus on the mechanisms of achieving a healthy body. Across the globe there is a focus on cultivating healthy bodies through proper nutrition and sufficient exercise. In a recent event organised by Tehran Municipality, around 7,000 senior citizens gathered in Velayat Park in southern Tehran to promote health week.[18] While in the early 1990s, the Jane Fonda Workout videos were found only in the well-to-do houses, there are now thousands of yoga and aerobics classes across the country, including in religious cities like Mashhad, Isfahan and even Qom (Moaveni 2008, 2009). In this case, the Iranian state uses the 'unhealthy' bodies of Iranian women – allegedly the result of compulsory veiling – to justify the 'need' for the opening of women-only parks. The undisciplined subjects of Iranian women with their unhealthy bodies come to signify simultaneously the failure and the success of the system (Foucault 1980: 195–6).

Mansoureh, one of the female exercise instructors of Tehran Municipality, states in her interview with me that the municipality aims to 'provide' women with one women-only park in each district of Tehran. 'Women want more of these parks,' Mansoureh rightly claims. When I shared this news with a group of women in the Mothers' Paradise, they all welcomed the 'much-delayed' initiative. Women want more of what the state wants them to want. However, there is more at stake here than internalising the norms of the Islamic Republic. As Moruzzi and Sadeghi (2006) point out: 'The decline of formal traditionalism has meant that gender inequality has evolved into specifically modern forms: sexual harassment on the street, gender discrimination in the workplace.' In their interviews with young women across the religious spectrum, many have complained of the sexual saturation of the youth public sphere, including the real spaces of parks and shopping areas. Thus, there is a small step from this reality to the state posing as women's protector.

In the process, the line between 'interest at the level of the consciousness of each individual' and 'interest considered as the interest of the population' becomes blurry (Foucault 1991: 100). This completes the process through which, in dealing with women's outdoor exercise and activities, the Iranian state shifted from relying on its sovereign power to prohibit to using its governmental power to provide and produce. Instead of prohibiting outdoor exercise in the name of Islam, it produces new spaces, and it 'rationalises' and 'justifies' the need for these segregated spaces by drawing on modern authoritative concepts and discourses such as urban justice, women's rights and public health. In doing so, the state ultimately enables its desired behaviours and practices, such as women exercising separately from men, not through coercion and prohibition but through protection and provision. Basically, showing that no regime is insulated from the need to retain legitimacy and manufacture consent.

Conclusion

The Mothers' Paradise stands on top of the Abbas Abad hills as a sign of the productivity of state power in Iran and the rulers' pragmatism and flexibility trying to contain a society through consent rather than naked coercion. Instead of being the product of a coercive and vertical state initiative founded on religious justifications, this park is the product of a consensual state initiative which draws on various justificatory discourses that permeate the boundaries of state and society. The state officials mobilised a variety of authoritative modern discourses (for example, public health and the 'right to the city') on both local and global scales and with both Islamic and secular orientations to promote women-only parks and to secure women's support for them. The fact that Iran is an Islamic republic does not mean that it can only have recourse to Islamic arguments: women as healthy citizens and mothers of the nation is old in Iranian nationalism and certainly predates the Islamic Republic (Amin 2009; Najmabadi 1999). Therefore, the state officials could revive this repertoire when needed.

The story of the creation of the Mothers' Paradise reveals shifts in the Islamic state's modes of governance, from its reliance on the application of prohibitive measures to the development of productive measures. I argue that three major factors contributed to this shift: first, after the stage of revolutionary exceptionalism passed, and post-revolutionary fatigue prevailed, the Islamic Republic had to conform to expectations, both at home and globally, about 'modern' states. In the early days after the revolution, the newly formed state was concerned with establishing its control over the Iranian territory and developing an Islamic order. But once the state was consolidated, and after the end of the eight-year war with Iraq, it found itself caught up in a web of unexpected consequences resulting from its earlier policies of compulsory veiling and its policies of urban development. Tehran had turned into a jam-packed, polluted and depressed city of more than eight million. Women's reported mental and physical health problems, which were associated with veiling and the depressive, confined lifestyle promoted by the state, pointed to the failures of a system that promised women dignity and integrity.

Second, the state found it futile to try and impose a gender-segregated spatial order in the face of bottom-up pressures. Women's disregard of the bans on women's exercise in public places and their continuous presence in mixed-gender parks pointed to the ineffectiveness of the state's prohibitive and disciplinary measures (Amir-Ebrahimi 2006; Bayat 2010). Moreover, women's rising levels of education and the fact that they had become more economically active by necessity, led to them developing a sense of entitlement to city spaces and voting with their feet. Their demands for broader access to public spaces could no longer be dismissed or overlooked. Finally, it had become difficult for the state to keep global influence at bay and insulate women from global trends. With the globalisation of cultural and political products and practices, Iran found itself in a disadvantageous position vis-à-vis the West, in which the banning of Western products was no longer feasible.

It was against this background that Iranian state power was reconfigured into a more effective and productive form. This transformation was achieved by reorganising everyday life, an attempt that was partially carried out through the reconfiguration of space along gender lines and the provision and production of new (although still separate) spaces for women. Various scholars (Abrahamian 1982, 1993) have pointed out that the populist streak was very strong in the revolution from the start, therefore the Islamic Republic has to constantly find ways of satisfying the populations' aspirations and demands. But, as shown in this chapter, the state's ability to do so depends on the resources at its disposal and the mechanism of redistribution they use. If these start falling apart, especially in a failing economy, as Keshavarzian (2015) points out, the state could find itself deprived of the compliant citizenry it craves.

Notes

1. This chapter is a revised version of an earlier, much shorter, article published in the *Journal of Middle East Women's Studies*, 10: 3 (Fall 2014), pp. 87–108.
2. Veiling in Iran is compulsory by law. All women (of any religion or nationality) must cover their hair and wear some type of outer garment over their clothes when appearing in public.
3. For an exception, see Le Renard (2014).
4. See also Corrigan and Sayer (1985), Joseph and Nugent (1994) and Ong (2006).
5. This chapter is based on a larger research project on the politics of gender segregation in Iran. The data presented here is based on sixteen months of fieldwork in Tehran, Iran, between 2008 and 2013. During my fieldwork, I conducted participant observation, interviews and archival study. For this chapter, I conducted a total of eighty-two formal and informal interviews with women I recruited from convenience samples. I also reviewed 153 newspaper clippings and government documents on gender segregation from 1979 to 2011.
6. For a different take on Islamic city, see AlSayyad and Massoumi (2010).
7. See Abu-Lughod (1987).
8. For an analysis of similar effects in higher education, see Mehran (2003).
9. Scholars (Koolaee 2014; Paidar 1997) have argued that while the Iran–Iraq war

had a significant impact on women's lives and in many ways opened up the space for their social participation (that is, providing logistic support in the headquarters, charity work, and so on), women's employment rate during the 1980s declined, mostly because of the decline in private sector jobs that, particularly in rural areas, provided women with low-skill job opportunities such as handicrafts (Bahramitash and Salehi Esfahani 2011).

10. Until 1999, the mayor was appointed by the Ministry of Interior. In 1999, Iran held its first-ever elections to the city and village councils. Since then, the city councils have been responsible for electing the mayor.
11. Ayatollah Ruhollah Khomeini was the leader of the 1979 revolution. Following the success of the revolution, he became the country's supreme leader. He died on 3 June 1989 and was succeeded by Ali Khamenei.
12. Saturdays are not a part of the weekend in Iran.
13. For an account of how some government-initiated programmes similarly encouraged women's activism, see Homa Hoodfar's article on health workers in Iran (2010).
14. For more on urban development, see Ehsani (1999).
15. Note the transformation of 'schoolgirls' into 'mothers'. It seems that women could only be provided for as 'mothers'.
16. Zahra Shojaee, the director of the Presidential Centre for Women's Affairs, claimed that women's main demand was employment and not entertainment (*Shargh* 2003).
17. See also Kurzman (2008) and Moruzzi and Sadeghi (2006).
18. Available at <http://ipsf.ir/fa/news/nte41871> (last accessed 25 February 2014).

Bibliography

Abrar (2008), 'How much fun we could have, without men!' (in Persian), 13 November.
Abrahamian, Ervand (1993), *Khomeinism: Essays on the Islamic Republic*, Berkeley: University of California Press.
—— (1982), *Iran between Two Revolutions*, Princeton: Princeton University Press.
Abu-Lughod, Janet (1987), 'The Islamic city-historic myth, Islamic essence, and contemporary relevance', *International Journal of Middle East Studies*, 19: 2, pp. 155–76.
Adelkhah, Fariba (2000), *Being Modern in Iran*, New York: Columbia University Press.
Agence France-Presse (2008), 'Iranian women strip down in "Mothers" Paradise', 17 June 2008.
AlSayyad, Nezar and M. Massoumi (2010), *The Fundamentalist City? Religiosity and the Remaking of the Urban Space*, New York: Routledge.
Amin, Camron M. (2009), *The Making of the Modern Iranian Woman: Gender, State Policy, and Popular Culture*, Gainsville, FL: University Press of Florida.
Amir-Ebrahimi, Masserat (2006), 'Conquering enclosed public spaces,' *Cities*, 23, pp. 455–61.
Andrews, Abigail and Nazanin Shahrokni (2014), 'Patriarchal accommodation: women's mobility and politics of gender difference from urban Iran to rural Mexico', *Journal of Contemporary Ethnography*, 43: 2, pp. 148–75.
Arjomand, Said Amir (1988), *The Turban for the Crown: the Islamic Revolution in Iran*, Oxford: Oxford University Press.
—— (2009), *After Khomeini: Iran under His Successors*, Oxford: Oxford University Press.

Bahramitash, R. and Hadi Salehi Esfahani (eds) (2011), *Veiled Employment: Islamism and the Political Economy of Women's Employment in Iran*, Syracuse: Syracuse University Press.

Banuazizi, Ali (1994), 'Iran's revolutionary impasse: political factionalism and social resistance', *Middle East Report*, 191, pp. 2–8.

Barry, Andrew, Thomas Osborne and Nikolas Rose (eds) (1993), *Foucault and Political Reason: Liberalism, Neo-Liberalism, and Rationalities of Government*, Chicago: University of Chicago Press.

Bayat, Asef (2010), *Life as Politics: How Ordinary People Change the Middle East*, Stanford: Stanford University Press.

Behdad, Sohrab (2001), 'Khatami and his 'reformist' economic (non-)agenda', *Middle East Report Online*, 21 May, <http://www.merip.org/mero/mero052101> (last accessed 25 February 2014).

Block, Fred (1987), *Revising State Theory: Essays in Politics and Postindustrialism*, Philadelphia: Temple University Press.

Boroujerdi, Mehrzad (2004), 'The reformist movement in Iran', in D. Heradstveit and H. Hveem (eds), *Oil in the Gulf: Obstacles to Democracy and Development*, London: Ashgate, pp. 63–71.

Carnoy, Martin (1986), *The State and Political Theory*, Cambridge: Cambridge University Press.

Chehabi, H. E. (1991), 'Religion and politics in Iran: how theocratic is the Islamic Republic?' *Daedalus*, 120: 3, pp. 69–91.

Corrigan, Philip and Derek Sayer (1985), *The Great Arch: English State Formation as Cultural Revolution*, New York: Blackwell Publishing.

Dean, Mitchell (1999), *Governmentality: Power and Rule in Modern Society*, New York: Sage Publications.

Ehsani, Kaveh (1999), 'Municipal matters: the urbanization of consciousness and political change in Tehran', *Middle East Report*, 212, pp. 22–7.

Ettelaat (2004), 'There are controversies around the construction of women-only parks' (in Persian), 17 May.

Evans, Peter (1995), *Embedded Autonomy: States and Industrial Transformation*, Princeton: Princeton University Press.

Evans, Peter, Dietrich Rueschemeyer and Theda Skocpol (eds) (1985), *Bringing the State Back In*, Cambridge: Cambridge University Press.

Ferguson, James and Akhil Gupta (2002), 'Spatializing states: toward an ethnography of neoliberal government', *American Ethnologist*, 20, pp. 981–1002.

Foucault, Michel (1980), *Power/Knowledge: Selected Interviews and Other Writings: 1972–1977*, New York: Vintage.

—— (1991), 'Governmentality', in Graham Burchell, Colin Gordon, and Pete Miller (eds), *The Foucault Effect: Studies in Governmentality with Two Lectures by and an Interview with Michel Foucault*, Chicago: University of Chicago Press, pp. 87–104.

—— (1995a), *The Birth of Biopolitics: Lectures at the Collège de France 1978–1979*, Basingstoke: Palgrave Macmillan.

—— (1995b), *Discipline and Punish: the Birth of the Prison*, New York: Vintage.

—— (1995c), *Security, Territory, Population: Lectures at the Collège de France 1977–1978*, Basingstoke: Palgrave Macmillan.

Harris, Kevan (2017), *A Social Revolution: Politics and the Welfare State in Iran*, Berkeley: University of California Press.
Hoodfar, Homa (2010), 'Health as a context for social and gender activism: female volunteer health workers in Iran', *Population and Development Review*, 36: 3, pp. 487–510.
Hoodfar, Homa and Samad Assadpour (2000), 'The politics of population policy in the Islamic Republic of Iran', *Studies in Family Planning*, 31: 1, pp. 19–34.
Iran (2001), 'A proposal for giving girls the freedom to exercise' (in Persian), 2 July.
—— (2007), 'Women's safe territory' (in Persian), 1 July.
Javan (2003), 'Greeting the sun yet again' (in Persian), 8 December.
Jessop, Bob (1990), *State Theory: Putting the Capitalist State in Its Place*, University Park: Pennsylvania State University Press.
Joseph, Gilbert M. and Daniel Nugent (eds) (1994), *Everyday Forms of State Formation: Revolution and the Negotiation of Rule in Modern Mexico*, Durham, NC: Duke University Press.
Kandiyoti, Deniz (1988), 'Bargaining with patriarchy', *Gender and Society*, 2: 3, pp. 274–90.
—— (ed.) (1991), *Women, Islam and the State*, Philadelphia: Temple University Press.
—— (2014), 'Contesting patriarchy-as-governance: lessons from youth-led activism', *Open Democracy*, <https://www.opendemocracy.net/5050/deniz-kandiyoti/contesting-patriarchy-as-governance-lessons-from-youth-led-activism> (last accessed 22 December 2014).
Karshenas, Massoud and Hashem M. Pesaran (1995) 'Economic reform and the reconstruction of the Iranian economy', *Middle East Journal*, 49: 1, pp. 89–111.
Keshavarzian, Arang (2005), 'Contestation without democracy: elite fragmentation in Iran', in M. P. Posusney and M. P. Angrist (eds), *Authoritarianism in the Middle East: Regimes and Resistance*, Boulder: Lynne Rienner Publishers.
—— (2015), 'The Iran deal as social contract', *MERIP*, <http://www.merip.org/mer/mer277/iran-deal-social-contract> (last accessed 18 February 2018).
Khatam, Azam (2009), 'The Islamic Republic's failed quest for the spotless city', *Middle East Report*, 250, <http://www.merip.org/mer/mer250/islamic-republics-failed-quest-spotless-city> (last accessed 22 December 2017).
Koolaee, Elaheh (2014), 'The impact of Iraq–Iran war on social roles of Iranian Women', *Middle East Critique*, 26: 1, pp. 5–24.
Kraus, Christopher (2010), 'The sources of anti-Americanism in Iran: a historical and psychological analysis', *Valley Humanities Review*, Spring, <http://portal.lvc.edu/vhr/2010/Articles/krause.pdf> (last accessed 31 March 2018).
Kurzman, Charles (2008), 'A feminist generation in Iran?' *Iranian Studies*, 41: 3, pp. 297–321.
Ladier-Fouladi, Marie (2002), 'Iranian families between demographic change and the birth of the welfare state', *Population*, 2, pp. 361–70.
Le Renard, Amelie (2014), *A Society of Young Women: Opportunities of Place, Power, and Reform in Saudi Arabia*, Stanford: Stanford University Press.
Lemke, Thomas (2001), '"The birth of bio-politics": Michel Foucault's lecture at the Collège de France on neo-liberal governmentality', *Economy and Society*, 30, pp. 190–207.

Massey, Doreen (1994), *Space, Place, and Gender*, Minneapolis: University of Minnesota Press.

Mehran, Golnar (2003), 'The paradox of tradition and modernity in female education in the Islamic Republic of Iran', *Comparative Education Review*, 47: 3, pp. 269–86.

Meyer, John (1999), 'The changing cultural content of the nation-state: a world society perspective', in George Steinmetz (ed.), *State/Culture: State-Formation after the Cultural Turn*, Ithaca: Cornell University Press.

Miller, Kristin J. (1996), 'Human rights of women in Iran: the universalist approach and the relativist response', *Emory International Law Review*, 10, pp. 779–928.

Miller, Peter and Nikolas Rose (1990), 'Governing economic life', *Economy and Society*, 19: 1, pp. 1–31.

Mir-Hosseini, Ziba (1999), *Islam and Gender: the Religious Debate in Contemporary Iran*, Princeton: Princeton University Press.

Mitchell, Timothy (2005), *Rule of Experts: Egypt, Techno-Politics, Modernity*, Berkeley: University of California Press.

Moaddel, Mansoor (1986), 'The Shi'i ulama and the state in Iran', *Theory and Society*, 15: 4, pp. 519–56.

—— (2010), 'Religious regimes and prospects for liberal politics: futures of Iran, Iraq and Saudi Arabia', *Futures*, 42, pp. 532–44.

Moallem, Minoo (2001), 'Transnationalism, feminism and fundamentalism', in E. A. Castelli and R. C. Rodman (eds), *Women, Gender, Religion: a Reader*, New York: Palgrave Macmillan.

—— (2005), *Between Warrior Brother and Veiled Sister: Islamic Fundamentalism and the Politics of Patriarchy in Iran*, Berkeley: University of California Press.

Moaveni, A. (2008), 'Should a pious Muslim practice yoga?' *Time*, 30 November, <http://content.time.com/time/world/article/0,8599,1862306,00.html> (last accessed 27 April 2014).

—— (2009), 'How to work out while Muslim and female', *Time*, 16 August, <http://content.time.com/time/magazine/article/0,9171,1924488,00.html> (last accessed 27 April 2014).

Moghadam, Valentine (1988), 'Women, Work, and Ideology in the Islamic Republic', *International Journal of Middle East Studies*, 20: 2, pp. 221–43.

Moruzzi, Norma C. and Fatemeh Sadeghi (2006), 'Out of the Frying pan, into the fire: young Iranian women today', *Middle East Report*, 241, pp. 26–7.

Najmabadi, Afsaneh (1999), 'Hazards of modernity and morality: women, state, and ideology in contemporary Iran', in Deniz Kandiyoti (ed.), *Women, Islam and the State*, Philadelphia: Temple University Press, pp. 48–77.

—— (2013), *Professing Selves: Transsexuality and Same-Sex Desire in Contemporary Iran*, Durham, NC: Duke University Press.

Ong, Aihwa (2006), *Neoliberalism as Exception: Mutations in Citizenship and Sovereignty*, Durham, NC: Duke University Press.

Osanloo, Arzoo (2009), *The Politics of Women's Rights in Iran*, Princeton: Princeton University Press.

Paidar, Parvin (1997), *Women and the Political Process in the Twentieth Century*, Cambridge: Cambridge University Press.

Resalat (2006), 'The launching of a 25-hectare park for women in Tehran' (in Persian), 17 May.
Saghafi, Morad (2005), 'Three sources of anti-Americanism in Iran', in T. Judt and D. Lacorne (eds), *With Us or Against Us: Studies in Global Anti-Americanism*, New York: Palgrave Macmillan, pp. 189–206.
Salam (1999), 'The president: "our society needs conviviality now more than ever"' (in Persian), 12 February.
Shams, Alex (2015), 'Urban space and the production of gender in modern Iran', *Ajam Media Collective*, <https://ajammc.com/2015/02/23/urban-space-production-gender-iran/> (last accessed 22 December 2017).
Shargh (2003), 'Female MPs comment on the women-only parks' (in Persian), 6 December.
Steinmetz, George (1999), *State/Culture: State-Formation after the Cultural Turn*, Ithaca: Cornell University Press.
Takeyh, Ray (2006), *Hidden Iran: Paradox and Power in the Islamic Republic*, New York: Henry Holt Publishers.
Tehran City Council (2002), The 'women-only parks' bill (in Persian).
Tohidi, Nayereh (2007), '"Islamic feminism": negotiating patriarchy and modernity in Iran', in I. M. Abu-Rabi (ed.), *The Blackwell Companion to Contemporary Islamic Thought*, Oxford: Blackwell Publishing.
Zan e Rooz (1986), 'An interview with Dr Ghafourifard, the Head of the National Olympic Committee' (in Persian), 7 March.
—— (1993), 'The allocation of Taleghani Park to women's sports' (in Persian), 11 June.

Chapter 4

Saudi Women: Between Family, Religion and State

Madawi Al-Rasheed

They took my passport and locked me up for thirteen hours ... if my family comes they will kill me. If I go back to Saudi Arabia I will be dead. Please help me. (Dina Ali, April 2017)

Thousands of miles away from Saudi Arabia, Dina Ali, a twenty-four-year-old woman, was arrested at Ninoy Aquino International Airport in Manila while she was in transit to Sydney. Two uncles, who arrived to return her to Saudi Arabia, kidnapped her from the airport. She screamed and kicked as they forced her to board Saudia flight SV871 to Jeddah. The Philippines authority, a signatory to the 1951 United Nations Convention on Refugees, denied that it had cooperated with the Saudis in this case. But forcing an adult to enter an aeroplane against her will is not easily accomplished without the cooperation of the police and the airport immigration officers. In Dina's case, airline security officials and two men secured her forced repatriation to Saudi Arabia, according to eyewitness accounts.[1]

While in the airport transit hall, and just before she was kidnapped, Dina had borrowed the phone of Meagan Khan, a Canadian woman traveller whom she had befriended while waiting for her own flight to Sydney. She recorded her final words before she was forced to board the Saudia flight. She may have realised that she was being followed and that her journey to Sydney would be cut short. She used the borrowed phone to tell her story. She knew that if she was arrested, her own phone would be immediately confiscated. She said that she had left Saudi Arabia to escape a forced marriage. Should she be made to return, she would face death for leaving the country without the permission of her male guardian.

Social media played an important role in publicising Dina's case. Within hours of recording the video, friends and sympathisers on Facebook and Twitter posted it across continents. Meagan Khan helped Dina at the airport and must have played an important role in making the short recording available. Saudi women activists and others immediately set up a hashtag on Twitter under the title 'SaveDinaAli'.[2] Online mobilisation, as we shall see later in this chapter, has become the only means to publicise abuse, seek help and enlist other women and men in the fight against domestic violence in Saudi Arabia.

In the same month, this time inside Saudi Arabia, anti-guardianship campaigner Maryam al-Otaibi left her abusive family in Ras, a small town in the central region of Qasim, and moved to Riyadh to work as a cashier.[3] On Monday, 17 April 2017, two officials and a woman approached her while she was working. After verifying her identity, the officials informed her that she was to be arrested. She was told that her family had filed a 'runaway report' with the authorities for leaving the family home in Ras and being absent from home without the consent of her father. They told her, in front of eyewitnesses, that they were acting on behalf of her family, and were at the Riyadh supermarket to arrest her and take her back to them.

Maryam's father and brother were the principal actors in this domestic drama that went global. Saudi state agencies cooperated with the family to enforce their control over their runaway daughter. In Ras, Maryam had been subjected to abuse by her younger brother, who had encouraged another brother to go to Syria and join Islamic State (IS) in 2013. He became more abusive as videos of the brother's death flooded social media only weeks after he made the journey to Syria. The brother who was still in Saudi Arabia wanted to 'purify the family home from sins', thus imposing strict rules on all members of the family, including Maryam. According to one source, this brother had always put pressure on the father to restrict Maryam's movement in order to protect the family honour and demonstrate its commitment to Islam and tradition.[4] After the 'martyrdom' of the young brother, he became more disturbed. He told the family that they should all purify the 'house of the martyr'.

In the past, the defiant Maryam had occasionally confronted her brother and reminded him that their father was her guardian, *wali al-amr*, implying that the brother had no authority over her. The brother became more aggressive and abusive, and started threatening the father. He told his father that if he did not honour his responsibility as the legal guardian of the girls in the family, he too would migrate to Syria and join IS. The father felt scared of the prospect of losing another son to the jihad in Syria, and so he succumbed to this blackmail and filed a complaint about his daughter, who had already left Ras to work in Riyadh.

After her arrest, Maryam languished in al-Malaz Prison in Riyadh. The brother continued to put pressure on the father to return Maryam to the family home. He also told his father to take her to court and accuse her of *uquq* (disobeying her parents), including her male guardian, and *hurub* (absconding from the family home), two serious accusations for a twenty-nine-year-old single woman in Saudi Arabia.

Informal local women's groups and government human rights organisations[5] initially declined to take on her case while she was in prison, but a group of women activists found a lawyer to represent her in court after her story went viral on social media. However, after reading the details of the story, the lawyer too declined to take the case, and eventually disappeared. Women activists contacted other social and welfare organisations to help, but they all hesitated on the pretext that this is 'a family matter' in which the state had already intervened.

Maryam's case became famous thanks to social media, as activists had no way of reaching out to the public except through Facebook and Twitter. Several Twitter hashtags, such as 'we are all Maryam al-Otaibi', were created both inside and outside Saudi Arabia. Of course, such hashtags are full of the contributions both of supporters and of those who condemn the girl for defying her family. However, the case became notorious and earned publicity.

In May 2017, only a month after the above two cases erupted and became hotly debated in the Saudi press and globally, two sisters, Ashwaq and Arij, fled to Turkey to seek asylum, according to several brief videos they recorded on their mobile phones. They posted the videos online and claimed that their family had abused them physically and forced them to live as prisoners in their own home. According to one report, the Turkish authorities detained the runaway sisters, aged eighteen and nineteen, after their family put a request through the Saudi Embassy to bring them back.

After the girls' videos were circulated, Arij's literature professor and activist, Sahar Nasif, recognised the girls and admitted on Twitter that she had listened to Arij talking about her abusive family in her university office:

> Areej was my student. I can't forget her innocent eyes as she was sitting in my office relating her dad's continuous abuse ... Every other day there are girls escaping for their lives, or dying or suffering greatly ... Why would a girl escape to a foreign country at a great risk without knowing anyone unless her conditions are so dire?[6]

The cases of Dina, Maryam, Ashwaq and Arij confirmed a persistent narrative about the plight of Saudi women who are constrained by family, religion, state and culture, and now the cooperation of foreign governments. The above cases were all related to the guardianship system, which is perhaps the most restrictive in the Muslim world when it comes to women's autonomy, freedom and choices.

The guardianship (*wilaya* or *wisaya*) system is 'not legally codified but is enacted through a series of informal and formal bureaucratic arrangements that stipulate that a father, husband, brother, or even son has complete authority to approve matters that dictate the daily lives of women'.[7] A comprehensive study of the *wilaya* in Jordan explains that it gives legal authority over a person without her consent (al-Jabiri 2016). In Saudi courts, judges who apply sharia law according to the most restrictive Hanbali interpretations side with male relatives and uphold the *wilaya* system. State institutions (hospitals, schools, universities, employers, and so on) continue to demand the approval of male guardians before they deal with women. Education, health, travel, employment and marriage, among other domains, all require the approval of the guardian.

Politics, Society and Religion

To answer the question why many Saudi women have increasingly fled the country – often to be forcibly returned – we must examine the intersection of several important contributing factors. At the heart of this problem, which is symptomatic of wider and pervasive gender inequality, is the way politics, society and Islam work together to impose the most oppressive regime on women. Restrictions on movement, the guardianship system, disenfranchisement, forced marriages and unfavourable divorce laws are but varied manifestations of general discrimination against women.

In its official narratives, the Saudi state portrays itself as a benevolent, paternalistic agent, supporting women via extensive welfare provisions (in health, education, social benefits and employment). The state enforces a type of patriarchy that is neither entirely private nor public but where the two spheres complement and reinforce each other (Walby 1990). This patriarchy easily and comfortably moves from the family domain to the public sphere where state agencies monitor its contours and reproduce both the dominant ideology – for example, in the schools' religious study curriculum and the various official *ulama* fatwas – and the practices that keep it intact. For several decades, the state employed religious vigilantes, called locally *al-haya* (the Committee for Commanding Right and Prohibiting Vice) in public places to ensure that women and men abide by the rules of appropriate behaviour. They are accompanied by police officers who are entrusted with arresting transgressors.[8] This type of policing has become a marker of so-called Islamic rule, for example in the Islamic caliphate (Mosul and Raqqa), Nigeria, Somalia and Pakistan, among other places.

Discrimination and marginalisation are perpetuated in Saudi Arabia because the state, the family and religious institutions and figures cooperate to restrict women's choices and perpetuate their dependency. Often this starts within the confines of the household. If a woman experiences abuse and restrictions within her own family, she has no recourse. In the four cases of the runaways mentioned above, state agencies inside Saudi Arabia and outside it (embassies) promptly became accomplices of the crimes perpetrated by family members. This happened despite the fact that the Saudi Council of Ministers passed a draft law to criminalise domestic abuse in 2013; it was not clear, however, which state agency is to enforce the law, thus making it ineffective and ambiguous. The Islamic judiciary usually is expected to cooperate and issue legal rules to return such girls to their abusive families. Running away from an abusive family is a crime, punishable by detention, enforced by state agencies, and sanctioned by strict religious interpretations of Islamic law. State, society and religion work together to maintain gender inequality.

The state provides prison-like shelters that most abused women prefer not to be taken to. Poor conditions and restrictions on their freedom inside the shelters, combined with the stigma of being in these places, make women hesitate to seek help from such badly run institutions. While many remain silent, a few women have gone public with their cases of abuse. Almost a decade after famous television presenter Rania al-Baz was badly abused and disfigured by her alcoholic husband and struggled to free herself from him, many younger women are now seeing no alternative but to flee. Al-Baz's case was taken up by a charitable organisation under the patronage of a princess. Only when the presenter was seriously disfigured, was she saved and treated in hospital. This happened only after a crime of passion became, in her own words, a 'state affair'. She then went to France, where her memoirs were published in 2005. Despite her injuries, her prompt flight to France gave her an opportunity to register her presence as an abused Saudi woman: 'The idea of this voyage to France lifts my morale, but the prospect of exposing myself in public brings me abruptly back to reality: "Am I presentable?"' (al-Baz 2005: 63).

Saudi Arabia faces a serious social problem, referred to as *haribat* (runaway girls). Ironically, many badly paid and overworked Asian domestic workers who are brought to London on holiday with Saudi and other Gulf families escape their employers' luxury apartments in Kensington and Knightsbridge, leaving their passports and other personal documents behind. The employers of such women often lock them in their apartments and hold their travel documents, but some manage to escape. They often leave in the middle of the night when their employers are asleep, or when they are sent to buy groceries or accompany children in parks. They seek shelters run by women's groups, the Catholic Church, or born-again Christians, who specifically target Filipinos. They are given housing and legal support and they get introduced to previous runaways, who host them while solicitors deal with their immigration status. Their embassies usually cooperate by issuing new travel documents to replace the ones held by their employers.[9]

In contrast, Saudi 'runaways' are brought back to their families by the Saudi government and foreign agencies in countries where women seek asylum or refuge, for example the Philippines and Turkey in the above cases, thus demonstrating the high level of cooperation between Saudi authorities and other governments. Contrasting the domestic-worker runaway with her Saudi counterpart demonstrates the commonality and differences, but above all it exposes discrimination across ethnic and class divides. The plight of domestic workers and Saudi women can only be understood if we go beyond divides that are meant above all to mask discrimination against all women in Saudi Arabia. In Saudi discourse about its women nationals, words such as 'queens', 'jewels', 'privileged' and 'protected' create the illusion that they are above the foreign domestic workers employed in their houses. The reality is that both, when abused, seek the same escape route, as other means remain unavailable or difficult.

Sociologists and social welfare services in the kingdom do not provide accurate statistics, but according to one sociologist the number of 'runaways' is rising. According to one source, over a thousand women flee the kingdom every year,[10] while more escape Riyadh for Jeddah, the kingdom's more liberal coastal metropolis. Others escape from rural areas to Riyadh. Running away from an abusive family to an overseas destination seems to be a final solution, but other women find ways to 'escape' Saudi Arabia in less dramatic ways.

Marrying someone who lives abroad, prolonging overseas study time, or simply returning after graduation to other Arab capitals, for example Dubai, to seek jobs have all been deployed as strategies to avoid returning to Saudi Arabia. On finishing their education inside Saudi Arabia or abroad, many women try to find jobs in neighbouring Gulf states in order to leave the country. An increasing number of Saudi women students seek asylum in countries where they had been studying, on the grounds of conversion to another religion, a relationship with a non-Muslim man, or pregnancy outside wedlock, each of which constitutes a serious crime in Saudi Arabia that is punishable by death.[11] Canadian, British and American immigration lawyers, among others, deal with such cases and seek expert reports from professionals, academics and Islamic law experts to ensure that such women are not deported back to Saudi Arabia. Of course there are no reliable statistics on Saudi women asylum seekers, as they would be a serious embarrassment in a country where state legitimacy is built on both piety and generous welfare given to women.[12] The reputation of women asylum seekers abroad is deliberately tarnished, as they are often accused of dishonouring their families and running away from punishment, even if they have not committed a crime. They are often described as immoral women who seek sexual freedom abroad.

Other women choose to leave Saudi Arabia and work abroad, especially after they become active in calling for the right to drive, to abolish the guardianship system or simply being different. Among others, Manal al-Sharif, a divorced thirty-three-year-old mother, an established computer engineer at the Saudi oil company ARAMCO, and an activist, encouraged women to drive, and posted videos of herself driving with her brother in al-Khobar. She was arrested, humiliated and treated like a criminal by the police, intelligence services and her employer. She spent nine days in a prison infested with cockroaches. She was released and later left the country to work in Dubai. She eventually married an Australian man and moved to Sydney where she wrote her memoirs, *Daring to Drive*, a book full of pain, psychological trauma and real scars of abuse, including a horrific circumcision episode when she was eight years old in Mecca (al-Sharif 2017). Exhausted, humiliated and scarred, at the end she chose flight instead of fight. She remains active online, mobilising from abroad and documenting the stories of others.[13]

Novelist Badriyya al-Bishr, who is married to a famous comedian, voluntarily moved to Dubai with her children after a death fatwa was issued against her husband for his role in a television series that mocked radical religious scholars.[14] She later became a presenter at a Saudi-sponsored television station based in Dubai that openly adopts a liberal stance on gender, while other Saudi television stations preach piety continuously and broadcast the most restrictive fatwas on gender.

Contradictions in the Saudi-sponsored media that target women are symptomatic of troubled and contradictory legitimacy narratives and nation-building projects. In the media, different princes sponsor channels with contradictory messages, from the most conservative to the most liberal.[15] The state combined its commitment to Islam with a commitment to a truncated hypermodernity in which success is measured by listing the incorporation of the latest technology in the public sphere, some of which is used to restrict women (Al-Rasheed 2013). However, full citizenship and equality remain excluded from the selective modernity of the state. In an authoritarian regime, any call for equality, representation and rights threatens to open a Pandora's box.

The Paradoxes of the Guardianship System

Upholding the guardianship system fails to take into account abusive male relatives who should not be entrusted with the responsibility of being the first arbiters in a woman's life. In 2017, the government waived the need for a guardian's approval for a woman to work as a shop assistant, cook or attendant. Seeking healthcare is also now exempt from the guardianship requirement. This proves that the state is the main arbiter of religious requirements and can waive the guardianship requirement in a selective and flexible way. But the majority of women still cannot travel outside the country without the approval of their guardians. Enlightened fathers sometimes give their approval for a period of five years, but they receive text messages from immigration officers at airports every time their daughters or wives leave the country. The technological aspects of modernity are double-edged in Saudi Arabia. At one level, technology helps to enforce an archaic system and perpetuates the denial of women's freedom of movement. However, when the state allowed male lecturers to teach on a video circuit in order to reach girls' classes, many in Saudi Arabia were overwhelmed with joy, as this gave women an opportunity to pursue higher education at a time when there was a shortage of women lecturers.

This is a truncated modernity in which technological innovations such as smart phones, surveillance cameras and video recordings can work in contradictory ways both against and for women. Women can publicise their plight and mobilise others to help them using the Internet and social media; yet they can also be controlled by the same enabling technology. A wealthy government obsessed with controlling its population can invest heavily in modern technology in the interests of general surveillance, including the maintenance of patriarchy and sex segregation.

In Saudi Arabia, women are symbols of piety and modernity in the process of nation-building (al-Fassi 2011). The state is therefore compelled to uphold the honour of men, restrict women under the guise of protecting them and keep them under control on behalf of those men, even if they physically abuse their women, force them into unwanted marriages, or refuse to divorce them when they seek divorce. I argued in 2013 that neither Islam nor culture alone explains the severe gender inequality in Saudi Arabia (Al-Rasheed 2013). While the role of the state is paramount in resisting change and perpetuating the current discrimination, it is also the main force in society that can change the situation, at least at the legal level.

Several changes with regard to gender came about as a result of royal decrees, mainly the king's orders. The latest change is the revocation of the ban on women driving in September 2017 when King Salman issued a decree instructing state agencies to issue driving licences for women. Many Saudi *ulama* used the principle of *sad al-tharai* (prohibiting conditions that can potentially lead to sin) to justify the ban. But the king decided to ignore this old prohibition when the appropriate domestic and international contexts arose. I do not propose to overstate the role of the state, but focusing on its role as the most powerful agent in society, in conjunction with Islam, culture and oil wealth, is still a relevant theoretical framework to explain both gender inequality and change in the Saudi case. As I have argued elsewhere, the 'woman question' in Saudi Arabia cannot be understood unless we take into account the role of the state, the conversion of Wahhabiyya into a religious nationalist movement, the impact of the oil economy, and cultural norms. None of these factors alone explains why Saudi women were subjected to a strict regime of control (Al-Rasheed 2013: 1–42).

The Gender Order and the State

It seems that the role of the state cannot be ignored – especially its project of nation-building and the centrality of gender in this project (Charrad 2001). Gender, politics, society and Islam are intimately connected not only in the narrative about the creation of the state but also in its everyday functioning. Gender is central to managing the image of the state domestically and globally. The Islamic legitimacy narrative, development projects and, more recently, its drive to move into a neo-liberal technology-based market economy less dependent on oil revenues have all shaped the way women are constructed. The state now wants to shrink welfare benefits and increase its global outreach through capital transfer and investment. For all these projects, women are the cornerstones of state identity and the project of building a non-oil-based economy.

Even when the state launches wars against its enemies, it is compelled to enlist women. This is a recent development in Saudi Arabia, in which women are drawn into a new kind of state-led militarised nationalism as the state has adopted a more aggressive regional foreign policy in the context of the Saudi war on Yemen (from 2015). Women journalists were expected to write supportive articles on the war, and even appeared among the soldiers on the southern border in military attire (Doaiji 2018).

In all these projects, gender remains central to defining the identity of the state and society in the past, the present and the future. While the Saudi case is not exceptional, it has nevertheless granted a special privileged place for Wahhabi interpretations in its legal system, discourses, policy and practices, forging a kind of religious nationalism out of these interpretations as a moral agency to bind the fragmented nation together. Women can potentially either threaten its integrity or promote its piety and purity. This remains a constant feature of the kingdom despite the recent promotion of women's rights under King Salman's rule. Perhaps this is also why Saudi Arabia remains a unique case in the discussion about gender in Muslim-majority countries.

The religious nationalist framework espoused by both the regime and its loyal Wahhabi clerics dominated the social and political scene throughout the turbulent 1990s. But it almost disappeared from state rhetoric after 9/11 when Saudi Arabia, along with its Wahhabi religious tradition and treatment of women, became increasingly scrutinised by both local women activists and international human rights organisations. In the post-9/11 era, the globalisation of human rights discourse and UN charters on gender discrimination[16] led to international non-governmental organisations producing several reports on the plight of Saudi women.[17] Their status as minors, restricted participation in the labour force, exclusion from limited municipal elections, the ban on driving and the guardianship system in which women are denied a legal persona were among the urgent issued highlighted in NGO reports, many built on the participation of Saudi women activists, especially the young connected generation of social media.

During King Abdullah's reign (2005–15), the state dealt with this deluge of damning international assessments of the status of women with a counter-narrative, orchestrated by the regime and its media. The modernism and cosmopolitanism of Saudi women, in addition to the achievements of individual women, became central news, which was fed to the international media. Women who espoused the distorted state feminism that highlighted the merit of appointing a selected female elite to high positions in government as deputy ministers, directors of banks and chambers of commerce began to publicise their achievements without adopting a critical position on whether such high-profile appointments easily lead to empowerment. Hind Al-Sudairy, a comparative literature professor at a women's university in Riyadh and a member of the privileged and elite Al-Sudairy maternal family of several kings, including the current one, dedicated a whole monograph to demonstrating the achievements of several Saudi women in government, sport, literature and medicine. While she acknowledges that there are still challenges and obstacles to full emancipation, she regards the state as the most important agent in women's empowerment. She invokes a nativist approach, stipulating that only an insider Saudi woman like herself can understand gender in Saudi Arabia (Al-Sudairy 2017).

Under King Abdullah, the two contradictory frameworks for gender, namely religious nationalism and truncated cosmopolitan modernity, coexisted and often collided. As a result, Saudi women were pulled in opposed directions and were caught in the contradictory frameworks through which their rights and citizenship can be comprehended and defined. These contradictory narratives also had an impact on women's struggles as two camps emerged and spent much energy fighting each other. Islamist and liberal women engaged in a fierce battle over their rights while the majority of Saudi women did not fall within the boundaries of either of these two well-defined yet informal groups. The majority of women remained oblivious to the internal battles within the women's camp, mostly led by educated middle-class women.

As a result of the increasing promotion of women in state narratives and the expansion of their role in the labour force, the employment of women rose to 21 per cent by 2017. Specific programmes were introduced to boost women's employment, for example the feminisation of lingerie shops and cashier jobs in supermarkets. The gradual shift from a state-centred capitalist economy to open liberal trade culminated in the appointment of several women to high-ranking positions in both government bureaucracy and the Consultative Council (Majlis al-Shura), in addition to their election to Chambers of Commerce and public- and private-sector institutions and businesses. In 2015, women were finally allowed to participate in municipal elections, both as voters and as candidates. By the time King Abdullah passed away in January 2015, his reputation as the 'King of Humanity' had already been fixed in the imagination of women. Many saw him as a benevolent, paternalistic father figure not only of the nation but specifically of its women. While the legal restrictions on women remained intact, like King Faisal before him, King Abdullah's propaganda as the emancipator of women was well established by the end of his reign.

Women themselves have been active in endorsing their own modernity, which they have articulated through the increased publication of novels and literature, op-eds and blogs. King Abdullah's reign coincided with the advent of the Internet, which initially brought about an explosion in debating forums and personal blogs, and later social media from Twitter to Facebook. During this period (2005–15), daring cosmopolitan women were tolerated and even celebrated as icons of modernity, progress and achievement. Their voices found a niche in liberal forums. Similarly, Islamist women began to participate in Islamist Internet forums alongside men.

The only women who got into trouble and were occasionally detained were those who incited other women to engage in collective action and mobilise against some existing restrictions, for example the ban on driving or support for political prisoners. As long as women dramatised their plight in fiction and urged other women to call for representation in minor municipal elections or greater job opportunities, they remained safe – and even protected by the state. So Rajaa al-Sani's famous novel *The Girls of Riyadh* was endorsed by a government minister, who praised her for her courage and literary insight into the lives of young Saudi women (al-Sani' 2008). Al-Sani' was subjected to damning criticism, and there were even calls by a consortium of Islamists and activists to punish her, as she was accused of sensationalising the city's young women. However, she remained secure from harassment, and even sold her novels at the various Saudi book fairs. Such contradictions reflect the fragmented and opposing views prevalent among men in different government ministries and institutions.

After 2005, when women were excluded from the first municipal elections, academic and prolific writer and activist Hatoon al-Fassi organised a series of events to train women for future elections, raise awareness and call for the inclusion of women in municipalities in the context of the Baladi campaign. She ran a monthly informal Sunday women's group (al-Ahadiyya), to discuss women's issues and mobilise them to demand more rights.[18] Such mobilisation was accepted by the state as it endorsed a gradual reform under the aegis of the state rather than outside its agenda. On the other side of the fence, women who called for an Islamic feminism and a return to 'true' Islam in which women had greater rights were also tolerated. Key to this toleration was the fact that they refrained from calling for actual mobilisation, such as demonstrations, sit-ins, strikes or civil action.

However, the situation was different when women activists abandoned their virtual resistance and moved to the real world. Wajiha al-Howeider, Manal al-Sharif (mentioned earlier) and Lujain al-Huthlul were among the activists who were inspired by the 2011 Arab uprisings and started to intensify their mobilisation against the ban on driving. They were behind the Campaign2Drive and the 26 October movement with their strong presence online calling on other women to drive. But women who violated the ban on driving and drove their cars with male relatives as passengers, such as Manal al-Sharif, ended up in prison, and according to her were treated like criminals. The details of her famous case are narrated in her memoirs. She describes her ordeal:

> I walked with Halimah and the security guard, a man, into prison, it was an old place, with high walls, and to get to the main prison we had to cross a huge yard that was all dirt. No tiles . . . just bare earth. The walls were filled with plastic bags, filled with partly eaten bread, plastic spoons, and more clothes . . . and everywhere there were cockroaches. Thousands and thousands of cockroaches scurried across the floors, the walls. Cockroaches on the bed, on the floor, on the food. (al-Sharif 2017: 19–33)

Lujain al-Huthlul has so far taken the fight-rather-than-flight option. The first wave of arrests of women drivers in 2011 did not deter her. In 2014 she drove her car from Dubai to the Saudi border, as she holds a full driving licence issued abroad. The Saudi border police forced her to stay in her car in the heat for twenty-four hours. While stranded on the Saudi border, her friend Maysa al-Amoudi joined her in solidarity. Within two hours, both al-Huthlul and al-Amoudi were arrested and taken to Riyadh in a police car. Al-Amoudi was immediately put in prison, as she was above the age of thirty, while al-Huthlul was detained in Muassasat Dar Ri'ayat al-Fatayat (a detention centre for minors) for women under the age of thirty. She was released after seventy-three days. During the 2015 municipal elections, al-Huthlul was banned from standing as a candidate because she had a 'criminal' record.

Other activists who worked on social issues, such as Wajiha al-Howeider and Fawziyya al-Ouyouni, were accused by the courts of helping women to become more vocal, and even to escape from abusive husbands and guardians.

Al-Howeider and al-Ouyouni were in fact sheltering abused women and providing support, especially for those subjected to violence by family members. Instead of pushing women to flee like the young girls mentioned above, the two activists wanted to create a safe space for abused women, a kind of sanctuary where they could be helped and given legal advice. However, interfering in what is considered a 'family matter' remains a dangerous endeavour that puts their helpers in a compromising situation: they become accomplices in an ill-defined crime, namely disobeying the male guardian and escaping the family home.

Some religious scholars and anti-women-driving campaigners used social media to tarnish the reputation of women activists, who were described online as immoral Westernised whores determined to create chaos in the community. This latest episode, which coincided with the post-2011 driving campaigns, was reminiscent of the 1990 incident in which around forty-seven women academics and professionals drove their cars in Riyadh and were taken to interrogation centres. Many of these women lost their academic jobs at that time and were deliberately marginalised.

After the 2011 Arab uprisings, women who supported political organisations such as the Saudi Association for Civil and Political Rights (ACPRA), an independent human rights and political organisation, or demonstrated against the indefinite detention of their male relatives, received harsh treatment at the hands of the security forces (Al-Rasheed 2016). Such defiant women did not fit the tame modernity narrative that the state wanted to project. They were defined either as terrorists or as sympathisers with terrorism. The state publicised the trials of famous women, for example those who were allegedly supporters of al-Qaida and the Islamic State in Iraq (IS), in order to justify the detention of peaceful women activists. The latter demonstrated in support of political prisoners and wrote blogs about the detention and trials of peaceful political activists.

Under a New King

Women in Saudi Arabia will remember King Salman's reign (2015–) as a period that ushered in two types of feminism that are variations on the previous state-led religious nationalism and truncated cosmopolitan modernity. Salman has already become known as the 'King of Decisiveness', a title that replaced the 'King of Humanity' adopted by his predecessor, King Abdullah (d. 2015). The shift to a masculine decisiveness has important repercussions for women's status and gender relations in the kingdom.

In the past, officials claimed that religious and social reasons prevent women from driving, but finally since 2015 the regime has begun to acknowledge that there might be no Islamic foundation to support the driving ban. Several senior princes always claimed that the state should not interfere in the ban on driving, as this is a social issue that should be resolved by society. In this spirit, the state allows the local press to post articles debating the issue. Opinions are often polarised. In his 2016 interview with *The Economist*, Prince Muhammad ibn Salman, now the crown prince, asserted that society is not ready for such a revolutionary step, and that women should wait until the right moment to drive.[19] The 'right moment' for any gender issue is always determined by the state, despite the claim that the ban is a social issue. But, as mentioned earlier, in September 2017 the king lifted the ban by royal decree, thus ignoring previous opinions by Islamic scholars. This shows that state requirements trump the assumed dictates of Islam in Saudi Arabia despite the rhetoric used.

King Salman wanted to distance Saudi Arabia from IS and anchor the country into a seismic economic shift, the success of which is bound to be tangled up with real social change. A combination of low oil prices and greater international media interest in the similarity between the treatment of women by IS and in Saudi Arabia led to new shifts in the treatment of the latter.[20] In these comparative contexts, gender issues are central in Saudi Arabia as much as they are in Western capitals, among IS recruiters and supporters, and elsewhere.

To push for a new Saudi image, after becoming king, Salman immediately reappointed thirty women to the Majlis al-Shura, thus honouring the pledge of his predecessor to empower women through appointment. He also issued a royal decree to restrict the powers of the Committee for Commanding Right and Prohibiting Vice (*al-haya*). This committee had harassed women as much as men, and there had been well-publicised cases of young men and women challenging members of the committee in public and resisting arrest. Women celebrated their defiance in the face of *al-haya* by posting video-clips on YouTube in which they appear to be chasing *al-haya* men from shopping centres rather than *al-haya* succeeding in controlling women in such precincts. As restrictions on Saudi women began to appear similar to those practised in the cities of Raqqa and Mosul in Syria and Iraq respectively that had fallen under the control of IS militants, the Saudi regime desperately tried to alter perceptions of the status of women inside the kingdom.

In 2016, Crown Prince Muhammad ibn Salman introduced Vision 2030, a Western management consultant's blueprint that shifts the state-centred Saudi oil capitalism towards a new liberal market economy and aims to lessen Saudi Arabia's dependence on a single commodity. The new blueprint drawn up by the McKinsey Global Institute was followed by the implementation of a Saudi National Transformation Programme with many chapters related to gender and social issues.[21]

Both Vision 2030 and the National Transformation Programme received broad coverage and praise in the local press. But exiled Saudi activist and asylum seeker Hala al-Dosari posed a legitimate question: how in a national workforce largely composed of men and foreign workers can economic reform ensure women's participation? Would legal restrictions on women's autonomy be considered in the reform plans?[22] She argues that neither religion nor conservative culture inhibit women's participation in the workforce. Rather, it is the problem of transport, together with the ban on driving, that deters women from seeking employment outside the house. Transportation is under the control of the state; hence while the state wants to promote women's employment, it assists in restricting its possibilities for realisation. The neo-liberal transformation may stumble and prove to be limited in increasing women's participation in society if the social controls remain in place, with women unable to secure their own freedom of movement.

Conclusion

Saudi Arabia has a long way to go before it actually integrates women as equal citizens. Gender inequality is perpetuated not only because of state legitimacy, the state protecting the interests of conservative men or simply religious restrictions. Depriving women of basic rights is a reflection of how much the state fears the language of rights in an authoritarian and undemocratic context like that of Saudi Arabia. While both men and women are disenfranchised and deprived of political and civil rights, women tend to suffer double discrimination. As women, they are subjected to the strictest legal constraints that deprive them even of the right to move freely in their own country. As citizens, they share with men their marginalisation and disenfranchisement in the absence of meaningful political participation. Both men and women remain unrepresented in an elected national assembly in Saudi Arabia. Despite the surge in propaganda highlighting the achievements of super-heroic Saudi women and the celebration of their educational achievements and contribution to society, women in general remain hostage to both their own male guardians and evolving state projects, serving only those who design them.

The grand state narrative about the emancipation and modernity of Saudi women aims to draw them into changing state agendas and the project of nation-building, which has gone through several transformations. While there is no single factor that may explain why Saudi women continue to live under the strictest codes, this chapter has shown that interconnected factors contribute to perpetuating the situation. This indicates that women's rights cannot be granted under an undemocratic and authoritarian regime.

The state promoted women as guardians of the nation's morality, piety and modernity. However, the majority of Saudi women are oblivious to such grand designs, and a minority chose flight as a final solution to their trauma, as this chapter has shown. As oil revenues decline, new taxes are introduced, employment in the public sector is frozen, the welfare state shrinks, and salaries are cut, women will find themselves the most negatively affected by Vision 2030 and the Transformation Programme. The welfare state that they had depended on is gradually but steadily being eroded by austerity measures that will be detrimental to the most vulnerable amongst them, for example young women, widows, divorcees and the unmarried. In a neo-liberal economy, prioritising the protection of women against abuse in the workplace, family home and elsewhere is paramount. Without adequate legal mechanisms put in place, Saudi women will be drawn further into dangerous spaces.

Notes

1. Human Rights Watch, 'Fleeing woman returned to Saudi Arabia against her will', 14 April 2017. Available at <https://www.hrw.org/news/2017/04/14/fleeing-woman-returned-saudi-arabia-against-her-will> (last accessed 9 September 2017). Further details of Dina's story are constructed out of several tweets that she initiated while in detention.
2. The kidnapping and detention story of Dina unfolded from 14 April until the present. Available at <https://twitter.com/hashtag/SaveDinaAli?src=hash>. See also BBC, 'Flying without a man: the mysterious case of Dina Ali'. Available at <http://www.bbc.co.uk/news/blogs-trending-40105983> (last accessed 9 September 2017).
3. Details of Maryam al-Otaibi's story was reported on 30 July 2017 by the BBC: 'Maryam al-Otaibi: Saudi anti-guardianship campaigner freed from detention'. Available at <http://www.bbc.co.uk/news/world-middle-east-40770776> (last accessed 10 September 2017).
4. Activist Manal al-Sharif documented the details of the story. Available at <https://manal-alsharif.com> (last accessed 18 September 2017).
5. Saudi Arabia has an official human rights organisation that often deals with cases of abuse, but on this occasion they did not respond promptly, as the government agencies interfered.
6. See Maryam al-Otaibi @MERIAM_AL3TEEBE and Sahar Hasan Nasif @Da7eyatAlmojtam. In the international press, see Mona Eltahawi, 'Why Saudi women are literally living the "Handmaid's Tale"', *New York Times*, 24 May 2017. Available at <https://www.nytimes.com/2017/05/24/opinion/why-saudi-women-are-literally-living-the-handmaids-tale.html?mcub> (last accessed 7 September 2017).
7. Human Rights Watch, *Boxed In: Women and Saudi Arabia's Guardianship*, 16 July 2016. Available at <https://www.hrw.org/report/2016/07/16/boxed/women-and-saudi-arabias-male-guardianship-system> (last accessed 15 September 2017).
8. In 2016, King Salman issued a royal decree to take away *al-haya*'s right to chase people and arrest them in public places. This happened after several car crashes and deaths resulted from the spectacle of chasing allegedly immoral people on the roads of the major cities. Now *al-haya* is deprived of some but not all powers, as the state wants to project a new liberal outlook and assure foreign investors that there is a

degree of freedom and privacy in the shopping centres of the capital and other cities. *Al-haya* supporters flooded the Internet with objections when King Salman issued his decree to limit its powers. They forecast the end of morality, the corruption of the pure and puritanical society and the general debauchery of the Muslim nation. Their noise did not make any difference, and the government agencies went ahead and applied the king's orders.

9. During research on the health of immigrants in west London, I came across several Filipinos who told me their stories of flight from abusive employers. The conversation took place over several months in 2000. It is estimated that 5,000 maids run away from Saudi families every six months. See Beatrice Thomas, '5000 maids run away in Saudi in 6 months,' *Arabian Business*. Available at <http://www.arabianbusiness.com/5-000-maids-run-away-in-saudi-in-6-mths-552603.html> (last accessed August 2017).
10. 'Some Saudi women are secretly deserting their country', *The Economist*, 16 March 2017. Available at <https://www.economist.com/news/middle-east-and-africa/21718871-women-are-fed-up-being-treated-children-some-saudi-women-are-secretly> (last accessed 18 August 2017).
11. I was involved in providing expert reports to lawyers dealing with such cases in the US, Canada and the UK. In the last decade, and since the introduction of government scholarships to study abroad in 2005, the number of women seeking asylum abroad has increased.
12. Moudhi al-Johni exposed the plight of Saudi women asylum seekers as she talked to the press: see Aya Batrawy, 'Saudi women plea for asylum', *Huffington Post*, 16 March 2017. Available at <http://www.huffingtonpost.ca/2017/04/16/saudi-runaway-asylum_n_16049164.html> (last accessed 9 September 2017).
13. See Manal al-Sharif's interview, available at <https://www.c-span.org/video/?429968-2/qa-manal-alsharif> (last accessed 16 September 2017).
14. My full interview with Badriyya al-Bishr is in Al-Rasheed (2013).
15. On the contradictory Saudi media projects, see Mellor (2008).
16. On the international and global human rights regime, see Massad (2015); on the globalisation of gender rights and issues, see Abu-Lughod (2013).
17. Human Rights Watch 2008; Human Rights Watch, *Boxed In* (see Note 7).
18. Conversation with Hatoon al-Fassi, London 2017. See also al-Fassi (2015).
19. Interview transcript, *The Economist*, 6 January 2016. Available at <http://www.economist.com/saudi_interview> (last accessed 7 September 2017).
20. Saudi Arabia criminalised comparisons in the press that find any common ground between the country and IS in Mosul and Raqqa. See BBC, 'What happens after one man compares Saudi Arabia to Islamic State,' 1 December 2015. Available at <http://www.bbc.co.uk/news/blogs-trending-34966066> (last accessed 4 September 2017).
21. McKinsey Global Institute, 'Moving Saudi economy beyond oil', 2015. Available at <https://www.mckinsey.com/global-themes/employment-and-growth/moving-saudi-arabias-economy-beyond-oil> (last accessed 1 February 2018).
22. Hala al-Dosari, 'The Saudi National Transformation Program: what's in it for women?' Available at <http://www.agsiw.org/the-saudi-national-transformation-program-whats-in-it-for-women/> (last accessed 7 March 2017).

Bibliography

Abu-Lughod, Lila (2013), *Do Muslim Women Need Saving?* Cambridge, MA: Harvard University Press.
Al-Baz, Rania (2005), *Défigurée: quand un crime passionnel devient affaire d'état*, Neuilly sur Seine: Michel Lafon.
Charrad, Mounira (2001), *States and Women's Rights: the Making of Postcolonial Tunisia, Algeria, and Morocco*, Berkeley and Los Angeles: University of California Press.
Doaiji, Nora (2018), 'From Hasm to Hazm: Saudi feminism beyond patriarchal bargaining', in M. Al-Rasheed (ed.), *Salman's Legacy: the Dilemmas of a New Era in Saudi Arabia*, London: Hurst & Co., pp. 117–47.
Al-Fassi, Hatoon (2011), 'Saudi women: modernity and change', in J. F. Seznec and M. Kirk (eds), *Industrialization in the Gulf: a Socioeconomic Revolution*, London: Routledge, pp. 157–70.
—— (2015), 'Sunday Women Group', *Journal of Middle East Women's Studies*, 11: 2, 242–3.
Human Rights Watch (2008), *Perpetual Minors: Human Rights Abuses Stemming from Male Guardianship and Sex Segregation in Saudi Arabia*, New York: Human Rights Watch.
Al-Jabiri, Afaf (2016), *Gendered Politics and Law in Jordan: Guardianship over Women*, London: Palgrave.
Massad, Joseph (2015), *Islam in Liberalism*, Chicago: University of Chicago Press.
Mellor, Noha (2008), 'Bedouinisation or liberalisation of culture? The paradox of the Saudi monopoly of the Arab media', in M. Al-Rasheed (ed.), *Kingdom without Borders: Saudi Arabia's Political, Religious and Media Frontiers*, London: Hurst & Co., pp. 353–74.
Al-Rasheed, Madawi (2013), *A Most Masculine State: Gender, Religion and Politics in Saudi Arabia*, Cambridge: Cambridge University Press.
—— (2016), *Muted Modernists: the Struggle over Divine Politics in Saudi Arabia*, London: Hurst & Co.
Al-Sani', Rajaa (2008), *The Girls of Riyadh*, Beirut: Saqi.
Al-Sharif, Manal (2017), *Daring to Drive: a Saudi Woman Awakening*, New York: Simon & Schuster.
Al-Sudairy, Hind (2017), *Modern Women in the Kingdom of Saudi Arabia: Rights, Challenges and Achievements*, Cambridge: Cambridge Scholars Publishing.
Walby, Sylvia (1990), *Theorizing Patriarchy*, London: Blackwell.

CHAPTER 5

Against All Odds: the Resilience and Fragility of Women's Gender Activism in Turkey

Deniz Kandiyoti

Introduction

This chapter explores the evolution of women's movements in republican Turkey from a relatively narrow base among the educated urban elite into a diversified mass movement that cuts across divides of class, religiosity and ethnicity. Historically, the relationships between women's movements and the state have been troubled and paradoxical. Indeed, my contribution to *Women, Islam and the State* (Kandiyoti 1991), titled 'End of Empire', ended rather ominously in 1935 when the Turkish Women's Federation disbanded itself only a fortnight after it had successfully hosted the 12th Congress of the International Federation of Women in Istanbul. The rationale for this self-elimination was announced by the president of the Federation, Latife Bekir, who declared that the Kemalist reforms had granted women complete equality with full constitutional guarantees, making the Federation redundant. This move was clearly prompted by leaders in Ankara who were displeased with the fact that the Turkish delegates were swayed by the pacifist appeals of American, British and French women on the eve of World War II. Thus began a bumpy trajectory of collaboration, co-optation, resistance and dissent that marks different moments of women's struggles for their rights.

'End of Empire' was a text of its time. It was an attempt to bring the role of the state and the vagaries of nation-building projects to the fore at a point in time when there was a dominant tendency to read off women's status in Muslim-majority countries from the presumed dictates of Islam. In the intervening quarter of a century, it became self-evident that the politics of gender[1] is inevitably mediated by systems of governance and processes of political contestation that may deploy Islam in diverse ways at subnational, national and transnational levels. There has, nonetheless, been a relative lack of systematic engagement with the links between the politics of gender and the nature of political regimes in Muslim-majority countries. In Turkey, this manifested itself in two parallel tracks of enquiry that seldom intersected or entered into dialogue with one another: on the one hand, attempts at identifying Turkey's evolving regime type and, on the other, analyses of discourses and policies in the domains of sexuality, reproduction, marriage and the family. I argued elsewhere (Kandiyoti 2016) that gender is intrinsic rather than incidental to a characterisation of Turkey's regime under the Justice and Development Party (Adalet ve Kalkınma Partisi – AKP hereafter) in at least three crucial domains since its rise to power in 2002: first, in shoring up a populism that privileges gender as a marker of difference, pitting an authentically national 'us' against an 'anti-national' (*gayri-milli*) 'them'; second, in the marriage of convenience between neo-liberal welfare and employment policies and a new biopolitics of (neo-)conservative familism; and finally, in the 'normalisation' of violence in everyday political discourse and practice manifested through soaring levels of gender-based violence and relative impunity for perpetrators.

Whatever the merits of this approach, it suffered from important limitations. It remained mainly state-centric to the extent that the politics of gender was principally analysed in relation to the ruling party's evolving political goals. The agency of social actors and of social movements was left out of this account making it difficult to explain the longevity, increasing diversity and resilience of women's activism in Turkey, even on the most inhospitable political terrain.

This chapter attempts to address this partial neglect by analysing the pathways of women's gender activism from the 1980s onwards, chronicling the diversification of its actors and charting its changing relationships with state power. By opting for the term 'gender activism' I simply aim to signal the existence of a broader register of collective action encompassing all types of mobilisation around gender by religious or secular constituencies, or by men, women, gays, transgender or queer individuals. By focusing on women's gender activism, I am limiting myself to a subset of issues within a much broader political field.

'There Are Women Everywhere':[2] a Tale of Presence and Persistence

Some selected episodes may serve as a guide to the range and scope of women's mobilisation in post-1980s Turkey.

On 17 May 1987, Istanbul was witness to the first mass demonstration after the 12 September 1980 military coup.[3] During this period of severe repression, a group of women, many drawn from the ranks of the Turkish left, started organising explicitly as feminists. What galvanised them into action was an infamous court ruling refusing to grant divorce to a pregnant mother of three who was the victim of systematic domestic violence. The closing statement by the prosecutor read: 'Do not leave a woman's belly without a foal, nor her back without the rod.' The women who initially and unsuccessfully tried to prosecute finally created the 'Solidarity Against Battering' platform and applied for permission to march. What they initially expected to be a small demonstration swelled into thousands. To this day, the event is widely recognised as a turning point in women's activism in the post-1980s, and its chants, slogans and colourful banners still live on.

Again under the military regime, a regulation was published in 1981 prohibiting the headscarf in public institutions. In 1982, the Higher Education Council, a new body created to oversee education, banned the headscarf in universities.[4] This occasioned acts of civil disobedience and passive resistance by veiled students who saw their equal rights to education and public presence imperiled by these regulations. However, the harshest measures against the wearing of headscarves and public expressions of religion came after the military intervention (or so-called post-modern coup) on 28 February 1997. This marked the beginning of the 'February 28 Process', which consisted of efforts by the state and the military to contain Islamist politics, which eventually led to the closure of the Welfare Party[5] (Cizre and Çınar 2003). This period represented the zenith of Islamic constituencies' sense of grievance, and its central mobilising trope was the headscarf.

In 1998, the hand-in-hand protest (*El ele eylemi*) was a nationwide mass mobilisation against the headscarf ban where women and men formed a human chain. Initially organised by students of the Faculty of Medicine at Istanbul University, almost three million people are alleged to have taken part. The Islamic women's movement that had been gaining momentum since the 1980s (Acar 2010) came into its own as the headscarf ban fostered the mobilisation of young generations of Muslim women which, in turn, stimulated the growth of new civil society organisations (Aksoy 2015).

Forced disappearances and political murders were rife during the military coup-era of the 1980s and the so-called 'dirty war' against the Kurds in the 1990s. Kurdish women initiated the Saturday Mothers (Cumartesi Anneleri), reportedly inspired by the Mothers of the Plaza de Mayo in Argentina. They held their first sit-in on 27 May 1995 and gathered at 12 noon every Saturday for half an hour in the Galata district of Istanbul, holding photographs of their 'lost' loved ones. Mainly composed of mothers of victims, they became a model of civil disobedience, combining silent sit-ins with communal vigil as their method of protest, aiming to raise awareness of state-sponsored violence and militarism in Turkey. Amid consternation, their 700th meeting on 25 August 2018 was banned and police used tear gas to disperse protesters.

As will be explained in detail below, the late 1990s and early 2000s were a period of flowering of civil society organisations in general and women's civil society activism in particular. However, the spaces opened by legal reforms and 'democratisation packages' linked to the EU accession process were to be short-lived. After the second electoral victory of the AKP in 2007, the erosion of civil liberties and of women's rights gathered pace, culminating in regime change after the June 2018 elections from a parliamentary democracy to an executive presidency that concentrates all powers in the person of the president.

During this protracted process, the failed military coup of 15 July 2016 stands out as a dramatic watershed, providing President Erdoğan with the means to totally liquidate the influence of an erstwhile political ally, the Fethullah Gülen community, (dubbed as FETÖ, the Fethullah Terror Organisation, or PYD, the parallel state structure) accused of mounting the coup and using it to suppress any form of dissent. The ensuing crackdown has been unprecedented in its scale and ferocity. A state of emergency declared on 21 July 2016 and extended seven times until 19 July 2018 authorised rule by decrees not subject to parliamentary scrutiny or judicial appeal. There has hardly been a more inimical and perilous time for protest or civil disobedience. Yet there has been a continuing presence of women on the streets, protesting violence and retrogressive social policies.

Emboldened by a laissez-faire atmosphere to women-bashing,[6] the number of attacks against women in public places took an alarming turn. On 12 September 2016, a nurse coming off duty who boarded a bus in her shorts was assaulted by a man who kicked her in the face. This was followed by spate of incidents of verbal abuse and physical assault; in the summer of 2017 a university student was slapped on a bus by a man who considered her outfit 'shameful', and a woman in a park in Istanbul was told to leave by a private security guard for wearing immodest clothes. These and similar events triggered a national mobilisation by women throughout the summer of 2017 under the slogan 'Don't mess with my outfit'.[7] All the demonstrations featured a minority of headscarf-wearing women and girls. Women were on the streets again on 25 November 2017 on International Day for the Elimination of Violence against Women with their chants, banners and slogans protesting the soaring levels of violence in Turkey. 'We won't obey, we are not afraid, we won't be silent', chanted thousands of women on 8 March 2018, International Women's Day, in the largest and most vibrant demonstration in recent memory.

What unites these disparate instances of women's militancy despite the diversity of their interests, political goals and modes of organisation is the remarkable persistence of women's activism over the last four decades, even during times of repression and adversity. In what follows, I attempt to chart the process of diversification of women's activism, the interactions between their movements and their evolving relationships with the state.

Dissent, Dialogue and Cooperation: Evolving Pathways and Uneasy Encounters

Until the 1980s, ideological divergences between mainstream Kemalist women, socialist feminists and a budding radical feminist movement could be discerned through their varied platforms, activities and sometimes short-lived publications (Arat 1994; Sirman 1989; Tekeli 1986; Diner and Toktaş 2010). Especially after the 1990s, women's activism took a turn towards identity politics against the background of, on the one hand, the consolidation of Islamic politics and, on the other, the demands for national recognition and autonomy of Turkey's Kurds.[8] This new conjuncture placed secular, Islamic and Kurdish women of various persuasions in complex relationships of conflict, dialogue, and cooperation with one another. These encounters meant that they made constant incursions into each other's ideational terrains, creating tensions between women's groups and splits within them.

A few examples should suffice to illustrate this point. The headscarf ban was fought over the question of freedom of attire and was defended as a human right since it was presented as a restriction on Muslim women's rights to study and work. The right to wear the headscarf was, thus, explicitly put on the agenda as a question of access to the public domain. This demand created splits within the secular feminist movement between those who opposed the ban as an infringement of human rights (such as the feminist periodicals *Pazartesi* and *Amargi*) and those who treated the headscarf issue as the stalking horse of a process of insidious attack on women's existing rights (Kadıoğlu 2005; Marshall 2005; Turam 2008; Saktanber 2006; Diner and Toktaş 2010).

Mobilisation around the headscarf also had the potential to create unease among more conservative Muslim women (and men), who wondered whether stepping out onto the domain of human rights, although tactically productive, was missing the point and diluting the issue. After all, wasn't covering up first and foremost a religious obligation? But if one moved in that direction, then why stop with the headscarf? What about more contentious issues such as polygyny and unilateral divorce? Venturing onto that slippery terrain, however, would not only confirm the worst fears of already sceptical secular feminists and secularists more generally but also meet with resistance from Muslim women who lived comfortably with the existing civil code.[9] Despite the scarcity of data on this question, there are indications that although religious women recognise Islam as a source of law, religious families resort to a hybrid system in the fields of property and inheritance that may circumvent secular laws but also allows them to pick and choose the mechanisms that best suit their interests, needs and motivations (Toktaş and O'Neil 2015).

After the AKP government weathered the crisis of threatened closure of the party in April 2007, it gained an even greater electoral majority in July 2007. Abdullah Gül was installed as president with a covered first lady in the face of fierce resistance by the military and some secular opposition groups. A more confident regime started adopting increasingly authoritarian policies. Among other things, frequent intrusions into citizens' and young people's lifestyles, such as interventions into the sale of alcohol, attempts to ban mixed residence halls in universities and to regulate allegedly 'indecent' behaviour in public spaces, started to elicit sporadic bouts of youth protest (Kandiyoti 2014). The Gezi protests of the summer of 2013, triggered by the violent police crackdown against a peaceful sit-in by environmental activists resisting the transformation of a public park into a shopping mall in Istanbul, expressed a mood of open defiance and rebellion (Özkırımlı 2014). It was now the turn of some Muslim youths (including women) to feel conflicted, some overtly siding with the protesters.[10] However, Prime Minister Erdoğan used polarising and provocative language to stoke popular fears by denouncing the alleged harassment of a covered woman by demonstrators in a bid to demonise them.[11]

Meanwhile, the Kurdish women's movement which had been gaining momentum since the 1980s presented conundrums for Turkish women activists across the board. Kurdish women were speaking from the position of an oppressed ethnic minority revealing the dark underbelly of modern nation-building in Turkey: its corporatist, homogenising drive to assimilate its diverse citizenry into a monolithic nation. The irony, of course, was that the Turkish modernisation project that presented itself as the vanguard of women's emancipation during the early years of the republic was now being upstaged by a Kurdish movement which, both at the level of rhetoric and in its governance practices, appeared to place gender equality at the heart of its political project. Çağlayan (2013) offers a sensitive analysis of the transformations of the movement and the place of women within it by tracing how the Kurdish myth of identity shifted to the invocation of an egalitarian, matriarchal national past. This account made the liberation of the Kurdish nation and of its women coterminous. In her evaluation of independent feminist initiatives among Kurdish women, Açık (2013) points to the diversity of their positions in terms of their willingness to combat patriarchy alongside fighting for the national cause, reminding us that the place of women as authentic bearers of the nation continues to loom large.

Especially during the period of the so-called 'Kurdish Opening', which started officially in June 2009 to resolve a conflict which had already claimed an estimated 40,000 lives, both secular and Islamic women's NGOs participated in meetings with their Kurdish counterparts. These encounters undoubtedly sensitised women's groups to each others' perspectives and demands. For instance, the broad-based Women's Initiative for Peace (Barış İçin Kadın Girişimi, or BIKG) which was founded in 2009, acted as a bridge between Turkish and Kurdish feminists (Al-Ali and Taş 2017). Yet, many Turkish feminists attributed the predicament of their Kurdish sisters to a combination of underdevelopment and patriarchal customs (Yüksel 2006), misconstruing a struggle for recognition as an issue of redistribution and development. Both secular and Islamic women's NGOs cooperated with ÇATOMs (Multi-Purpose Community Centres – Çok Amaçlı Toplum Merkezi), state-sponsored organisations for women that provide Turkish literacy courses and training in health education programmes that include family planning and income generation. These attempts were critiqued by some Kurdish women for having an 'assimilationist' bias (Çaha 2011). Küçükkırca (2015) argued, however, that the Turkish and Kurdish women's movements which entered into conflictual relations in the 1990s, when the former tended to downplay the realities of war, matured into more affirmative relationships of both solidarity and coalition-building in the 2000s.

These encounters were mediated in complex ways by the Turkish state, its various bureaucratic apparatuses and international organisations such as the UN, the EU and the bilateral and multilateral donor community. Women's grass-roots movements and organisations worked, as we shall see below, at the interstices of changing priorities of state, regional and global actors, attempting to make strategic use of potential allies both domestically and among international bodies (Kardam 2005; Marshall 2013).

Confrontation and Co-optation: Working With and Against the State

Turkey is singled out as the first Muslim-majority country with a secular constitution and a civil code (adopted in 1926) that breaks with the sharia. Women were accorded the vote in 1934, well before some European countries, and reforms in the fields of education and employment boosted their public presence. I argued elsewhere that 'the republican regime opened up an arena for state-sponsored "feminism" but at one and the same time circumscribed and defined its parameters' (Kandiyoti 1991: 42).

Şirin Tekeli (1982) was the first scholar to critically probe into the strategic goals of the Kemalist regime. Alongside eliminating the remnants of the Ottoman *ancien régime* and enlisting women in a national modernisation drive, she suggested that presenting Turkey as a democratic nation electing its women to parliament at a time when dictatorships held sway over some European states (namely in Nazi Germany and Fascist Italy) was a clear priority. However, while the republican reforms accorded women equal rights *de jure* some of the fundamental cultural premises underlying gender relations and sexuality remained untouched (Kandiyoti 1987; Durakbaşa 1998). Indeed, Tekeli (1986) asserted that the image of the self-sacrificing wife–mother–sister defined the attitude of most women's organisations. It fell to a new generation to interrogate the Kemalist legacy and probe its limits.

The vanguard of second-wave feminism in the 1980s consisted of secular women who had benefited from the educational and employment opportunities afforded by the Kemalist reforms. Many were members of the Turkish left. The break of feminists from movements on the left bore striking resemblances to second-wave feminisms in Europe and the US which were the earlier products of the students' movements of the late 1960s. From then on, we would witness both continuities with the earlier Kemalist project in renewed efforts to deepen legal reforms as well as important new departures in the recognition of previously taboo issues of body politics, gender-based violence and sexualities (Arat 1994; Berktay 1998). Second-wave feminism also signalled an important moment of institution building. Organisations such as the Women's Library and Resource Centre (Kadın Eserleri Kütüphanesi) founded in 1990, the Purple Roof Women's Shelter Endowment (Mor Çatı) founded in the same year to offer shelter and protection to abused women, and KADER founded in 1997 to support women's political representation, were legacies of this period (Bora and Günal 2014).

The late 1990s and early 2000s were periods of great ferment for the women's movement. According to the statistics of the feminist NGO, the Flying Broom Association (Uçan Süpürge), whereas there were only ten women's organisations between the years 1973 and 1982, these rose to sixty-four between 1983 and 1992, and by 2004 there were over 350 women's organisations. Networking and advocacy efforts culminated in a major campaign initiated by over 120 women's NGOs from across the country to eliminate any remaining discriminatory clauses in the civil code. The new code, passed in November 2001, abolished the supremacy of men in the conjugal union and established the full equality of men and women with respect to rights over the family abode, marital property, divorce, child custody, inheritance and rights to work and travel.

This was followed by another vigorous three-year campaign between 2002 and 2004, led by a coalition of women's and sexual liberties groups – The Platform for the Reform of the Turkish Penal Code – that resulted in the adoption of the draft law on 26 September 2004. Amendments were put in place to prevent sentence reduction for 'killings in the name of customary law' (or so-called honour killings); marital rape was criminalised; the article foreseeing a reduction or suspension of the sentence of rapists and abductors marrying their victims was abolished; sexual offences, such as harassment at the workplace, were criminalised and the discrimination between virgins and non-virgins, married and unmarried women in sexual crimes was abolished.

The momentum behind these initiatives was undoubtedly bolstered by the administrative and ideational infrastructure that grew around global advocacy for women's rights throughout the UN decades for women and through the process of EU accession after Turkey was accepted as a candidate for membership in December 1999. Feminists seized the moment and made the most of these new spaces for claim-making. No sooner had Turkey ratified the United Nations Convention on the Elimination of all Forms of Discrimination Against Women (CEDAW) in 1985 that a petition signed by 7,000 women was presented to parliament in 1986 demanding that Turkish laws be made compliant with its stipulations. As a requirement of CEDAW, the Directorate on the Status and Problems of Women was established in 1990 as a new national machinery tasked with monitoring the progress of the country. This necessitated new forms of expertise and accountability. Over the years, the directorate became responsive to the demands of feminist organisations and adopted some of their concepts and terms. The expertise and labour of academic feminists working in research centres on women's issues and departments of women's studies (currently numbering around ninety throughout the country) were pressed into service creating a complex landscape of relationships between state bureaucracies, academic institutions, research and consultancy outfits, NGOs and women's grass-roots initiatives (Kandiyoti 2010).

As elsewhere, women's NGOs became recipients of donor funding from organisations ranging from the World Bank and the UN and its specialist agencies to a variety of bilateral donors. Pre-accession assistance by the EU, the largest donor to civil society in Turkey, also spurred the growth women's NGOs in the context of democracy promotion and peace-building. This meant that the agenda of women's NGOs was influenced, if not often set, by donor priorities. The global critiques of the 'NGOisation' of women's movements (Alvarez 1990; Jad 2004) found their echo in Turkey where these developments accrued the derogatory label of 'project feminism' (Bora and Günal 2002; Diner and Toktaş 2010; Üstündağ 2006).

Donor-funded projects carried the risk of depoliticising feminist demands by translating them into technocratic fixes within a broadly neo-liberal agenda and of driving a wedge between the 'gender literate' experts and the grass roots. Nonetheless, women's donor-backed activities also resulted in the diversification of women civil society actors, the spread of rights discourses and new forms of service delivery outside metropolitan centres.

Enabling international conjunctures (such as the EU accession process) also created new opportunity structures for women's collective action and opened up spaces for solidarity and coalition building in the 2000s. This, however, built upon the experience and infrastructure created by first-generation republican women. For instance, women's professional associations such as the Women Jurists Association (Hukukçu Kadınlar Derneği) played active roles in following through on the expectations raised by Kemalist legal reforms. It took decades of invisible behind the scenes work on the remaining discriminatory clauses of national legislation to prepare the ground for the legal reforms of the 2000s. Thus, neither the opportunities offered by global conjunctures nor donor-supported democratisation packages can account for this deeper seam of entirely home-grown activism around women's rights that has shown resilience across generations.

The threats to women's rights platforms and civic spaces were starkly exposed after the AKP government gradually started implementing a project of radical change that set out to capture civil society and refashion the gender regime of the republic. The AKP's stated aim of raising a 'pious generation' targeted gender relations and the family in direct and explicit ways. Furthermore, this shift which started a decade ago is now taking place in an international climate marked by the global ascendance of right-wing populisms and of an illiberal turn that signals that norms of gender equality, however patchily applied, can no longer be taken for granted. Açıksöz and Korkman (2017) suggest, in fact, that an over-visibility of masculinity (and hyper-masculinised leaders) have become a constitutive part of the political repertoire of the contemporary right-wing populist wave. Turkey now finds itself at the epicentre of this wave.

THE REGIME STRIKES BACK: INSTRUMENTALISM AND SOCIAL ENGINEERING

Turkey provides excellent examples of the instrumentalisation of women's rights. Like many countries jumping on the women's rights bandwagon for geopolitical advantage, Turkey made the most of the legal advances of the early 2000s during the first term of the AKP (2002–7) when EU accession was still high on the policy agenda. As a result, women's NGOs played an active role in advocacy and policy formulation and in the representation of Turkey in international fora. Turkey was also the first country to ratify the Council of Europe's Convention on Preventing and Combating Violence Against Women and Domestic Violence (CAHVIO), the Istanbul Convention, in 2012.

Under this facade of compliance with international standard-setting instruments, new political messages had started circulating. One of the first shocks came at a consultation meeting with women's NGOs (where some sixty organisations were present) on 18 July 2010, where then Prime Minister Erdoğan declared that he did not believe in the equality of men and women. Women's principal, and preferably sole vocation, should be home-making and motherhood in accordance with their divinely ordained nature (*fitrat*).[12] It is worth noting that some of the eighty-odd attendees were members of NGOs with known feminist credentials whose sense of consternation was in no small measure related to the fact that they had long been working within state structures and representing Turkey on a variety of international platforms.

This situation was further aggravated when the embarrassing Uludere incident in December 2011 (where thirty-four Kurdish smugglers were killed near the Iraqi border after the Turkish military allegedly thought them to be Kurdistan Workers' Party (PKK) militants) was rather unexpectedly turned into a debate about a Turkish woman's right to choose. Speaking to a meeting of the AKP's women's branches in Ankara on 26 May 2012, Prime Minister Erdoğan told the assembled women that he considered abortion as murder and suggested that abortion and Turkey's high rate of caesarean section births were part of a hidden plot to reduce Turkey's population. Similar pronouncements and a pronatalist insistence on at least three children per woman have followed with regularity.

Institutional changes followed. The General Directorate of Women's Status and Problems was abolished in 2011 and replaced by the Ministry of the Family and Social Policies. Women were now being cast primarily as objects of 'protection' alongside children, the disabled and the elderly rather than fully fledged bearers of rights. The Directorate of Religious Affairs (Diyanet İşleri Başkanlığı) started operating in tandem with the Ministry of Family and Social Policies with an enhanced mandate and an enlarged budget, aiming to refashion gender relations and family life. The outreach mechanisms of the directorate involved a significant feminisation of its cadres through the employment of female preachers (*vaize*) who reach women at the grass roots in diverse contexts (Hassan 2011). The directorate also fields a network of family guidance bureaus in all provincial capitals and numerous sub-districts to offer religious guidance on family and other personal matters. Again, the target audience is predominantly female, as are the majority of the counsellors (Sancar 2016). Adak (2017) argues that this penetration of the private sphere by state institutions acts as a key agent of desecularisation, despite a nominally secular constitution.

Gender issues were constantly kept on the agenda by systematic attempts to roll back the gains of the 2001 Civil Code and the 2004 Penal Code. A case in point was the work of an investigative commission established on 14 January 2016 by the Turkish parliament on 'Protecting the Integrity of Family', with the purpose of investigating the causes of allegedly high divorce rates.[13] The draft report of the commission, nicknamed the 'Divorce Commission', lowers legal marriage age from eighteen to fifteen. If minors (those below fifteen) engage in sex with adults there is no charge of paedophilia if they decide to get married and if the marriage shows no evidence of physical violence for five years. This proposal was castigated on Turkish social media as the 'marrying your rapist' law and street demonstrations followed. The report also proposes a system of mediation in cases of domestic abuse (with hardly any mention of shelters for abused women), limits the payment period of alimony and recommends the mediation of family counsellors from the Directorate of Religious Affairs in preference to divorce proceedings in open court.

Despite fierce protests by thousands of women in thirteen cities in October 2017, an amendment called the 'mufti marriage' bill was passed into law allowing muftis (state-employed Sunni clerics) to issue civil marriage licences. Women's rights groups expressed concerns that this legislation initiates a dual track marriage certificate system that may carry the risk of making child marriages easier.

This state-directed effort at re-educating women and closing off avenues of survival outside the family has direct repercussions on civil society which is now populated by a myriad of government-organised NGOs (or GONGOs). Many are active under the umbrella organisation of the Turkish Family Platform (TÜRAP) whose mission statement includes the protection and elevation of the family and of general morality. Funding flows are directed towards 'government-sponsored' civil society such as the Women and Democracy Association (KADEM), whose deputy chair is Erdoğan's younger daughter Sümeyye Erdoğan Bayraktar. Although Turkey remains a signatory of CEDAW, an alternative approach to gender justice through the 'complementarity' of the sexes has now become official state ideology.[14]

The hijacking of women's initiatives by ruling elites in authoritarian Arab states where the wives, daughters and close kin of heads of state or ruling dynasties headed government-sponsored women's organisations is a familiar pattern and one that led to the discrediting of women's rights platforms in the immediate aftermath of the Arab uprisings (Kandiyoti 2012a). This type of co-optation did not characterise the political landscape of Turkey. Indeed, Turkey exhibited the full range of modes of operation detailed in Molyneux's (1998) influential typology that distinguishes between independent, associational and directed organisations. Although 'official' state-sanctioned women's organisations have always collaborated with governments, and women's branches of political parties and labour unions have always acted as their auxiliaries, there was also a space in civil society allowing for the independent articulation of women's gender interests (as demonstrated by the lobbying activities that led to legal reforms in 2001 and 2004). These spaces have now left their place to government-dependent clientelistic networks that are part of a broader process of capture of civil society by the state in the service of a totalistic vision for a 'new Turkey'.

Whilst overtly targeting feminist organisations, the top-down policies of the state have also exerted a demobilising effect on Islamic women's NGOs and had a crippling effect on Kurdish women's civil society initiatives. The first run-in between the male AKP leadership and Muslim women's organisations came when they demanded parliamentary representation in the run-up to the 2011 elections. It suited male members of the AKP to keep militancy around the headscarf ban alive while they were in the process of consolidating their grip on power. However, the 'No Vote If There is No Candidate with a Headscarf!'

campaign elicited a lukewarm if not an outright hostile response. Some columnists even took religious women to task for betraying their god-ordained mission as mothers and home-makers, going as far as slandering them as 'fifth columnists' who aim to destroy the Muslim community from within. Ruşen Çakır (2000) offered a harsh evaluation of the relationships between Islamic parties and their female following (first in the case of the Welfare Party and then the AKP), arguing that the only deal the male leadership was prepared to make was one where women could be deployed as trump cards to further their common cause but only on condition that they made no demands of their own.

It was not until 2013 that four women lawmakers appeared in parliament in their headscarves. This was to have paradoxical effects. The 'victimhood' narrative of the AKP rested in no small measure on the fact that veiled women were debarred from public service and the parliament. This victory, in conjunction with the government's increasingly top-down, and interventionist approach, had a demobilising effect on Muslim women activists. This may also have signalled a parting of the ways for the different constituencies that the headscarf ban had held together. Fully co-opted individuals, groups and organisations received the material payoffs of working in well-resourced think tanks, NGOs and media outlets. Those, on the other hand, who exhibit more pluralistic leanings and feel discomfort with the increasing authoritarianism of the regime, risk marginalisation and exclusion.[15]

If the authoritarian policies of the government had a paralysing effect on secular groups and a demobilising effect on Muslim women activists, the consequences for Kurdish actors in both political and civil society have been nothing short of devastating. By the end of 2014 the Kurdish peace process was all but shattered by events in neighbouring Syria where the IS siege of the border city of Kobane and its environs and the Turkish government's seemingly complacent attitude to the massacre of its civilians galvanised riots and protests in the Kurdish south-east. The climate deteriorated even further after the June 2015 elections when the Kurdish-led People's Democratic Party (HDP) garnered 13 per cent of the national vote, denying the governing Justice and Development Party (AKP) an absolute majority. Heavy-handed and polarising election tactics in the run-up to repeat elections in November 2015 secured the AKP's single-party majority at the cost of an alliance with a nationalist bloc that vehemently opposes the Kurdish peace process. In the run up to the 16 April 2017 constitutional referendum on an amendment that would transform Turkey from a parliamentary democracy to an executive presidential system, the People's Democratic Party (HDP) and its regional sister party the Democratic Regions Party (DBP) were directly targeted, removing them from the political field altogether and jailing many of its members (including the chair and co-chair) under charges of terrorism. The cross-border military operations in Syria aiming to annihilate the PKK have contributed to a frenzied mood of nationalism that denounces any form of dissent as treason. The June 2018 elections have further cemented the alliance between the AKP and the ultra-nationalist MHP (National Movement Party) providing both the necessary votes to enact regime change and make up for the AKP's shortfall in achieving a parliamentary majority. The fragile threads binding civil society actors across ethnic and religious divides are now moribund.

In this dispiriting political landscape, women's rights activists appear to have no foothold left in either state or civil society. They have to resort to ad hoc organising, reactive, issue-based mobilisation, new forms of expression on the Internet and social media[16] or engaging in the 'unruly politics' (Tadros 2011) of the street which carries major risks. Nonetheless, unlike women's rights platforms that were confined to an educated secular urban elite in the early years of the republic and for many decades to follow, we are now witnessing a mass movement that cuts across many social divides and mobilises women from all walks of life. Arat (2016) is entirely justified in arguing that women's movements have been central to the deepening of democracy in Turkey by keeping egalitarian and emancipatory values alive. I would like to conclude by speculating on their prospects for survival under a regime that is intent on closing off all avenues of claim-making and dissent.

Conclusion

Women's struggles in Turkey have been rich in paradoxes. The republican reforms of the 1920s and 1930s were enacted in an impoverished, war-weary, predominantly rural and illiterate society at a point in time when sociological realities were not aligned with the possibilities offered by new legislation. These top-down reforms initially remained a dead letter outside a relatively thin layer of urbanites and failed to elicit popular buy-in from conservative strata of society. Nonetheless, the cadres of professional women nurtured by the republic created social expectations and an infrastructure of institutions that would serve as a baseline for future mobilisation. Since the 1980s, second generation feminists took up the challenge and were joined by religious and Kurdish women struggling to carve out their own space and find their own voices within their respective movements.

Throughout the 1990s and early 2000s there was a steady process of diffusion of gender equality norms in political society, in popular culture and in everyday life. Paradoxically, this coincided with the simultaneous 'Islamisation' of public space and the normalisation of public expressions of piety. This co-existence of lifestyles, a booming economy and a polity that seemed headed in a more pluralistic direction in the early days of European accession, inspired the label

'Turkish model': an 'Islamic liberalism' based on 'the marriage of formal democracy, free market capitalism and (a toned down) conservative Islam' (Tuğal 2016: 112). Yet behind this facade of democratisation, lauded by international observers and Turkish liberals alike, breaches of the rule of law, show trials and a culling of secular military and bureaucratic cadres were being orchestrated by the AKP and their erstwhile Gülenist allies who had infiltrated state apparatuses at every level. The conventional narrative of authoritarian secularism versus liberalisation led by Muslim 'conservative democrats' (Kandiyoti 2012b) acted to obfuscate a sustained and systematic process of embedding of unaccountable and illiberal actors into the polity. The failed military coup of 15 July 2016, the unprecedented purges that followed, the constitutional referendum of April 2017 that marked the shift to an executive presidency and the June 2018 elections that institutionalised one-man rule were milestones on the road to regime change. Moreover, these transformations took place against the background of both rising levels of coercion and the constant deployment of a highly polarising discourse that excludes any dissenters from national belonging.

The rapid unravelling of the 'Turkish model' in the aftermath of the 2011 Arab uprisings and the Gezi protets of the summer of 2013 represented a turning point that pushed the regime to intensify its authoritarianism and conservatism further. The spectacle of allegedly apolitical millennials joining the protests and its diffusion across all provinces (where university campuses now exist) inflamed the government who lashed out in fury, further antagonising educated urban youth. What made this type of youth protest particularly subversive is that it destabilised dominant political culture by exposing the patriarchal pretensions of power. Dissenting youth explicitly targeted an idiom of power that transcends the secular/Islamic divide and traverses diverse mainstream political parties: an authoritarian conservatism that is prone to the cult of the patriarch/ruler.[17] This resilient strain in political culture combined with a masculinist militarism that is touted as a key ingredient of national identity (Altınay 2004), is now fully installed and erects formidable hurdles to any gender egalitarian or, indeed, any emancipatory project. The safeguard of male privilege – whether in the name of religion, the maintenance of social order or the integrity of the 'national' family – is integral to this package. Well-educated young professionals who came of age under AKP rule (known as the 'Gezi generation') are rejecting this new order by voting with their feet and leaving Turkey in what has become the largest brain drain in generations (Gursel 2018).

There are, however, important sources of instability inherent to this gender regime. First, we have the irony that it is precisely at a point in time when substantial societal transformations have heightened youth expectations concerning their levels of education, their lifestyles, life prospects and choices in marriage and divorce (Özyeğin 2015) that gender relations and women's rights are being made an active subject of contention and the object of heavy-handed social engineering. Decades of changes in consumption and leisure patterns, in family structures and lifestyles mean that notions of female subordination are no longer securely hegemonic. This is precisely what mandates reliance on a new politics of masculinist restoration as a blunt tool for the maintenance and reproduction of patriarchy. This politics requires systematic indoctrination, greater surveillance and higher levels of intrusion into citizens' lives. Yet there is both an irony and a paradox in the fact that a form of rule that explicitly targets the private and the policing of gender relations risks bringing personal liberties and gender issues closer to the heart of democratic struggles than ever before. This may unexpectedly give rise to new coalitions and cross-gender alliances in recognition of the fact that the politics of gender has now become a key stake in anti-authoritarian resistance. There is little doubt that the staying power and resilience of women's movements in Turkey will play a central role in any future struggles for democracy.

Dedication and Acknowledgement

This chapter is dedicated to the memory of Şirin Tekeli whom we lost in June 2017. She was a pioneer of second-wave feminism in Turkey who left us with a rich intellectual legacy and a deep influence on numerous institutions and campaigns she helped to promote. Her integrity and commitment continue to inspire us. I owe a debt of gratitude to Yeşim Arat and Fatmagül Berktay for encouraging me to persevere with this chapter at a time when I was wavering. I also owe thanks to Sevgi Adak, Ceren Lord, Merve Kütük-Kuriş and Zühre Emanet for their thoughtful comments on an earlier draft.

Notes

1. I define this term to broadly denote processes of appropriation, contestation and reinterpretation of positions on gender relations, women's rights and sexual liberties by state, non-state and global actors.
2. This is the refrain of a song written by Filiz Kerestecioğlu on the occasion of the demonstration of 17 May 1987 protesting violence against women. It has since become Turkey's feminist anthem.
3. Political instability and violence in the 1970s, including ideological confrontation between leftist and right-wing groups, served as justification for military intervention. In the aftermath of the coup, all political parties were closed down (except for newly founded ones vetted by the military), many leaders of the political parties, labour unions and political organisations were banned from politics and a new constitution was adopted in 1982, severely curtailing individual rights and freedoms.
4. This ban, which was inconsistently applied until the 1990s, was only lifted in universities in 2008 and fully for all public-sector personnel in 2013.

5. The Welfare Party (Refah Partisi), an Islamic Party with leanings similar to the Muslim Brotherhood, participated in successive coalition governments from 1991 until it became the largest party in 1996 under the leadership of Necmettin Erbakan.
6. Outrageous pronouncements concerning women became increasingly commonplace. The cases mentioned here merely represent some examples. A functionary of the Greater Istanbul municipality (who was eventually sacked) declared after the presidential referendum of April 2017, won by a slim majority in favour of an executive presidency, that 'the women and girls of those who voted No are now booty (*ganimet* – the term used to indicate loot after a victory) to us'. Available at <http://www.hurriyet.com.tr/skandal-paylasim-sonrasi-aciga-alindi-40426547> (last accessed 14 April 2017). A local *müftü* (religious functionary) created an outcry by using his Facebook account to declare in September 2017 that 'merchandise with faulty packaging sells at half price' in an allusion to women who go around uncovered. Available at <http://www.hurriyet.com.tr/muftunun-sosyal-medya-hesabindan-yaptigi-paylasim-tepki-cekti-40586255> (last accessed 21 September 2017). The pro-regime theologian Hayrettin Karaman accused covered women who smoke of indecent conduct and immodesty. The first reaction came from an AKP minister whose covered daughter is a smoker and a deluge of other protests followed. Available at <http://www.internethaber.com/hayrettin-karaman-sigara-icen-basortulu-kadinlar-icin-boyle-dedi-1797672h.htm> (last accessed 3 August 2017).
7. Documentary footage is available at <https://www.youtube.com/watch?v=4XbfX-Rt5j00> (last accessed 20 August 2018).
8. The Kurdish conflict flared up in 1984 when the Kurdistan Workers' Party (Partiya Karkerên Kurdistanê – PKK hereafter) mounted an insurgency against the Turkish state. The PKK declared a unilateral ceasefire until 1999 when the PKK leader Abdullah Öcalan was captured. Hostilities resumed on 1 June 2004. In 2013, the Turkish Government and the jailed PKK leader started talks. On 21 March 2013, Öcalan announced the 'end of armed struggle' and a ceasefire accompanied by peace talks. This paved the way for the so-called 'Kurdish opening'. On 25 July 2015, the PKK cancelled their 2013 ceasefire after a year of acute tensions.
9. According to a Pew Research poll the proportion of those who wish to see sharia as 'the law of the land' in Turkey make up some 12 per cent of the population, in contrast to 84 per cent in Pakistan and 74 per cent in Egypt. Available at <http://www.pewforum.org/2013/04/30/the-worlds-muslims-religion-politics-society-overview/> (last accessed 10 August 2018).
10. Noteworthy among these was the Emek ve Adalet Platformu (Platform for Labour and Justice) representing the views of Muslims dissatisfied with the excesses of neo-liberal policies under the AKP. An open-air *iftar* (evening meal breaking the Ramadan fast) that was open to all was held as an act of pluralistic conviviality that seemed like a living reproach to the polarising and belligerent discourse of the government.
11. An alleged attack on a veiled woman in front of Istanbul's Kabataş dock at the height of the Gezi protests during the summer of 2013 had the prime minister fuming over the affront to 'our sister' that demonstrated the violent and anti-religious disposition of the protesters. The incident was later challenged by CCTV footage as possibly

bogus. The same applied to the alleged consumption of beer and alcoholic beverages by the demonstrators inside a mosque where they took shelter. Nonetheless, a group of Muslim women (Kadına Karşı Şiddete Karşı Müslümanlar İnisiyatifi – Muslim Initiative Against Violence Against Women) held a march from Kabataş to Taksim where they were met by feminists in a show of solidarity and recognition of their common plight.

12. 'Kadınla Erkek Eşit Olamaz', *Vatan*, 20 July 2010. Available at <http://www.gazetevatan.com/haber/kadinla-erkekesit-olamaz/318006/9/Siyaset> (last accessed 10 July 2013).
13. In fact, compared to most countries in the Middle East, divorce rates in Turkey are relatively modest at 1.7 per cent as compared to a 7.7 per cent annual marriage rate. Rates of violence against women, on the other hand, are of epidemic proportions.
14. KADEM's Journal of Women's Studies (bilingual in Turkish and English) is the academic arm of the Association that promotes a gender order that is in harmony with the government's ideological and cultural goals. The Family Academy Association (Aile Akademisi Derneği), a member of TÜRAP, also disseminates materials that challenge the concept of gender equality that underwrites CEDAW. See for instance <http://aileakademisi.org/sites/default/files/arastirma_kadin_erkek_farkliliklari.pdf> (last accessed 10 March 2017).
15. It is, for instance, hard to imagine that some of the fleeting openings that occurred in the past could recur. After the lifting of the headscarf ban in universities a group of women created a blog under the rubric *We Are Not Yet Free* (available at <www.henuzozgurolamadik.blogspot.com> (last accessed 11 March 2016)) with a petition stating that, as women who had been discriminated against, they would not be happy to attend universities with their headscarves until Kurdish and Alevi rights are also recognised. Another blog in the same period *We Look Out for Each Other* (available at <http://www.birbirimizesahipcikiyoruz.blogspot.com> (last accessed 11 March 2016) was a call for solidarity across women of different persuasions in recognition of their common predicament. These initiatives which required courage and were quite marginal at the time have become inconceivable in the current climate.
16. The blogosphere features sites such as Reçel, 5 Harfliler and Çatlak Zemin, which express the sensibilities of a new generation of young women who refuse to be dictated to and insist on choice and inclusivity.
17. The president is called Reis (chief) by devoted followers and now poses as the *pater patriae* (father of the nation) alongside Atatürk, the founder of the republic.

Bibliography

Acar, Feride (2010), 'Kadın Dergileri ve Bir Grup Üniversite Öğrencisi Üzerine Bir İnceleme', in Ş. Tekeli (ed.), *1980'ler Türkiye'sinde Kadın Bakış Açısından Kadınlar*, Istanbul: İletişim Yayınları, 5th edition.

Açık, Necla (2013), 'Re-defining the role of women within the Kurdish national movement in Turkey in the 1990s', in C. Güneş and W. Zeydanlıoğlu (eds), *The Kurdish Question in Turkey: New Perspectives on Conflict, Representation and Reconciliation*, London: Routledge, pp. 114–36.

Açiksöz, Salih Can and Zeynep Kurtuluş Korkman (2017), 'Grab 'em by the patriarchy', *Anthropology News*, 8 May 2017, <http://www.anthropologynews.org/index.php/2017/05/08/grabem-by-the-patriarchy/> (last accessed 10 June 2017).
Adak, Sevgi (2017), 'Turkish secularism revisited', *The Middle East in London*, 13: 5, pp. 11–12.
Aksoy, Hürcan Aslı (2015). 'Invigorating democracy in Turkey: the agency of organized Islamist women', *Politics & Gender*, 11: 1, pp. 146–70.
Al-Ali, Nadje and Latif Taş (2017), '"War is like a blanket": feminist convergences in Kurdish and Turkish women's rights activism for peace', *Journal of Middle East Women's Studies*, 13: 3, pp. 354–75.
Altınay, Ayşe Gül (2004), *The Myth of the Military Nation: Militarism, Gender, and Education in Turkey*, New York: Palgrave Macmillan.
Alvarez, Sonia (1990), *Engendering Democracy. Women's Movements in Transition Politics*, Princeton: Princeton University Press.
Arat, Yeşim (1994), 'Women's movement of the 1980s in Turkey: radical outcome of liberal Kemalism?', in F. Müge Göçek and S. Balaghi (eds), *Reconstructing Gender in the Middle East: Tradition, Identity and Power*, New York: Columbia University Press, pp. 100–112.
—— (2016), '1980 Sonrası Kadın Sorunları ve Kadın Hareketi', in M. Kabasakal (ed.), *Türkiyede Siyasal Yaşam: Dün, Bugün, Yarın*, Istanbul: Bilgi Üniversitesi Yayınları.
Berktay, Fatmagül (1998), 'Cumhuriyet'in 75 Yıllık Serüvenine Kadın Açısından Bakmak', in A. B. Hacımirzalıoğlu (ed.), *75 Yılda Kadınlar ve Erkekler*, Istanbul: İş Bankası ve Tarih Vakfı, pp. 1–11.
Bora, Aksu and Asena Günal (eds) (2014), *90'larda Türkiye'de Feminizm*, Istanbul: İletişim, 5th edition.
Çağlayan, Handan (2013), 'From Kawa the Blacksmith to Ishtar the Goddess: gender constructions in ideological–political discourses of the Kurdish movement in post-1980 Turkey', trans. C. Evren, *European Journal of Turkish Studies* [Online], 14 | 2012, online since 18 January 2013, <http://ejts.revues.org/4657> (last accessed 1 November 2017).
Çaha, Ömer (2011), 'The Kurdish women's movement: a third-wave feminism within the Turkish context', *Turkish Studies*, 12: 3, pp. 435–49.
Çakır, Ruşen (2000), 'Dindar kadının serüveni', *Birikim Dergisi*, 137, September, pp. 27–35.
Cizre, Umut and M. Çınar (2003), 'Turkey 2002: Kemalism, Islamism and politics in the light of the February 28 process', in S. Irzık and G. Güzeldere (eds), *Relocating the Fault Lines: Turkey Beyond the East–West Divide*, The South Atlantic Quarterly, 102: 2–3, pp. 309–32.
Diner, Çağla and Şule Toktaş (2010), 'Waves of feminism in Turkey: Kemalist, Islamist, and Kurdish women's movements in an era of globalization', *Journal of Balkan and Near Eastern Studies*, 12: 1, pp. 41–57.
Durakbaşa, Ayşe (1998), 'Cumhuriyet Döneminde Modern Kadın ve Erkek Kimliklerinin Oluşumu: Kemalist Kadın Kimliği ve Münevver Erkekler', in A. B. Hacımirzaoğlu (ed.), *75 Yılda Kadınlar ve Erkekler*, Istanbul: Tarih Vakfı, pp. 29–50.
Gürsel, Kadri (2018), 'Gezi generation' fleeing Turkey', *Al-Monitor*, 21 September,

<http://www.al-monitor.com/pulse/originals/2018/09/turkey-brain-drain-young-generation-fleeing.html#ixzz5RwJJq6Ed> (last accessed 10 December 2018).

Hassan, Mona (2011), 'Women preaching for the secular state: official female preachers in contemporary Turkey', *International Journal of Middle East Studies*, 43: 3, pp. 451–73.

Jad, Islah (2004), 'The NGO-isation of Arab women's movements', *IDS Bulletin*, 35: 4, pp. 34–42.

Kadıoğlu, Ayşe (2005), 'Civil Society, Islam and democracy in Turkey: a study of three Islamic non-governmental organizations', *Muslim World*, 95: 1, pp 23–41.

'Kadınla Erkek Eşit Olamaz', *Vatan*, 20 July 2010, <http://www.gazetevatan.com/haber/kadinla-erkekesit-olamaz/318006/9/Siyaset> (last accessed 10 July 2013).

Kandiyoti, Deniz (1987), 'Emancipated but unliberated? Reflections on the Turkish case', *Feminist Studies*, 13: 2, pp. 317–38.

—— (1991), 'End of empire: Islam, nationalism and women in Turkey', in D. Kandiyoti (ed.), *Women, Islam and the State*, London: Macmillan, pp. 22–47.

—— (2010), 'Gender and women's studies in Turkey: a moment for reflection?', *New Perspectives on Turkey*, 43, Fall, pp. 165–76.

—— (2012a), 'Disquiet and despair: the gender sub-texts of the "Arab spring"', *Open Democracy*, 26 June, <https://www.opendemocracy.net/5050/deniz-kandiyoti/disquiet-and-despair-gender-sub-texts-of-arab-spring> (last accessed 1 October 2017).

—— (2012b), 'The travails of the secular: puzzle and paradox in Turkey', *Economy and Society*, 41: 4, pp. 513–31.

—— (2014), 'Contesting patriarchy-as-governance: lessons from youth-led activism', *Open Democracy*, 7 March, <http://www.opendemocracy.net/5050/deniz-kandiyoti/contesting-patriarchy-as-governance-lessons-from-youth-led-activism> (last accessed 1 October 2017).

—— (2016), 'Locating the politics of gender: patriarchy, neoliberal governance and violence in Turkey', *Research and Policy on Turkey*, 1: 2, pp. 103–18, DOI: 10.1080/23760818.2016.1201242 (last accessed 1 October 2017).

Kardam, Nükhet (2005), *Turkey's Engagement with Global Women's Human Rights*, Aldershot: Ashgate.

Küçükkırca, İclal Ayşe (2015), 'Coalition or solidarity? Or maybe a different approach: the relationality between the free women's movement of Kurdistan and the feminist movement in Turkey', *Trespassing: Gender*, 5, Fall, pp. 38–58, <http://trespassingjournal.com/Issue5/TPJ_I5_Kucukkirca_Article.pdf> (last accessed 15 October 2017).

Marshall, Gül Aldıkaçtı (2005), 'Ideology, progress, and dialogue: a comparison of feminist and Islamist women's approaches to the issues of head covering and work in Turkey', *Gender & Society*, 19: 1, pp. 104–20.

—— (2013), *Shaping Gender Policy in Turkey: Grassroots Women Activists, the European Union, and the Turkish State*, Albany, NY, SUNY Press.

Molyneux, Maxine (1998), 'Analyzing women's movements', *Development and Change*, 29: 2, April, pp. 219–45.

Özkırımlı, Umut (ed.) (2014), *The Making of a Protest Movement*. London: Palgrave Macmillan.

Özyeğin, Gül (2015), *New Desires, New Selves: Sex, Love and Piety among Turkish Youth*, New York and London: New York University Press.

Sancar, Serpil (2016), 'Diyanet'in 'Kadınlaşması': Diyanet İşleri Başkanlığı'nın Yeni Kadın ve Aile Politikası', in Ç. Kağıtçıbaşı, D Barlas, H. Şigma, M. Önok and Z. Gülru Göker (eds), *Kadın Odaklı: Koç-Kam Araştırmaları Dizisi 1*, Istanbul: Koç Üniversitesi Yayınları.

Saktanber, Ayşe (2006), 'Women and the iconography of fear: Islamization in post-Islamist Turkey, *Journal of Women in Culture and Society*, 32: 1), pp. 21–31, http://vc.bridgew.edu/cgi/viewcontent.cgi?article=1151&context=jiws> (last accessed 1 February 2019).

Sirman, Nühkhet (1989), 'Feminism in Turkey: a short history', *New Perspectives on Turkey*, 3, pp. 1–34.

Tadros, Mariz (2011), 'The Politics of Unruly Ruptures', *UNRISD*, 5 December, <http://www.unrisd.org/80256B3C005BE6B5/search/6CACEA99340950AAC125795D00581C33> (last accessed 1 February 2019).

Tekeli, Şirin (1982), *Kadınlar ve Siyasal Toplumsal Hayat*, Istanbul: İletişim.

—— (1986) 'Emergence of the new feminist movement in Turkey', in D. Dahlerup (ed.), *The New Women's Movement: Feminism and Political Power in Europe and the USA*, London: Sage, pp. 179–99.

—— (ed.) (1995), *Women in Modern Turkish Society: a Reader*, London: Zed Books.

Toktaş, Sule and Mary Lou O'Neil (2015), 'Competing frameworks of Islamic law and secular civil law in Turkey: a case study on women's property and inheritance practices', *Women's Studies International Forum*, 48, pp. 29–38.

Tuğal, Cihan (2016), *The Fall of the Turkish Model: How the Arab Uprisings Brought Down Islamic Liberalism*, London: Verso.

Turam, Berna (2008), 'Turkish women divided by politics: secularist activism versus pious non-resistance', *International Feminist Journal of Politics*, 10: 4, pp. 475–94.

Yüksel, Metin (2006), 'The encounter of Kurdish women with nationalism in Turkey', *Middle Eastern Studies*, 42: 5, pp. 777–802.

Üstündağ, Nazan (2006), 'Türkiye'de projecilik üzerine eleştirel bir değerlendirme', *Amargi*, Winter 4, pp. 23–4.

Chapter 6

Discrete Moves and Parallel Tracks: Gender Politics in Post-2001 Afghanistan

TORUNN WIMPELMANN

Introduction

Few places have been so central to the debate about the relationships between gender, Islam and Western power in recent decades as Afghanistan. In late 2001, following the 9/11 terrorist attacks in the US, Afghanistan's Taliban government was overthrown by the US and its allies, in an invasion partially justified by the need to liberate Afghan women from Taliban oppression. A post-9/11 grand narrative of 'women's localized oppression and foreign saving' (Fluri and Lehr 2017) produced harrowing accounts of the subjugation of Afghan women at the hands of the Taliban, followed by celebrations of their new-won freedoms and public visibility under the new order. Central to this grand narrative was a radio address made by American First Lady Laura Bush in November 2001, a few weeks after the first bombs were dropped on Afghanistan. The First Lady famously declared that:

> Because of our recent military gains in much of Afghanistan, women are no longer imprisoned in their homes. They can listen to music and teach their daughters without fear of punishment... The fight against terrorism is also a fight for the rights and dignity of women.

Not surprisingly, triumphalist accounts such as these were soon countered by sharp denunciations of feminism that aligned itself with Western military imperialism (Abu-Lughod 2002; Hirschkind and Mahmood 2002; Butler 2004), drawing on parallels with colonial tropes of 'saving brown women from brown men' (Spivak 1988). These critiques problematised simplistic equations of veiling and the burka as an indicator of Afghan women's agency and status (Abu-Lughod 2002), and the reduction of multiple causes of suffering – war, displacement, poverty – to Taliban gender oppression (Daulatzai 2008; Kandiyoti 2007). They also pointed to the glossing over of earlier US support to Afghan Islamists – the *mujahedin* – with gender policies resembling those of the Taliban (Hirschkind and Mahmood 2002). The critiques provided important correctives to simplistic and instrumental notions of Afghan women being 'saved' by the military removal of the Taliban.

At times, however, the debate risked being reduced to 'moral posturing' (Abu-Lughod 2010), in which post-2001 Western models and their effects on gender politics in Afghanistan was declared either wholly emancipatory – or wholly imperialist. Certainly, the preoccupation with interrogating the premises for Western claims of 'saving Afghan women' have tended to overshadow (or even detract from) examinations of actual, subsequent developments of gender politics in Afghanistan. In this chapter, I demonstrate how such a detailed exploration unsettles notions of Western interventions into gender politics in Afghanistan as either the unambiguous liberation of its women, or a simple tool of imperialism. I show how both local and external visions of women's positions and entitlements were multiple and contradictory.

Western countries, for instance, would vacillate between the promotion of universal frameworks for women's rights, on the one hand, and concessions to sharia or to 'cultural sensitivities' on the other. Nor did the Afghan government enforce a singular gender regime. The many gender orders envisioned by Afghan officialdom ranged from socialist-inspired state paternalism to dogmatic enforcement of sharia to a socially conservative recognition of patriarchal authority.

In fact, contemporary orders of governance in Afghanistan themselves defy conventional labels such as the Afghan 'state' or the 'international community'. Post-2001 Afghanistan must be understood as a site of competing claims of governance, transnationally, nationally and locally configured and working through state structures to various degrees. In other words, I contend that we cannot undertake a meaningful analysis of the specific relationship between governance, Islam and gender politics in the case of Afghanistan if governance is equated with state projects or 'the Afghan state'. I lay out throughout this chapter how this fragmentation becomes visible through its consequences for gender politics and gender regimes. I focus, in particular, on women's legal rights and the governance of gender through evolving legal configurations.

Histories of Governance, Gender and Islam in Afghanistan

As argued by several contributors to this volume, the relationship between gender and Islam is inextricably shaped by the political alignments of a given setting. In Afghanistan many recent configurations in the domain of gender have appeared as dramatic shifts imposed by the political center in a top-down manner. Much like the broader political projects they were part of (communism, Islamism, liberal democracy), these configurations failed – sometimes rather spectacularly – in consolidating themselves. The first Afghan ruler to place the status of women at the forefront of his political agenda was Amanullah Khan (r. 1919–29). Inspired by Ataturk's Turkey, reformist Islam and nationalism, the king's vision for his country centred on education, the rule of law and the emancipation of women (Olesen 1995). Having promulgated a number of legal reforms that restricted polygamy, child marriage and generally curtailed the power of the Islamic clergy, Amanullah faced increasing hostility from conservative forces. His lack of political and coercive power, as well as his increasingly authoritarian approach (Nawid 1999) left him ill-equipped to face the revolts that eventually forced him to abdicate the throne. In significant parts of Afghan historiography, the case of Amanullah is employed to suggest that the perennial sensitivity of the Afghan male population to any outside attempts at reforming gender relations makes such undertakings doomed (Wide 2016). At the same time, Amanullah's anti-imperialist credentials combined with his ability to articulate a vision of gender relations less patriarchal and nonetheless rooted in Islam scriptures mean that he remains an icon to many progressive Afghans.

Having revoked Amanullah's most radical reforms, subsequent Afghan rulers largely refrained from intervention in the domain of women's status and rights. By the 1970s, the development of a small urban middle class saw women entering the universities and many professional fields, albeit in small numbers (Dupree 1984). Legal reforms enacted in 1977, under the authoritarian government of Daoud Khan (r. 1973–8) (after a short period of parliamentarianism), introduced some of the same reforms that Amanullah had attempted five decades earlier. They included the prohibition of underage marriage, restrictions on polygamy and provisions for divorce. Half a century of social change and a different political context meant that these reforms were now less controversial. But the country was about to enter several decades of war and political upheaval, where questions of gender would again come to the forefront. Less than two years later the communist Peoples Democratic Party of Afghanistan (PDPA) seized power through a violent coup and sought to dismantle what they considered the vestiges of feudal power in Afghanistan through land reforms, debt cancellation, literacy programmes and changes to marriage practices (Dorronsoro 2005). These latter were promulgated in the government's Decree Number 7, which made forced and underage marriage, as well as excessive wedding celebrations and dowries, criminal offences (Malikyar 1997).

Like Amanullah's reform attempts half a century earlier, Decree Number 7 was framed by its critics as a misguided foray into the sensitive domain of the family and was singled out as a key explanation for the government's unpopularity and eventual downfall (Malikyar 1997). A more convincing argument, however, is that in both cases the 'woman question' served as rallying cry against rulers who had attacked a series of vested interests from a very narrow power base (Ahmed 2017), and in the case of the PDPA, through unprecedented violent repression. When, in December 1979, Soviet military forces invaded the country to prevent the new government from collapsing into vicious infighting, the military resistance against the communist government was further galvanised. It was soon framed primarily in religious terms, as a jihad against the Soviet occupying power and their local collaborators (Dorronsoro 2005). The *mujahedin* fighters, as they became known, were supported by the US, Saudi Arabia and Pakistan, and promoted an Islamist ideology. The *mujahedin* controlled the refugee camps in Pakistan, where they enforced strict gender seclusion, eventually banning Afghan refugee women from working for humanitarian organisations and girls from attending school (Billaud 2015). In 1992, the *mujahedin* finally succeeded in driving the communist rulers out of Kabul. They sought to cleanse Afghan society from the depredations of communist rule, partly through the imposition of a gender regime radically different from that of their predecessors. Women's mobility, visibility and access to work and education would no longer be left to the discretion of their families but become subject to the uniform dictates of the government. Among other things, all female public servants were dismissed (Billaud 2015), and women were mandated to fully veil and to refrain from using perfume or noisy jewellery, walking in the middle of the pavement or leaving home unless absolutely necessary (Wimpelmann 2017). However, the *mujahedin* government was unable to enforce these dictates since it soon collapsed into internal fighting, leaving large parts of the capital in ruins. The lawlessness of this period was one factor in the subsequent rise to power of the Taliban, who would control most of Afghanistan by 1996. Once in power, the Taliban's gender policies resembled those of the *mujahedin*, although in some respects, such as in their blanket ban on female employment or education, and in prohibiting women from venturing outside without a male relative, the Taliban went further. Moreover, in contrast to the *mujahedin*, the Taliban were able to enforce their strict measures fairly widely, relying on a mixture of vigilante justice and references to uncodified sharia.

The political order established in Afghanistan in the wake of the 2001 would contain significant structural tensions and competing priorities. On paper, Afghanistan was being 'reconstructed' in accordance with international best practices of post-conflict state-building, largely based on the economic, administrative and political blueprints of Western liberal democracies. At the same time, the US focused on capturing remaining al-Qaida and Taliban members, leading to alliances with a range of armed commanders and so-called strong men, alliances that clearly ran counter to attempts to centralise the means of coercion and build a unified state. Pledges towards enhancing women's rights, fighting corruption and establishing 'good governance' often had to cede ground to the demands of short-term political stability and intelligence gathering (Suhrke 2011).

Moreover, the US-led invasion had made allies of many former *mujahedin*, who would come to serve as important power brokers. They secured key positions in the security apparatus and many successfully ran for parliament in the 2005 elections. The *mujahedin* also dominated much of the ideological field in Afghanistan during the first decade of the post-2001 order. They claimed credit for the re-establishment of Afghanistan as an Islamic republic (as had been the case during their brief rule in the 1990s) and set themselves up as its vanguard, espousing a conservative gender politics and labelling dissent as blasphemy or foreign contamination. The apex of the *mujahedin*'s influence came in 2007, when they used their substantial representation in parliament to secure the passing of a law which provided full amnesty for war crimes committed during previous decades, protecting themselves from any future prosecution. In an oft-cited warning in defence of the Amnesty Law, former *mujahedin* commander and MP Abdul Rasul Sayyaf stated that 'whoever is against the *mujahedin* is against Islam, and they are the enemies of this country' (BBC 2007). To many, this statement crystallised the ideological climate of the Karzai presidency. Any public statements that could be interpreted as support for secularism or for the previous communist government, and by extension as a challenge to the position of the *mujahedin*, risked bringing upon its proponents' accusations of blasphemy and treason. More broadly, the alliances and policies that resulted from the continuing War on Terror acted to thwart rule-bound and more inclusive democratic politics. The latter would have been more enabling both of the enforcement of existing rights and the mobilisation of a women's movement. Instead, Karzai's presidency became characterised by attempts to placate conservative power bases as well as to accommodate the demands of women's rights advocates and international donors in a highly personalised and unpredictable way.

Emerging Women's Rights Infrastructure in the Post-2001 Order

Even though the promises to 'liberate' Afghan women were blatantly instrumental and steeped in colonial tropes, soon enough they gathered a momentum of their own. Looking back, more than fifteen years later, it is clear that a durable alliance around women's rights has consolidated among both with Western and Afghan constituencies (albeit with many problematic aspects). The first years after the overthrow of the Taliban government witnessed a number of formal achievements in terms of gender equality, many of which were realised with substantial involvement from the Western coalition. However, these gains were often in direct contradiction with other developments, setting the stage for a fragmented landscape. An early example of this fragmentation took place in March 2003, when Afghanistan ratified the CEDAW convention unreservedly, an unprecedented move for a country with sharia derived legislation (Kandiyoti 2009). Amongst other things, such ratification effectively committed Afghanistan to the revision of existing legal codes to ensure, inter alia, equal rights in marriage and divorce. Such rights ran counter to most conventional understandings of Islamic law – including the interpretations of Islamic law enshrined in existing Afghan codes. The CEDAW ratification came as a surprise, even to Afghan women's rights activists and officials in the Ministry of Women's Affairs, who reportedly had no idea that the Ministry of Foreign Affairs were pursuing this goal until the ratification took place (Chishti and Farhoumand-Sims 2011). It is difficult to avoid the conclusion that Afghanistan's CEDAW ratification was the impulsive act of a small group of individuals taking place 'under international persuasion or to win international support without taking into account the realities on the ground' (Shah 2005: 255).

The CEDAW ratification preceded the 2004 Constitution which, in turn, provided grounds to contest it. Having established Afghanistan as an Islamic Republic, the constitution went on to state that 'no law can be contrary to the beliefs and provisions of the sacred religion of Islam' (article 3), which would appear to block the possibility of the legal reforms that CEDAW ratification necessitated. But like many constitutions, the new Afghan constitution contained internal contradictions of its own. It also had articles stating that 'the Citizens of Afghanistan – whether male and female – have equal rights and duties before the law' (article 22) and that the Afghan state had an obligation to abide to the UN charter and international treaties and conventions it had signed, as well as the Universal Declaration of Human Rights (article 7). The constitution also contained other significant gender equality provisions such as quotas for women in parliament and in provincial councils. However, it also granted the Supreme Court the authority to review whether laws, legislative decrees, international treaties and international covenants were in conformity with the constitution (article 121). In the Supreme Court, conservative Islamic scholars held prominent positions, including that of chief justice.

Another noteworthy development in the early days of the new order was the establishment of the Ministry of Women's Affairs (MOWA). Rather ambitiously, it was mandated to ensure gender mainstreaming across the government. This proved a tall order in a ministry lacking qualified staff and political support, and in an overall setting where the fairly theoretical concept of gender mainstreaming[1] itself carried little resonance. Instead, the ministry, having had many of its positions filled by the protégés of male-led political networks, sought to carve out a role for itself by providing direct services to women. At the provincial level, its departments of women's affairs became a recourse for women facing wide range of problems, including family violence and civil disputes. In many areas, the possibility of such outside help was totally novel and important in a society where women's access to external support in cases of abuse could be non-existent. However, the general trend was for MOWA's local representative to fulfil this role in a conservative manner, acting with little regard for formal law and upholding the privileges of family elders to control young women. For instance, a number of cases ended in women reconciling with abusive family members, sometimes putting them in serious harm's way (Wimpelmann 2017).

The ministry developed a tense relationship with the 'civil society women'; activists mainly working as NGO leaders or at international aid organisations. Many had returned from exile in Pakistan and from work with women's NGOs there, having acquired both the motivation and the skills to enter the rapidly expanding women's rights sector in Afghanistan (Azarbaijani-Moghaddam 2006). As elsewhere, the inflow of donor funds led to a general 'brain drain' of qualified people to the aid industry away from the public sector. However, this dynamic was particularly evident in the women's rights field, since funding and donor interest was relatively high, and female levels of education comparatively low.

Arguably, violence has been the single most important issue for women's rights in the post-2001 era. Already in late 2002, the first shelter for women fleeing family domestic abuse was established in the capital by an Afghan activist (Wimpelmann 2017: 114). A couple of years later a commission for the elimination of violence against women was set up, and suggestions soon surfaced about having a law dedicated to the issue. Spearheaded by UNIFEM, whose country office in Afghanistan was its largest in the world, international agencies and embassies also made violence against women a central issue. In so doing the international actors in Afghanistan were able to draw upon established templates from the international women's rights arena, where violence against women has emerged as a central focus area since the early 1990s (Merry 2003). Apart from political and financial support to the drafting of the law addressing violence against women, international funds were channelled into shelters, advocacy, the training of legal officials, legal aid, and eventually, the establishment of dedicated units at the police, prosecutors' offices and the courts. Towards the end of the first decade after Taliban rule, violence against women, and women's access to the justice system more broadly was by far the field with most activity, both by aid donors and Afghan activists. At the heart of these activities was the Law on the Elimination of Violence Against Women (EVAW Law), which by early 2009 had been developed into a draft criminalising twenty-two acts of violence against women, including rape, beating, forced and underage marriage and certain forms of polygamy. The law thus confronted established notions that saw many of these acts as the legitimate prerogatives of husbands and fathers, rather than violations of women's rights mandating state intervention (Wimpelmann 2017: 70).

Meanwhile, in the Islamic Republic...

Whilst these efforts were underway, across many of Afghanistan's legal and institutional practices, as well as political discourse, rigid gender ideologies rooted in conservative Islam prevailed. A rude awakening, not only to embassies and Western politicians, but also to many local women's rights advocates, came in spring 2009, when it emerged that the parliament had passed a discriminatory family law for the country's Shia minority almost completely under their radar (Wimpelmann 2017). The law, which was a detailed codification of Jafari *fiqh*, sanctioned marriage with underage girls, made women's right to marry dependent on fathers' and grandfathers' permission and obligated women to obey their husbands or forfeit their right to financial maintenance. This law contradicted many points in the existing civil code (which prohibits underage marriage and recognises a women's right to choose her spouse, and presumably would now only apply to non-Shias). The new law was certainly a far cry from the progress that many women's rights activists felt was currently in the making, including the principles enshrined in the draft EVAW Law. The Shia Personal Status Law had passed through parliament in murky circumstances. It appeared that a bargain had been struck with conservative Sunni parliamentarians, according to a logic whereby the assessment of any law derived from sharia (such as family law) would be the exclusive domain of trained religious scholars of the relevant sect (Oates 2009). MPs lacking such background were not informed about the law and prevented from reviewing drafts.

When news about the Shia Personal Status Law broke it created something of a scandal in Western media, where NATO leaders were now held accountable for their inability to meet earlier pledges to liberate Afghan women. However, the response of the international actors and women activists was characteristic of the overall strategy they had adopted. Unwilling or unable to press for reform of all the problematic articles of the law, women activists and their international supporters opted instead to throw their support behind the new law proposal on the Elimination of Violence against Women (EVAW Law). They hoped that this law which, among other things, made underage marriage and the prevention of women's choice in marriage criminal offences, would counteract and somehow cancel out the Shia Personal Status Law (Wimpelmann 2017). Rather than going through the parliamentary process, the plan was to get the EVAW

Law enacted as a presidential decree. This was anchored in article 79 of the 2004 Constitution, which permits the president to enact laws as presidential decrees in emergency situations and during times when the parliament is in recess, although such decrees should be presented for ratification in parliament within thirty days. To President Karzai, the ability to pass the EVAW Law as a decree represented a possibility to placate two of his constituencies simultaneously: the women activists and the conservative Shia groups who resisted reform of the Shia Personal Status Law (Wimpelmann 2017). Both groups obtained their law, although it was not at all clear which of the two laws took precedence.

The status of the EVAW Law was further complicated by the fact that it was never ratified in parliament. Despite several attempts, a number of powerful MPs, many of them former *mujahedin*, denounced the law's criminalisation of underage marriage and of certain forms of rape, polygamy and beating as un-Islamic and questioned the Muslim credentials of those supporting it. Thus, the EVAW Law remained a presidential decree, coexisting with, and sometimes in contradiction with a number of other laws, such as the penal code, the civil code – and the Shia Personal Status Law. Despite its ambiguous status, the EVAW Law nonetheless gradually gained the status of a prominent accomplishment for women's rights in the post-2001 era or even as 'possibly the most monumental gain for women's rights in Afghan history' (Hudson and Leidl 2015: 245)

In the years that followed, this kind of parallel effort became the strategy of choice. Existing institutions and frameworks, such as national legislation, the parliament or judicial bodies were circumvented in order to achieve quicker results untainted by compromises. In this vein, a mode of intervention and activism evolved in which neither Islamist gender norms nor government practices were confronted head-on but sidestepped through the carving out of parallel arenas and domains. For instance, when a number of judges and prosecutors chose to ignore the EVAW Law, referring only to the existing, comprehensive penal code, donors and activists endeavoured to set up specialised prosecution units to apply the new law, regardless of the fact that the parliament, where conservative actors prevailed, refused to ratify it. The first such specialised unit was set up in Kabul in 2010.[2] It was staffed with close to a dozen dedicated prosecutors, who received top-up salaries[3] and technical support from the International Development Law Organization. Soon to be set up countrywide, the dedicated prosecution units were intended to provide an accessible and welcoming space for women to report violence. They also constituted a focal point for the channelling of funds and 'capacity-building', as well as monitoring and accountability by aid donors and supporters of the EVAW Law more generally.

By the time the dedicated prosecution units were set up, Western actors had been trying in vain to reform Afghanistan's legal system for years. Mainly unable to speak local languages and dependent on interpreters, they encountered a bureaucracy steeped in legal traditions which they had little comprehension of, entrenched institutional interests and complicated political alliances. Often, files of individual cases did not even exist, let alone information about judicial decisions or conviction rates. Decades of conflict and frequent political shifts had produced an extremely heterogeneous staff trained in different legal traditions and with low qualifications. The powerful Supreme Court,[4] staffed by a number of conservative Islamic scholars and in general highly sceptical of outside interference (Sarwari and Crews 2008: 328) proved particularly testing. However, other parts of the legal chain also represented challenges to Western reformers, or simply resisted the changes they proposed, some of which were ill-suited to local conditions and skills. In this context, establishing dedicated legal spaces for processing gender-based violence was a way of promoting results without having to address the structural, sector-wide difficulties of the justice system. Both donors and activists would have a focal point for advocacy and monitoring, with the overall objective of increasing the implementation of the EVAW Law and conviction rates for gender-based violence. However, like the EVAW Law itself, the outcome was a partial one. As my co-authors and I have explained in some detail elsewhere, the dedicated prosecution unit, at least in Kabul, became a place where women could negotiate a slightly better deal within abusive situations, or obtain leverage in disputes over civil matters (Shahabi et al. 2016). Criminal convictions were relatively rare and often not on the agenda of complainants either.

The reason for this state of affairs was the fact that broader social and legal practices proscribed female autonomy and reinforced women's dependence on their families. By referring to uncodified Islamic jurisprudence, the application of which was permitted in certain cases by the 2004 Constitution,[5] the mainstream justice system had long been routinely arresting and imprisoning women for the crime of 'running away from home' (*farar az manzel*), even though no such crime exists in codified law. Sometimes, women could be apprehended simply for travelling on their own. When challenged on the legality of this practice, the Supreme Court in 2010 issued a statement determining that women who run away from home for any reason including violence, and failed to go directly to a family member or a government office were all guilty of 'attempted adultery' and should be punished.[6] The stigmatisation of women's existence outside the control of family or public authorities was reflected in social and economic life as well. Single women, even in the cities, were hard-pressed to find accommodation and attracted malicious and sometimes threatening gossip. In this setting, the specialised prosecution units were operating within broader relations that prevented women from realising the rights granted to them by recent legislation. Women's ability to live and survive outside family settings was hampered by both legal and social regulations. Consequently, women who saw little prospect of surviving outside of their families were unlikely to press for the imprisonment of family members, even if they were culpable.

The new protective frameworks ushered in during the post-2001 order had limited anchoring in the Karzai government as a whole. Shored up by external funds and pressure, they constituted globalised zones of protection entangled in and modified to various degrees by local practices and modes of politics. This ring-fenced, transnationally constituted space was most pronounced in the case of the women's shelters. The shelters, which were run by Afghan or international NGOs and funded by international aid were a crucial haven for women who had escaped family abuse and were at risk of family reprisals or could not survive on their own. The shelters came under increasing attack by conservatives who perceived them as some kind of dangerous moral void where women could live unsupervised, outside the control of family or society and free of sanctions against improper behaviour (Wimpelmann 2017). In 2011, the Ministry of Women's Affairs, frustrated at its marginalisation from the women's rights field by the internationally funded NGOs who by now implemented most of the programmes in this field, announced that it would take over the running of the shelters. This would eradicate financial waste, secure the shelters a legitimate standing in Afghan society, and implement checks on women's modesty in the shelters, by subjecting residents to 'virginity testing' upon entry. However, the takeover was prevented through the mobilisation of international outrage by the NGOs running the shelters. Open letters, online petitions and other lobbying activities caused the consternation of Western politicians and diplomats and eventually led the Afghan government to back down. The shelters continued their existence as globalised zones of protection, in the sense of being spaces maintained and funded by transnational networks, insulated from the local dynamics of politics and gender.

The initiatives pursued by Afghan women activists and international actors, namely Afghanistan's CEDAW ratification, the EVAW Law, the dedicated prosecution units and the shelters, were far from inconsequential. However, they made for a capricious and fragmented gender regime, where women's rights were not politically or institutionally anchored, but instead secured through transnational alliances almost on a case by case basis, often discreetly in order not to attract too much resistance from conservative Islamic actors. These initiatives also supported an entire industry of monitors, trainers and awareness-raisers to the point that certain local actors developed a vested interest in the continuation of a specialised or parallel legal infrastructure, and a 'women, peace and security' industry more generally. Zooming out, it becomes apparent that these interventions were operating within an overall political landscape saturated by the logic of patronage. Justice, protection or entitlements were handed out as personal favours, rather than accessed as institutionalised rights.

The fates of individual women under this fragmented governance regime were highly unpredictable. For instance, women who 'run away' from abusive family situations could end up in prison on 'attempted adultery' charges or as plaintiffs in a trial against their abusers. In the former case, they could in turn find themselves freed under the yearly issuing of presidential pardons. In a number of individual cases of severe abuse, such as multiple rapes or torture, intense campaigning by local activists eventually forced official action, but perpetrators with political connections were often able escape punishment further down the line (Wimpelmann 2017: 45).

Moving to the Centre: Gender Politics during the National Unity Government

In November 2014, the government of Norway hosted a one-day 'High Level Symposium on Afghan Women's Rights and Empowerment' in its capital city, Oslo. The event attracted most of the well-known Afghan women's rights advocates and female MPs, Afghan government officials, such as the Minister of Women's Affairs, and various mid-level officials from NATO countries and beyond. The host government was represented both by the prime and foreign ministers and had hoped for the attendance of US Secretary of State John Kerry. In this they were disappointed (although Hillary Clinton appeared in the form of a pre-recorded video message). Instead, the star of the symposium was Rula Ghani, Afghanistan's new first lady. At that point she was a relatively unknown figure, but she would soon emerge as an influential and engaged ally to both Afghan women's rights workers and aid donors. The event featured two panels on economic, political and legal questions and was intended 'to provide an arena for discussing how Afghanistan can advance women's rights and empowerment, as well as how the international community can support the necessary reforms'. However, not much substantial debate was possible during the short time available, some of which was appropriated by Western officials keen to announce new funding schemes.

Above all, the symposium illustrated the extent to which Afghan women's rights had become a gate opener to diplomatic prestige. For years following the 2001 invasion, frequent warnings were made that Western governments would inevitably abandon their high-profile commitment to Afghan women's rights when politically convenient. But such warnings proved unwarranted. Instead the alliance around women's empowerment moved to the heart of Western and, eventually, Afghan government agendas. By 2014, it was clear that commitment to Afghan women had become a currency that could purchase meeting time in Washington. Hillary Clinton, when secretary of state, had taken a strong personal interest in the question of Afghan women. However, she was not alone –

over the years, a cross-partisan interest had evolved in the US capital, involving a number of politicians, diplomats and other figures, with a particular hub at the Georgetown University and through the US–Afghan Women's Council. As a result, many US-allied governments, including Norway, undoubtedly came to see the 'Afghan women question' as a useful way of attracting the attention of high-level US officials.

With the change of government in Afghanistan in 2014, they also found a different level of interest in their agenda in Kabul. During Hamid Karzai's presidency, whether brought up by Afghans or foreigners, women's rights were generally met by Afghan officialdom with polite interest at best. Typically, moderately feminist proposals were watered down into initiatives to 'help women' within socially prescribed gender roles in the context of a pervading sense of needing to tread carefully to avoid provoking a dangerous backlash. Much energy was spent on seeking to reverse government decisions that testified to limited commitment to gender equality in the presidential palace, for instance when the Afghan president endorsed a statement from the National Council of Religious Scholars asserting that women were secondary to men, or when he failed to appoint any women to official bodies or delegations.

The 2014 election (which Hamid Karzai was constitutionally barred from contesting) was marred by allegations of systematic and large-scale fraud, leaving election bodies unable to declare a winner. A national unity government – a de facto power-sharing arrangement – was finally agreed in September 2014 after US intervention. The two main contenders in the election, Ashraf Ghani and Dr Abdullah Abdullah, were to be president and chief executive officer respectively, and ministerial posts were distributed between the two camps. The new president, Ashraf Ghani, was a technocrat and moderniser intent on cultivating strong Western support. Under him, the official mood on women's rights changed. Already at his inauguration, Ghani signalled a new era, when he tearfully thanked his wife, present in the audience, for her lifelong support. To many Afghan women's rights supporters this was a promising sign of change, given that Karzai's wife had hardly been seen in public at all during his thirteen years as president. Indeed, under the present national unity government, reformist Islam in the tradition of Amanullah has received official sanction, and in some areas, such as the public visibility of women there has been a significant shift in the political and social environment. This sense of relaxation around women's comportment and appearance, combined with more merit-based recruitment to government positions have provided space for a new generation of women without links to male-based patronage networks to take up senior government posts. There have also been public debates on previously taboo issues such as routine 'virginity testing' of women coming into contact with the law. Sexual harassment at universities and workplaces, a topic previously downplayed out of fear that an acknowledgement of its widespread existence could lead to calls for gender segregation or to male kin prohibiting girls and women from attending work or studies, has become a mainstream government concern.

However, the political support to women's rights issues during the Ghani presidency has also had its downsides. With 'Afghan women' now a major part of the aid and diplomatic portfolio of most NATO countries, donors have been scrambling for initiatives and projects to support and often micro-manage processes that have little buy-in in Afghan institutions but tick the right boxes on key global blueprints. The production of Afghanistan's National Action Plan for Women Peace and Security, which was finalised in 2015 with extensive international involvement is a case in point.[7] The consolidation of political interest in women's rights led to an influx of politically ambitious actors (both male and female) with few feminist convictions and little interest in more transformative goals. With the Afghan first lady now a declared supporter of the cause, working on women's rights represented access to the presidential palace. By contrast, the Ministry of Women's Affairs, a ministry allocated to the camp of Chief Executive Dr Abdullah, did not promise similar political access and faced increasing marginalisation by international actors in Kabul.

In general, the women's rights agenda promoted by Western embassies was fairly delinked from broader political visions and movements. Instead it reinforced a form of 'quota politics' also espoused by many established activists of the 'Peshawar generation'.[8] For instance, position papers and publications by Afghanistan's most prominent women's network, the Afghan Women's Network, have in essence been lobbying papers for an increase of women in political and government positions.[9] The form of politics promoted through the alliance between Western embassies and established activists typically failed to connect with attempts at more fundamental change and younger, more radical generations who became more assertive and active during the Ghani presidency. To many of these younger women (and men) struggles for women's rights had to be rooted in broader visions of political and social change, which included democratic and transparent politics and the overcoming of ethnic cleavages and religious dogma. Not only did mobilisation around such visions run counter to entrenched modes of top-down, non-democratic governance, it was also hampered by the deteriorating security situation. By the mid-2010s, the Taliban and other insurgent groups contested government control across the country, besieging provincial towns and controlling some rural areas completely. The deteriorating security situation marginalised grass-roots activism and dramatically limited the impact of the shift in gender policies in Kabul.

Yet, despite its limitations, the shift in policies after Karzai suggested that that there had been no inevitability to the subdued women's rights agenda of the Karzai period. Rather, the atmosphere of restraint and caution of that period was kept alive by Karzai's personal disinterest in reform, the nature of his political power base and by donors' and activists' unwillingness or inability to confront Islamist discourses (or their proponents) head on. The more open and relaxed climate under Ghani testified to the political contingency of Afghan gender politics. In running for office, and in setting up his administration, Ghani mobilised young, reform-oriented urban groups. Whilst he did not shy away from making alliances with religious, tribal and *mujahedin* leaders, these actors were not as central to his power base as they had been to Karzai's. Moreover, assuming power at a time when Western support to Afghanistan's government, still heavily aid-dependent,[10] came with fewer guarantees, Ghani took pains to show himself a closer and more trustworthy Western ally than his predecessor. A more reform-oriented policy on women's rights was certainly an important part of this image. Finally, personal outlook doubtlessly also played a role. While few with knowledge of Ghani's biography would have described him as a feminist, the vision that he espoused for Afghanistan entailed the active and public participation of its women.

But as in earlier phases of Afghan history, the place and conduct of women continued to attract controversy and radically opposing views. In March 2015, the public murder of Farkhunda, a young woman accused of being an American agent and of burning the Qur'an (Nemat 2015), showed the continued existence of significant constituencies for the kind of misogynist sentiments that were espoused by the *mujahedin* in the name of Islam (Wimpelmann 2013b), perhaps appearing in even more radicalised forms. At university campuses and on social media it was abundantly clear that a new generation of extremists, IS-inspired young radicals, had gained a foothold in the country, often seeing 'corrupted', secularised women as key agents of Western aggression and moral degradation. As before, the particular ways in which Islam was used to sanction restrictions on women was not derived from 'traditional Afghan culture' but a product of transnational encounters and changing internal power balances.

Conclusion

It is difficult to overstate the prominence of Afghanistan in the literature critiquing colonial tropes of 'saving Muslim women'. When Laura Bush announced the liberation of Afghan women as one of the goals of the US and coalition invasion, many predicted a problematic and hollow imposition of 'Western'-style gender emancipation, followed by an inevitable retraction of principles as other political priorities eventually took precedence. However, the actual trajectories in Afghanistan over the last decade and a half show a more complex dynamic whereby external and Afghan agendas and governance claims coexisted in complicated and multiple entanglements, rather than as clearly distinguishable fronts. Indeed, a survey of the women's rights field in Afghanistan calls into question the very idea of state (or imperial) governance as a coherent project. There was a narrow field of intervention created by externally allied sections of the Afghan state apparatus and civil society in which a comparatively radical gender order was envisioned and enforced. However, in the same state apparatus, and in parliament and political discourse more generally, another type of gender regime was also in evidence. Rooted in a conservative understanding of sharia it placed women under the authority of husbands and fathers. Often, the eventual fates of individual women depended on the personal inclinations of the officials presiding over their cases which, in turn, was as likely to be swayed by private loyalties and influences as by ideological conviction.

Pinpointing Western (or imperial) influence in this landscape is less than straightforward. The official Western footprint was manifest in the infrastructure erected through the EVAW Law, the ratification of CEDAW, the dedicated prosecution units and courts, and the shelters for abused women. However, Western countries were equally implicated in core elements entrenching a more conservative gender regime, such as the rehabilitation of the *mujahedin* and the personalised, fragmented, unaccountable logic through which much of Afghan politics operated. During the height of the NATO war effort, Western military commanders also attempted to boost the position of tribal and traditional authorities, in a bid to create local allies against the Taliban (Hakimi 2013). Parts of the diplomatic community in Kabul even threw their support behind a proposal to incorporate so-called tribal councils into the formal legal system, much to the dismay of Afghan women's rights advocates (Wimpelmann 2013a).

Arguably, the case of contemporary gender politics in Afghanistan has been as much about discreet tactics, parallel domains and personal accommodations as it has been about direct religious and ideological confrontation. Many of the first post-2001 generation of women activists aligned themselves closely with Western embassies and aid organisations, affording them a measure of autonomy from local conservatives and leverage to push reforms through, often discretely and quietly. Partly as a result, the formal achievements of this period were weakly anchored, and the ability to call upon external support tended to detract from the need to mobilise local constituencies. With the coming of age of more radical and explicitly feminist generations, under a more supportive presidency, gains in women's rights could potentially consolidate and expand. At this point, however, much of the country is in turmoil as a result of armed conflict, and there is no predicting what new constellations of Islam, gender and governance might emerge in Afghanistan in the future.

Notes

1. An established term in international development practice, gender mainstreaming refers to the process of ensuring that both women and men's experiences and needs are integral to the design, implementation and assessment of any policy or programme. For an evaluation, see Larson (2008).
2. I was present at the opening ceremony in March 2010 in Kabul.
3. Personal communication with IDLO staff in Kabul, March 2015.
4. The Supreme Court is in charge of the administration and oversight of lower courts as well as the professional education for judges. It nominates judges for presidential approval, serve as the final court of appeal and is authorised to review laws, treaties and conventions for their compliance with the constitution.
5. Article 130 of the constitution permitted the application of Hanafi (Islamic) jurisprudence in cases where no written laws apply.
6. Approval number 572, 24 August 2010, High Council of the Supreme Court.
7. Since 2000, a remarkable momentum in rectifying the historical exclusion of gender issues from armed conflict and peace-making has taken place, centred on eight UN Security Council Resolutions on women, peace and security (Swaine 2017). National Action Plans on Women Peace and Security have become the main instrument for UN member states to implement and to signal commitment to this agenda. As Swaine argues, even if the adoption of such action plans are entirely voluntary, they have in effect become a way of signalling a country's 'modern status' (Swaine 2017: 10) and 'the provision of support for the development of [national action plans] have effectively become a . . . industry in itself . . . dominated by a number of international organisations (Swaine 2017: 22–3).
8. I use this term to refer to the first generation of Afghan women's rights advocates post-2001, many of whom had run relief organisations based in Peshawar, Pakistan, during the 1990s.
9. For a criticism of this numerical approach to gender equality in Afghanistan, see also Nijat and Murtazashvili (2015).
10. Afghanistan is one of the most aid-dependent countries in the world, with aid levels nearing 100 per cent of GDP at its peak years of 2009–11 (Byrd and Farahi 2018).

Bibliography

Abu-Lughod, Lila (2002), ' Do Muslim women really need saving? Anthropological reflections on cultural relativism and its others', *American Anthropologist New Series*, 104: 3, pp. 783–90.
—— (2010), 'The active social life of "Muslim women's rights": a plea for ethnography, not polemic, with cases from Egypt and Palestine', *Journal of Middle East Women's Studies*, 6: 1, pp. 1–45.
Ahmed, Faiz (2017), *Afghanistan Rising. Islamic Law and Statecraft between the Ottoman and British Empires*, Cambridge, MA and London: Harvard University Press.
Azarbaijani-Moghaddam, Sippi (2006), 'Gender in Afghanistan', *Publication Series on Promoting Democracy under Conditions of State Fragility, Issue 1: Afghanistan*, Berlin: Heinrich Böll Foundation, pp. 25–45.

BBC (2007), 'Afghan warlords in amnesty rally', 23 February, <http://news.bbc.co.uk/1/hi/world/south_asia/6389137.stm> (last accessed 13 October 2017).

Billaud, Julie (2015), *Kabul Carnival. Gender Politics in Postwar Afghanistan*, Philadelphia: University of Pennsylvania Press.

Butler, Judith (2004), *Precarious Life: the Powers of Mourning and Violence*, London: Verso.

Byrd, William A. and Shah Zaman Farahi (2018), 'Improving Afghanistan's public finances in 2017–2019: raising revenue and reforming the budget', *United States Institute of Peace Special Report*, 18 April, Washington, DC: USIP.

Chishti, Maliha and Cheshmak Farhoumand-Sims (2011), 'Transnational feminism and the women's rights agenda in Afghanistan', in Z. Jalaizai and D. Jefferess (eds), *Globalizing Afghanistan: Terrorism, War and the Rhetoric of Nation Building*, Durham, NC and London: Duke University Press, pp. 117–44.

Daulatzai, Anila (2008), 'The discursive occupation of Afghanistan', *British Journal of Middle Eastern Studies*, 35: 3, pp. 419–35.

Dorronsoro, Gilles (2005), *Revolution Unending. Afghanistan: 1979 to the Present*, London: Hurst & Co.

Dupree, Nancy Hatch (1984), 'Revolutionary rhetoric and Afghan Women', in N. M. Sharani and R. Canfield (eds), *Revolutions and Rebellions in Afghanistan: Anthropological Perspectives*, Berkeley: Institute of International Studies, University of California, pp. 306–40.

Fluri, Jennifer L. and Rachel Lehr (2017), *The Carpetbaggers of Kabul and Other American–Afghan Entanglements*, Athens, GA: University of Georgia Press.

Hakimi, Aziz A. (2013), 'Getting savages to fight barbarians: counterinsurgency and the remaking of Afghanistan', *Central Asian Survey*, 32: 3, pp. 388–405.

Hirschkind, Charles and Saba Mahmood (2002), 'Feminism, the Taliban, and politics of counter-insurgency', *Anthropological Quarterly*, 75: 2, pp. 339–54.

Hudson, Valerie M. and Patricia Leidl (2015), *The Hillary Doctrine: Sex and American Foreign Policy*, New York, Columbia University Press.

Kandiyoti, Deniz (2007), 'Old dilemmas or new challenges? The politics of gender and reconstruction in Afghanistan', *Development and Change*, 38: 2, pp. 169–99.

—— (2009), *The Lures and Perils of Gender Activism in Afghanistan*, The Anthony Hyman Memorial Lecture, 16 March, School of Oriental and African Studies, University of London.

Larson, Anna (2008), 'A mandate to mainstream: promoting gender equality in Afghanistan', *Issues Paper Series*, November, Kabul: Afghanistan Research and Evaluation Unit.

Malikyar, Helena (1997), 'Development of family law in Afghanistan: the roles of the Hanafi *Madhab*, customary practices and power politics', *Central Asian Survey*, 16: 3, pp. 389–99.

Merry, Sally E. (2003), 'Constructing a global law-violence against women and the human rights system', *Law & Social Inquiry*, 28: 4, pp. 941–77.

Nawid, Senzil K. (1999), *Religious Response to Social Change in Afghanistan, 1919–29: King Aman-Allah and the Afghan Ulama*, Costa Mesa, CA: Mazda Publishers.

Nemat, Orzala Ahraf (2015), 'Farkhunda paid for Afghanistan's culture of impunity', *Open Democracy*, 25 March, <https://www.opendemocracy.net/5050/orzala-ashraf-

nemat/farkhunda-paid-for-afghanistan's-culture-of-impunity> (last acccessed 16 October 2017).

Nijat, Aarya and Jennifer Murtazashvili (2015), 'Women's leadership roles in Afghanistan', *United States Institute of Peace Special Report*, Washington, DC: United States Institute of Peace, pp. 1–16.

Oates, Lauryn (2009). 'A closer look: the policy and law-making process behind the Shiite Personal Status Law', *Issues Paper Series*, September, Kabul: Afghan Research and Evaluation Unit.

Olesen, Asta (1995), *Islam and Politics in Afghanistan*, Richmond: Curzon Press.

Sarwari, Atiq and Robert D. Crews (2008). 'Epilogue: Afghanistan and the Pax Americana', in R. D. Crews and A. Tarzi (eds), *The Taliban and the Crisis of Afghanistan*, Cambridge, MA and London: Harvard University Press, pp. 311–55.

Shah, Niaz A. (2005), 'The constitution of Afghanistan and women's rights, *Feminist Legal Studies*, 13: 2, pp. 239–58.

Shahabi, Mohammad Jawad, Torunn Wimpelmann and Farangis Elyasi (2016), 'The specialized units for prosecution of violence against women in Afghanistan: shortcuts or detours to women's empowerment?' *Report in External Series*, Kabul and Bergen: Research Institute for Women, Peace and Security and Chr Michelsen Institute.

Spivak, Gayatri C. (1988), 'Can the subaltern speak?' in C. Nelson and L. Grossberg, *Marxism and the Interpretation of Culture*, Basingstoke: Macmillan Education.

Suhrke, Astri (2011), *When More is Less: the International Project in Afghanistan*, London and New York: Hurst/Columbia.

Swaine, Aisling (2017), 'Globalising women, peace and security: trends in national action plans', in S. Aroussi (ed.), *Rethinking National Action Plans on Women, Peace and Security*, Amsterdam: IOS Publishing, pp. 7–27.

Wide, Thomas (2016), 'Astrakhan, borqa', chadari, dreshi: the economy of dress in early 20th-century Afghanistan', in S. Cronin (ed.), *Anti-Veiling Campaigns in the Muslim World: Gender, Modernism and the Politics of Dress*, Abingdon and New York: Routledge, pp. 163–201.

Wimpelmann, Torunn (2013a), 'Nexuses of knowledge and power in Afghanistan: the rise and fall of the informal justice assemblage', *Central Asian Survey*, 32: 3, pp. 406–22.

—— (2013b), 'Problematic protection', *Open Democracy*, 29 November, <https://www.opendemocracy.net/5050/torunn-wimpelmann/problematic-protection-law-on-elimination-of-violence-against-women-in-afghan> (last accessed 16 October 2017).

—— (2017), *The Pitfalls of Protection: Gender, Violence and Power in Afghanistan*, Oakland: University of California Press.

CHAPTER 7

Palestine: Gender in an Imagined Fragmented Sovereignty

ISLAH JAD

INTRODUCTION

The aim of this chapter is to trace the effects of the fragmentation of the Palestinian national movement in the aftermath of the legislative elections of 2006 that led to the victory of the Islamic Resistance Movement (Hamas hereafter) and their takeover of Gaza in 2007. The ensuing political schism divided the Palestinian polity into the West Bank and Gaza governments, both operating with pretence of sovereignty. This has altered the priorities of women in the West Bank and Gaza and impaired their capabilities for mutual accommodation. I shall chart, in what follows, the ways in which a system of governance of the Occupied Territories endorsed by international players, coupled with donor-led agendas in the realms of gender and women's rights, displaced the struggle against colonial violence and aspirations for liberation, leading to the marginalisation of women's roles and agency in national resistance.

From the British Mandate (1920–48) onwards, Palestinian nationalism presented contradictory constructions of Palestinian women and their movements. On the one hand, women were seen as the modernisers, and the civilising agents of the long-awaited independent nation. This led to the opening up of spaces for the women's movement to grow, develop and become visible. On the other hand, Palestinian women were seen not only as the bearers of their nation's 'authenticity' (Kandiyoti 1991a), but as markers of their own social class. The elite background of participants in the early women's movement denied them a space for full and equal integration into the Palestinian nationalism of the 1930s and the 1940s, and in the structures and organisations of the national movement. Women were less mobile and disconnected from the wider constituencies due to social norms and class boundaries, therefore unable to enter the mainstream national movement or cultivate links with poorer or peasant women due to their confinement to their upper- or middle-class women's circles.

The emergence of the Palestinian Liberation Organization (PLO) based on a national, secular leadership, especially after the Arab defeat against Israel during the Six-Day War of 1967, played an important role in consolidating a national identity based on core principles of struggle, return and sacrifice (Schulz 1999). Again, Palestinian nationalism used contradictory tropes about women as 'traditional', 'self-sacrificing mothers' whose main role was to reproduce their nation by providing male fighters, and of 'revolutionary militants' prepared to join the struggle for national liberation shoulder-to-shoulder with their brothers. These images were contested by women activists who started to challenge the prevailing gender order by pressuring their national organisations for more equitable legislation and policies that redress gender inequality. Yet, the constant political upheavals that have marred the Palestinians and their leadership since 1947 has always militated against any serious push by women for social change.

The 'revolutionary' era in the diaspora and the Occupied Territories in early 1970s was an important phase in the development of the Palestinian women's movement that succeeded in bridging the gap between urban elite women, rural women and refugees. This represented an important shift to more broad-based organisation, the mobilisation of women at the grass-roots level and the formation of new cadres who, for the first time, did not come from a middle-class background. The broad popular base for women's organisations developed during the eighties reflected itself in the large numbers of women who were active in the first Palestinian uprising (intifada) in 1987. Empowered by their important role in organising women from all walks of life, Palestinian women were developing their own 'home-grown' feminism that combined the struggle for national liberation with their own gender interests (Molyneux 2001). They supported women in rural areas, refugee camps and in urban centres by providing childcare, job opportunities and consciousness-raising whilst recruiting them into their women's organisations.

Following the first Palestinian intifada (1987–91), which led to the Oslo Agreement (1993) between the PLO and the Israeli State, the Palestinians were assigned self-governance in the Occupied Palestinian Territories (OPT). The Oslo Accords in 1993 and 1995 were apparently designed to relieve Israel of the administration of the areas of highest Palestinian population density to maintain itself as a self-defined 'Jewish and democratic state' (Haddad 2010). In this respect, Oslo envisioned the establishment of a collaborator, helping Israel relieve itself of its Arab demographic 'burden'. Thus, the Palestinian Authority (PA hereafter), the self-governing Palestinian body established in 1994, became a de facto captive of Israeli policy. The Camp David peace negotiations between the PA and Israel collapsed in 2000 after failing to fulfil the most elementary of Palestinian historical rights (including an independent state within 1967 borders with East Jerusalem as its capital, and the right of return for Palestinian refugees). Israel, with the backing of the US, unleashed its military might against the PA and the Palestinian people at large, to eradicate the 'troublesome', resilient nationalist elements. The goal was to teach the Palestinians and the PA a lesson that there was no space for nationalist positions in 'Israel's backyard' or for resistance to Israel and the dictates of the US in general (Haddad 2010).

In the aftermath of the second al-Aqsa intifada[1] in 2000, Israel's scorched-earth policy resulted in roughly 6,000 Palestinian dead, 50,000 injured, 11,000 imprisoned and countless others forced to leave, seeking a more stable life elsewhere (Hanafi 2008). In 2004, Arafat was removed from office and his successor Mahmoud Abbas adhered to the terms of the Camp David peace negotiations as the only strategy to fulfil Palestinian national rights. Elections for the second Palestinian Legislative Council (PLC) were held on 25 January 2006 with the prompting of the US and Israel, resulting in a sweeping victory for Hamas, which captured 44.45 per cent of the votes. All attempts by Hamas to form a national unity government failed due to the reluctance of the PA (controlled by Fatah) and the pressure of the donor community represented by the Quartet.[2] After a period of harassment against Hamas leaders and militants, Hamas took over Gaza as a result of military conflict between Fatah and Hamas in the Gaza Strip between 10 and 15 June 2007. The economic siege of Gaza that followed under Hamas rule further reinforced Hamas' grip on power by broadening the constituencies dependent on them for sheer survival and tightened their control. In the West Bank, the US and the donor community worked to create a class with specific interests that organically tied sections of the Palestinian population to global and Israeli capital, and that would deliver stable disciplinary interests in a functioning, secure internal order (Haddad 2010; Hanafi and Tabar 2005).

In Gaza, the US and Israeli governments, and the donor community more generally, spared no efforts to make the Hamas government fail. Two massive wars were launched on Gazans in 2009 and 2014, alongside air, ground and sea blockades by Israel and Egypt, cutting off Gaza from the rest of the world (Haddad 2010). The head of the charitable societies in Gaza, Ahmed Al Kurd, announced at a press conference on 25 January 2018 that Gaza

> is considered a human disaster area at all levels, in that 40 per cent of children need health care, 80 per cent of students are from poor families in need of humanitarian aid, 95 per cent of Gaza's water is unsuitable for drinking, sewage water pumps have stopped working due to power failure caused by restrictions on fuel, 5,000 houses were destroyed after the 2014 war and

their residents still live in caravans because of restrictions on construction materials. (Almayadeen.net, 25.1.2018; PCBS 2015).

Governance in the West Bank and Gaza is shaped by complex international financial aid structures (see Figure 7.1) regulated by the Quartet, that dictates priorities and designates which territory, ministry or project should be funded (Khan and Hilal 2004). The besieged Gaza Strip, governed by Hamas, the first Islamic movement to control 'quasi-state' power before the so-called Arab Spring, aims to be self-reliant but is dependent on funding through some transnational Islamic networks conveying flows of cash and ideas.[3] The Trump administration's recognition of Jerusalem as the unified single capital of the state of Israel on 6 December 2017 forced the PA to reconsider its peace process strategy under US patronage and to reactivate the national unity government that was formed in 2014. This has progressed slowly due to many regional and international pressures obstructing any possible reconciliation. The stagnant political schism led the Hamas government in Gaza to launch, in March 2018, a massive protest civil movement, called the Great March of Return, urging hundreds of thousands of Palestinian refugees in Gaza refugee camps to cross the Israeli–Palestinian border back to their villages and homes.

Post-Oslo Transformations of the Palestinian Women's Movement: Demobilisation and Fragmentation

A brief history of the Palestinian women's movement and organisation before the Oslo Agreement in 1993 illustrates the transformation which occurred as regards the women's movement after this agreement. The role of these early NGOs, established before the Oslo Agreement, differed significantly from their role in the post-Oslo phase. Before the formation of the PA, Palestinian society was organised in and around political parties and grass-roots mass organisations. NGOs were connected to these parties under the umbrella of the PLO, which encouraged and financially supported the parties and their satellite organisations.

Although the PLO and its political parties were banned by Israel, their satellite organisations were to some extent allowed to operate, since they were seen as service providers. Between the end of the 1987 intifada and the signing of the Oslo Accords in 1993, the NGO sector was used as the main channel of foreign aid for delivering services at the grass-roots level. Services included clinics, kindergartens and income-generating projects. The result was that these NGO actors became important and acquired even more power than their parent parties.

The women's elite leading these organisations came from various social backgrounds, ranging from urban to rural or refugee, and the organisations (called *utor nassaweyya*) they led managed to bridge the divide between rural (now refugee) and urban women. They all managed to organise and mobilise a large number of women in different political activities during the first Palestinian intifada, beginning in 1987. It is the women in the latter, the *utor nassaweyya*, that I characterise as having been nationalist secularist. They were nationalist because they developed their activism under the aegis of the PLO, the leading organisation of the Palestinian national movement. They considered themselves secularist because they aimed to establish an independent Palestinian state founded on liberal or socialist principles, rather than on religious ones, and because they believed that religion should be separate from the state. Some of these organisations, especially the Palestinian Federation for Women's Action Committees (the PFWAC), had a clear feminist orientation, while others were in the process of developing feminist platforms in relation to PA policies.

Crucially, through their activism, leftist women's organisations developed their own brand of feminism, combining the struggle for national liberation with the struggle for women's emancipation. In the Palestinian case, women's activism and feminism have historically been the adjuncts of nationalism.

Troubled links between women and their national movements in Palestine are not dissimilar from experiences in other Third World countries in which the nationalist elite acted as the 'modernisers' for their nation and for 'their' women (Jayawardena 1986; Kandiyoti 1991a, 1991b; Molyneux 1998; Badran 1995; Chatterjee 1990, 1993; Mohanty 1991). Nationalist elites were driven by the paradoxical impulse to struggle against colonial domination while at the same time internalising and applying the modernist values of the coloniser (Mohanty 1991; Chatterjee 1993; Kandiyoti 1991b; Sharkey 2003).

Women had to forge a space for themselves in order to be able to join the national struggle on equal terms, perhaps especially in Palestine, where successive and ongoing forms of colonial oppression have made it particularly difficult to disengage a project for women's emancipation from one for national liberation. The construction of Palestinian nationalism was centred on the male fighter as the liberator of the nation, and on struggle and sacrifice as idioms of contribution to the nation. Women's activism introduced changes in the gender images of Palestinian nationalism whereby it became possible for women to be militant and activist without openly challenging the gender order. What women did was to identify with nationalism while also reconstructing it, through their activism, in an attempt to subvert its gender boundaries.

The Oslo Agreement and the emergence of the PA in 1994 triggered a shift in priorities whereby civil society organisations changed their goals from sustaining their communities to claiming citizenship rights (Jad 2011). This shift brought back to the fore the professional urban elites at the expense of the rural and refugee leadership. The merger between the structures of the PLO in exile with the PA led to the marginalisation and fragmentation of all grass-roots organisations and their leadership.

From 1988 onwards, particularly with the influx of funding from European women's organisations and international aid to support the first Palestinian intifada, a new type of women's organisation emerged in the form of NGOs. What became known as the 'gender agenda' was driven by a new rights-based approach premised on total equality principles. However, this took place against the background of a steady decline in women's capacity for political organisation and mobilisation (Jad 2008). The new women's organisations were situated mainly in urban centres and led by an urban middle-class female elite. Earlier discourses on modernising 'traditional' society, prevalent at the turn of the century, were resuscitated, now designating Islamist women as the traditional 'other'.[4]

After the establishment of the PA in 1994, yet another form of women's activism emerged, this time from within the quasi-state apparatus. Many formerly militant women, mainly from Fatah and the General Union of Palestinian Women (GUPW), were on the lookout for good job opportunities in the large Palestinian public sector; they were mostly assigned the task of 'developing women'. This task suited the modernising image of the new Authority as much as it suited donors who pressured the Authority to mainstream gender issues. These cadres were mostly nominated through patronage relations to different gender units in many Palestinian ministries.

The establishment of the Women's Affairs Ministry in 2003 was the result of demands by some older generation feminist militants who lobbied the then head of the PA, Yasser Arafat. They became the new 'femocrats', a term coined to denote feminists employed in bureaucratic positions in order to advance women's status through the development of equal opportunity (Eisenstein 1989; Yeatman 1990: 65). Palestinian femocrats were left without resources yet had to prove their professionalism in achieving gender mainstreaming through their ability to solicit donor funding to support their projects.[5] They were thus left in a precarious situation. They were incapable of fulfilling their new goals due to the lack of resources and of national security, while, at the same time, unable to resort to older forms of activism through the structure of the PLO, which had now merged with the PA. Islamist women's organisations were a recent addition to the field of women's activism in Palestinian society, starting from the 1980s. Following the path of earlier nationalist women's organisations, Islamists began by founding charitable societies and organising student units in universities (Jad 2005). I have argued elsewhere (Jad 2008) that the creation of 'new' NGOs and their co-optation of many of the leaders of the secular mass movement have inadvertently opened the way for the flowering of the Islamist women's movement.

The successive wars on the besieged Gaza reinforced the grip of Islamist governance on its population. Any 'dissident' voices from civil society in general, and women's organisations in particular, were denounced as 'traitors' who side with the Gazans' oppressors. This depiction was reinforced by the dictates of donor organisations refusing to support any section of civil society that cooperates with the Islamists in power. This gave the Gaza administration the opportunity to play up the links between women's rights and feminism with colonialism and imperialism, and to portray Islamist women as the nation's healers and saviours.

The ideological and political rifts between liberal national women's organisations (led by women in Fatah, in the GUWP and in the remaining left parties, such as the Democratic Front for the Liberation of Palestine, FIDA party, People's Party and women leaders in independent women's NGOs) and the Islamist women of Hamas, left the latter struggling to develop their own nascent notion of 'Islamic feminism' framed by their practical needs, on the one hand, and their political role in the national struggle, on the other. A new Islamic version of the Women's Charter that was developed by the national women's movement and the Women's Affairs Ministry in the West Bank became the locus of this struggle. The Islamic version of the Women's Charter, although not necessarily based on religious texts, reflected the difficult course Hamas women tried to steer in their attempts to placate their political leaders and differentiate themselves from other women's groups. However, liberal and national women's groups held fast to the original version of the Women's Charter and to many other strategies and plans enabled by transnational women's organisations and donor funding.

Thus, the Ministry of Women's Affairs became another site for power struggles between the liberal national agenda in the West Bank and its Islamist version in Gaza, designating gender, gender identity and gender justice as arenas of contested governance.

A Tale of Two Ministries: Fragmentation and Flawed Governance

Two case studies serve to illustrate the influence of global funding and donor-driven gender activism in shaping the Palestinian agenda. The first case chronicles the different phases that Ministry of Women's Affairs in the West Bank has gone through since 2000. The second case focuses on the Ministry of Women's Affairs in Gaza. This account is set against the background of the most important developments that influenced the political life of women in the Occupied Palestinian Territories (the West Bank and Gaza Strip, including Jerusalem).

The Ministry of Women's Affairs: gender mainstreaming in the context of schism and conflict

The trajectory of the Ministry of Women's Affairs can be analysed through three defining phases: the initial formative stage from 2003; the second phase that witnessed the political schism between the West Bank and Gaza governments from 2005 to 2007; and the third phase that entrenched this divide from 2007 onwards. I trace these influences through an analysis of key documents and plans of action produced by the minsistry.

During its formative stage, the Ministry of Women's Affairs based its 2004 plan on the 1997 National Strategy for the Advancement of Palestinian Women, which was based on international and regional conference documents, including the Convention on the Elimination of All Forms of Discrimination Against Women (CEDAW, 1979) and the resolutions of the 1995 UN International Women's Conference in Beijing. However, the 1997 strategy reflected the approach and vision of feminist activists and the General Union of Palestinian Women at the time, hence a continuing focus on national liberation, the role of women in opposing occupation, and the mobilisation of international cooperation and solidarity to expose the crimes of occupation against women in particular, and Palestinian people in general.

Prompted by the hope that the Oslo Agreement was a prelude to a Palestinian state, matters of governance came to the fore. Thus, a change in mission and vision regarding national liberation and gender mainstreaming led to a clear shift in emphasis towards 'construction and development of the democratic Palestinian homeland, and consolidation of an effective civil society governed by national, cultural and humanitarian values' (Ministry of Women's Affairs 2004). The three key objectives of the plan centered on a 'social agenda' consisting of securing a government commitment to mainstream gender, democracy and human rights in policies, plans and programmes of the various ministries, as well as in legislation and regulations; linking lobbying activities to the development of policies and laws; and building a network of relationships with governmental and international women's organisations and human rights groups to exchange experiences in applying international conventions on women and human rights, particularly the Convention on Elimination of all Forms of Discrimination Against Women (CEDAW) (Ministry of Women's Affairs 2004). The plan also focused heavily on the institutionalisation of the Ministry's work and on its incorporation within the body of government through an organisational structure, human resources and a budget, applying to Palestine the blueprint of inclusion into the international community with all its standard setting instruments.

The subsequent 2005–7 plan focused on educational, vocational and technical training of young women, support for women's access to decision-making positions, and tackling poverty of young women, especially heads of households. These goals were based on the Beijing Platform for Action adopted by the UN in 1995, as well as on consultation with governmental and other non-governmental institutions. Once again, this plan focused on development and capacity-building, with an emphasis on women's access to decision-making positions, which was a popular item among women working in the various ministries, supporting them in their efforts to improve their job prospects.

After winning the 2006 legislative elections (where Hamas garnered 44.45 per cent of the votes as compared to compared to Fatah's 41.43 per cent), Hamas formed a cabinet on 25 January 2007; it was dominated by Hamas members, but also included four independent members. This was the first Hamas-led PNA government in the Occupied Palestinian Territories; Fatah and other factions refused to join. The first Islamist Minister of Women's Affairs[6] set out to provide assurances that existing rights would be safeguarded. However, ambiguity or lack of clarity over the positions of Hamas vis-à-vis the demands of the feminist movement raised doubts in the minds of some activists. For example, several meetings were held for women leaders, coordinated by the Palestinian Initiative for the Promotion of Global Dialogue and Democracy (MIFTAH), to understand the reasons behind the political 'turning of the tables', namely, the Hamas electoral victory. The meetings called for a review of the work and discourse of women's organisations in order to extract lessons. The elitism of feminist work and its focus on educated groups of women in the central West Bank was criticised, emphasising a need to change the means of communication with women at the grass roots. There was no acknowledgement, however, of the importance of opening dialogue with the official newcomer (minutes of MIFTAH meetings, 2006).

The two Hamas ministers introduced amendments to the mission of the Ministry of Women's Affairs. A new element was introduced alongside the fight against discrimination, violence against women (VAW) and the need for legal reform, directing the work of the ministry towards support for certain groups of women, mainly young women and the wives and families of Palestinians killed in conflict (martyrs), detainees and prisoners. These changes focused on the national resistance agenda and its social ramifications for women and their families. This priority was to later become the main focus of the Ministry of Women's Affairs in Gaza after the split between Fateh and Hamas in June 2007. Islamist ministers' leadership of the Ministry of Women's Affairs led to paralysis resulting from internal conflicts that derived mainly from political rejection of the Islamist government and the Islamist women leading the ministry.

After the split between the PA and Hamas, and in a newly charged political environment, a fresh strategy for the Ministry of Women's Affairs was developed for 2008–10. The focus returned to earlier priorities, with an added new one: combating violence against women, mainly domestic violence, and building an appropriate strategy for the 2011–15 period. Plans, strategies and evaluation reports proliferated, funded by UNDP, UNWomen and many other donors who influenced the theoretical frames guiding the setting of priorities and goals. The UN Security Council Resolution 1325 adopted in 2000 surfaced as another blueprint to be applied to the Palestinian situation regardless of contextual factors. Under the terms of Resolution 1325, Palestinian women can file complaints concerning the violence of the Israeli occupation to international bodies, especially the International Criminal Court. The new strategy promoted government efforts to implement Resolution 1325 and its clauses related to the participation of women in conflict resolution and peace-building. However, the recommendations did not address how this goal might be achieved.

The political division between the PA and Hamas led the ministry to shift its focus away from the strategic needs of women (understood as legal reform and having an impact on policy-making) towards meeting their practical needs and implementing relief policies. This shift was reluctant since, according to the 2009 national report of the Ministry of Women's Affairs, such policies were considered to be 'often in conflict with "social justice"' and with the 'state building' aspirations of 'mainly secular [non-governmental organisations]' (Palestinian National Report Beijing +15 2009).

However, priorities soon changed again with the 2011–13 strategy, which reverted to national issues, envisaging support for women in Jerusalem and for women prisoners. The strategy included a number of sub-goals that were difficult to achieve within the specified period. Moreover, the priorities lacked consistency. Combating violence was directed at domestic violence, rather than violence perpetrated by the Israeli occupation. Furthermore, low budget allocations did not reflect a real commitment to national issues. Out of a total budget of NIS43,813,240 or about US$11 million, NIS200,000 or 2.74 per cent was allocated to family law and civil rights programming, while only NIS128,400 (0.29 per cent) was allocated to protecting the rights of women in Jerusalem and NIS53,000 (0.12 per cent) to supporting women prisoners.

Strategies of the Ministry of Women's Affairs were mainly based on the Declaration of Independence of 1988, Palestinian Basic Law, the Palestinian Women's Charter of 2008, and international conventions, particularly CEDAW and UN Security Council Resolution 1325 addressing women in conflict. The ministry made great efforts to raise awareness about these instruments, in particular Resolution 1325 and the Palestinian Women's Charter. It succeeded in several areas, the most important of which was the institutionalisation of gender and women's issues in various ministries. The Council of Ministers decision (15/12/09 M.W/A.Q) of 2005 urged ministries, particularly larger ones, to establish units for women's affairs, where needed and possible. However, this decision was not mandatory and remained unclear. The ministry later worked to amend it and specify clearer tasks and an organisational structure to match. On 28 July 2008, it succeeded in gaining approval for a name change for these groupings, from 'women's units' to 'gender units', in keeping with the gender mainstreaming objectives of the Beijing Platform for Action (Palestinian National Report Beijing +15 2009). Nonetheless, ministries are not required to establish such units.

There are currently twenty gender units in various ministries and official institutions. Their status varies from one ministry to another, depending on the capacity of staff, their positions and their influence, in addition to the overall vision of the ministry and the political will of the minister. Several continue to focus on women's access to decision-making positions, which translates to having more women in each ministry in senior or better positions. Some ministry units (such as in the Ministry of Labour and the Ministry of Local Government) have been active in forming coalitions with civil society activists in an effort to increase their influence, while others are still feeling their way.

The ministry also supported the establishment of women's 'communication' centres in key provinces (Hebron, Nablus, Bethlehem, Jenin and Ramallah) through partnerships with civil society, government, local, regional and international institutions designed to combat all forms of discrimination against women. According to documents issued by the ministry and the Palestinian Women's Charter, the aim is to empower women and enable them to participate in public life. However, these centres suffer from a lack of essential human and financial resources (Palestinian National Report Beijing +15 2009). In addition, women and children's departments were added on 4 April 2007 by presidential decree to the structures of the various governorates, with the aim of supporting and developing the capabilities of women and children. However, these units were not allocated budgets, making the implementation of plans, programmes and activities assigned to them problematic, as is the case with most of the structures that have been established to institutionalise and mainstream gender. The ministry's vision and goals are shared by many women's rights and women's empowerment organisations since some of the leading women's NGOs are part of the national team. Criticisms, however, come from a few academics and youth groups who see that most women's organisations follow the agenda set by donors who provide the funding for these activities.

The Palestinian Women's Charter: arena of contention and conflict

After the split, the Palestinian Women's Charter proved to be a point of contention and a source of conflict between the Ministries of Women's Affairs in the West Bank and Gaza. The West Bank ministry sought to entrench the document as a guiding beacon for achieving equality for women, while Gaza officials, who could not disregard it altogether, sought to adopt some of its contents but annul or reverse others to render them compliant with an 'Islamic' vision for achieving women's rights.

Since its founding in 2003, the Ministry of Women's Affairs sought to establish the Palestinian Women's Charter developed by the feminist movement in 1994, as a benchmark for policy-making and legislation. Based on the charter, the ministry proposed several amendments to legislation, especially in relation to combating violence against women and advocating rising sentences for honour crimes by classifying them as criminal offences. This came in response to several cases of femicide that shook public opinion (Hammami (forthcoming)).

Using the Women's Charter as a guide, the West Bank Ministry of Women's Affairs and women's organisations worked together and succeeded in lobbying for various legislative and policy changes. These include quotas for women in the electoral law, raising the marriage age to eighteen, approval for gender-responsive government budgets, cabinet approval for the establishment of units for women in the various ministries, and the implementation of UN Resolution 1325 by the Palestinian Authority. The ministry also prompted the president to adopt the Convention on the Elimination of All Forms of Discrimination Against Women (CEDAW) and in 2008 secured his blessing for the charter.

This did not, however, mean a commitment by the PA to abide by the charter as a point of reference in legislation and policy-making. Indeed, the document has faced major challenges due to a lack of general community consensus. For example, clerics and the Ifta Council[7] claimed that the document does not adopt Islam as its reference but is, instead, based on secular laws and international conventions that could rip the Muslim family apart. The document was opposed on the grounds that it includes infractions of Islamic law, such as the right of women to assume all public positions with no conditions or restrictions, equality between men and women in testimony before the courts (*shehadah*), denial of the right of husbands to discipline their wives, an increase in the marriage age to eighteen, abolition of a man's authority and the principle of guardianship (*wilaya*) over his wife, establishing the right of Muslim women to marry non-Muslims, codifying the right of women to obtain divorce, restricting polygamy, establishing a woman's right to seek compensation in cases of arbitrary divorce, and equality in laws pertaining to property and inheritance. The charter was considered 'part of the drive to westernize Muslim women and detach them from their religion and an assault on the basic tenets of Islam; hence abiding by it or even accepting it is prohibited by sharia law' (Hussein 2010: 17–18). The Ifta Council called the document blasphemous and appealed to the president not to endorse it. Women at the grass-roots level, as became apparent in several workshops arranged by women's organisations, had views similar to those of the clergy who considered the charter a violation of Islamic law. These criticisms and attacks ultimately prompted the ministry to stop implementing the charter (Hussein 2010).

The two Hamas-affiliated ministers of Women's Affairs in the 2006–7 government and in the 2007 national unity government adopted the Palestinian Women's Charter with reservations (Al-Quds 2006; Al-Hayat al-Jadidah 2007). However, after the post-June 2007 split, the content of the document was changed by the Gaza Ministry of Women's Affairs. Despite significant changes, the Gaza ministry retained the document itself, which indicates a recognition of injustice and a need to develop an integrated rights and political framework, albeit in an Islamic context. It also indicates the vacuum of a coherent Islamic position on what constitutes their gender agenda. Workshops were conducted to promote the contents of the sharply altered document. For example, in a workshop held on 5 June 2009, the official in charge of policy and planning in the Gaza ministry stated that the document serves as a legal base compatible with the special identity and culture of Palestinian society but that the original document promoted by the West Bank ministry is not based on Islamic law. He went on to say that

> 99 per cent of the previous document promoted Western thought that is incompatible with Islam ... being grounded in leftist thought based on secularism. The current ministry has modified it to bring it in line with Islamic law. Initial rewriting of the document will be accomplished through a series of workshops (26 workshops) to be held by experts to study and analyze various issues in the document. (Haroun 2009)

Thus, the charter could not be entirely ignored even if its contents were modified beyond recognition.

The main objection to the West Bank ministry's version of the document is 'that it was based on the concept of gender, since it deals with individual rights of women, thereby promoting conflict between men and women' (Al Sabti 2009). By advocating complete equality in all matters relating to gender, such as considering testimony of women in courts of law equal to that of men, that version of the document purportedly denies complementarity[8] between men and women (Al Sabti, 2009). Nonetheless, as Al Sabti explains, the Gaza ministry document advocates that Palestinian women have the right to vote and be nominated in general and at local elections, the right to equal access to all public offices according to Islamic law,[9] the right to form and join political parties, and the right to enjoy all educational, financial, health and social services granted to citizens by law. There is thus a contradiction between an avowed rejection of the principle of full equality and these entitlements that are based mostly on the principle of equality in civil rights and penal law. Foundational concepts, such as gender and gender-based equality, are rejected in the original document, largely because they touch on more threatening issues such as women's position in the family, especially their rights to divorce, custody of their children, inheritance rights and the rejection of polygamy. Nevertheless, there is serious work underway, albeit indirectly, aimed at mobilising women as community workers and engaging them in political, economic and social roles.

However, the political split in 2007 eliminated any possibility of engagement between Islamist women in Gaza and other feminist groups and organisations. Scepticism and hostilities manifested themselves in the sharp criticism of Hamas social policy by women's NGOs, a policy that required female lawyers to wear head coverings in courts and resulted in the harassment of one of the prominent women's NGOs in Gaza (the Culture and Free Thought Association) in 2008 (al-Saqa 2018, interview). Part of the antagonism was also related to the restrictions imposed by the PA in the West Bank and the donor community proscribing any relations with Hamas or Islamists in Gaza. The PA followed a non-cooperation policy with Hamas, forcing all government employees to quit their jobs or lose their salaries. This policy played into the hands of the Hamas government who immediately hired thousands of new graduates, thus enlarging its popular base. The war on Gaza in 2008–9 prompted several feminist women's organisations, such as the Culture and Free Thought Association, the Women's Affairs Centre and the Women's Affairs Technical Committee, to support, jointly with the Hamas government, the hundreds of thousands of people who were displaced after the Israeli bombardment of their homes. Confronting a common enemy helped some feminist organisations in Gaza to forge a mutual cooperation with Islamist women in the Gaza government based on respect and recognition.

The various benchmark documents produced by the Ministry of Women's Affairs over the years spelling out the guiding principles of women's 'advancement' were also contested. The West Bank Ministry, at least on paper, claimed to be in full compliance of the standards set by international conventions on women's rights and CEDAW and continued to submit an annual report on its progress to the UN commission on CEDAW. The Gaza ministry was freed from the pressure to compromise with the national and secular activists and their donor–driven gender activism. After the split, Aisha Al Shanti, the women's affairs minister, rejected CEDAW as a reference for Palestinian women's rights. Instead, the ministry in Gaza was struggling to formulate its own vision of what should constitute women's rights from an Islamic perspective, relying on its powerful Supreme Council for Women, the women's arm of Hamas. The council is headed by influential wives of martyrs serving a constituency of martyrs' families and the constituency of the Islamic movement. It is considered by some feminist NGO activists as the most powerful women's organisation in Gaza (al-Saqa 2018, interview). The Women's Council with the Women's Ministry provided vital support for young graduates by offering vocational training, counselling programmes for young couples, food coupons for poor families, allowances for martyrs' families and political prisoners, and job opportunities for new graduates. They also achieved some legal reforms related to the right to custody of young children of wives of martyrs until the age of marriage if they so wish and if the mother refrains from remarrying. The Women's Ministry also managed to nominate three female general prosecutors and formed a women's police.

Islamic women's activism largely took over the mantle of women in the national movement of the 1970s and 1980s with their emphasis on consolidating Palestinian national identity based again on its old core elements of struggle, return and sacrifice.[10] The Islamic version of Palestinian nationalism constructs women, yet again, through non-confrontational images of the 'traditional', 'self-sacrificing mother', whose main role is to reproduce her nation by providing male fighters and of the 'revolutionary militant' who joins the struggle shoulder-to-shoulder with her brothers to liberate the nation – but this time in 'traditional' dress and adhering to militant Islamic groups and militant Islam. Thus, the women's brigade of the Qassamiat (followers of Ezzel Din al-Qassam), formed in 2005, was the culmination of Islamist women's engagement in the militant resistance.

The National Unity Government and the Instrumentalisation of Gender Platforms

After the renewed attempt at national unity in 2014, the nominaton of a new minister from Gaza (Dr Haifa al-Agha) to run the Ministry of Women's Affairs in both the West Bank and Gaza was an important development. She was immediately accepted and welcomed by Hamas women running the ministry but was greeted with suspicion by some feminists in the West Bank, because they considered her to lack feminist knowledge and qualifications. She was rapidly put to the test on how to bridge the gap between the separate ministries of the West Bank and Gaza. Her attempts to include Hamas women cadres in the many national teams producing the different women's plans and strategies did not succeed. However, in the last strategy document (Partners in Construction 2017–22), a slight change was introduced in the definition of gender equality to signify equity defined as having equal access to resources and opportunities. The document emphasised with some ambiguity that equality does not mean that men are like women ... they could be treated the same sometimes or different at some other times, each according to his/her own needs, but in a way to guarantee equality in rights, privileges, commitments and available opportunities in the frame of development. (Ministry of Women's Affairs 2017–22: 8)

However, in the face of a pile of strategies and plans developed in the West Bank ministry,[11] there is no noticeable change when it comes to the top priority goals to be implemented. These goals were reducing violence against women (VAW) by half, increasing women in decision-making government and non-government bodies by 10 per cent, mainstreaming gender equality and justice in the different governmental institutions, enhancing women's participation in the economy, and improving the quality of life for poor and marginalised families. Most of these plans and coalitions formed around them (like the National Coalition for Combating Violence Against Women), are seen by the Gaza ministry as irrelevant to their realities on the ground (Ministry of Women's Affairs 2017–22: 30–6).

The goals of the Gaza women's ministry are quite different: improving the economic standards of poor families through small income-generating projects, consolidating the unity of the Palestinian family by raising consciousness about rights and duties, supporting martyrs' families, improving women's legal status, capacity building for women's organisations to equip young women with skills for leadership and labour force participation (Ministry of Women's Affairs 2018). With these emerging disagreements, the Gaza ministry could not fully escape the pressure from international organisations and was forced to deal with issues related to VAW, in the final narrative report on the Millenium Development Goals in the Occupied Palestinian Territories, drafted by many UN organisations such as UNDP/PAPP; UN Women; ILO; UNESCO; UNRWA; and UNFPA, which read:

The establishment of the Hayat multipurpose center (shelter) in Gaza, however, initiated a breakthrough in the Gazan society in the sense that the Hamas government was *forced* (stress added) to address GBV and VAW issues for the very first time at the national/policy level. (MDG 2013: 10)

However, disagreements persisted on the ideological reference point on means to empower women and defend their rights. According to the deputy adjutant minister in Gaza, Amira Haroun, Plan 1325 does not take the colonised reality of Palestine into consideration, nor the Israeli violence that destroys Palestinian livelihoods. Instead, according to Haroun:

> It is sad to see women activists driven by these plans in Gaza focusing on sexual harassment against women who still live in caravans after the destruction of their homes by Israeli bombs in 2014, and they don't see the violence against their lives, families and their homes. (Haroun 2018, interview)

Nonetheless, Haroun sees participation in these plans and strategies as a medium to politically recognise the Islamists in the ministry:

> We asked to be part of the national coalition to combat violence and the national strategic plan on violence, but our request was rejected by the cabinet in the West Bank; the same happened with our request to be part of the 1325 Plan, they did not include us in forming these plans and they don't want to include us. (Haroun 2018, interview)

Not surprisingly, the ministry in the West Bank presents the plans on their website, but they are not publicised online in Gaza.

Factional disputes have been reflected among the female cadres of the Ministry of Women's Affairs since 2014. Although Hamas cadres of MOWA do not recognise issues such as VAW as priorities for the Gazans, they nonetheless fight for representation on platforms that receive support and funding from international donors, suggesting that an instrumental engagement with these issues is important to their presence and legitimacy.

Donor-driven Gender Activism and the Saving of Palestinian Women

The rift between Islamist women in Gaza and feminist activists in the West Bank is to some extent, cemented by the discourse of donor-driven gender activism reflected in the plans and documents discussed throughout this text. We read, in many documents, as is the case with UN Women and other global institutions, that gender-based violence is singled out as the priority to be tackled to safeguard Palestinian women's rights. (MDG 2013: 6)

The attempts of a few Palestinian feminists to emphasise the structural limitations to the advancement of women's rights fell on deaf ears. Reem Al Botmeh, in her thorough analysis of the trajectory of legal reform in Palestine, showed, in a study commissioned by the UNDP, that legal reform has a limited impact from the women's rights perspective given the realities on the ground.

Reaching the same conclusion, the Ministry of Women's Affairs showed in its new Intersectoral Plan that women's participation in the labour market increased from 17.4 per cent in 2012 to 19.1 per cent in 2015. However, the total number of working women as a proportion of the total number of workers decreased from

18.1 per cent in 2012 to 16.8 per cent in 2015, while the percentage of unemployed women increased from 32.9 per cent in 2012 to 39.2 per cent in 2015. The reason given for this regression was related to structural constraints, such as limited job opportunities in the labour market, the political and economic siege on Gaza and the control of Area C in the West Bank that represents 60 per cent of its total space (Ministry of Women's Affairs 201722: 16).

As for the drive to combat VAW, Al Botmeh states that:

> while the PNA can pass legislation aimed at protecting the victims of domestic violence, it cannot enforce this legislation in the district of Jerusalem, which has been illegally annexed by Israel; neither can it send its police force to most of the West Bank to respond to an emergency call from a potential victim of violence without obtaining the prior permission of the occupier.[12] (UNDP 2012: 2–1)

The Intersectional Plan in its review of achievements since the previous plans, showed 'the data gathered did not show any progress in reducing violence against women' (Ministry of Women's Affairs 2017–22: 17). The reason given for the lack of progress was attributed to the lack of surveys on the number of women who asked for support from women's institutions or those who sought counselling.

In a thorough and profound examination of the genealogy of the global statistical norm for measuring VAW in the non-West and its consolidation into 'best practice' within institutions of global development funding under the guise of 'ethical considerations', Rema Hammami drew attention to what she calls 'statistical apartheid', according to which VAW as a social problem has been largely off-shored to the non-West where the normative measure can produce outcomes confirming its 'pandemic' proportions. Turning to the Palestinian case, Hammami concludes:

> Despite counter knowledge[13] being produced, it is unable to penetrate this dense discursive field. Even attempts by the Palestinian Central Bureau of Statistics (PCBS) technicians to counter it in the second survey (on VAW) undertaken in 2010 had no impact on its operations. Local activists get pulled into this vortex, in need of its resources to do the real work of treating actual victims of domestic abuse. But caught in its logics they constantly have to show their relevance to it that by providing evidence that perpetuates the need for more interventions . . . But while this is the everyday productivity of this power/knowledge formation, it is also accomplishing wider geo-political work. Most simply by 'domesticating' violence, it makes Palestine's 'violence problem' a Palestinian problem. (Hammami (forthcoming))

Hammami eloquently argues, that, thus, the burden of violence is taken off Israel and resituated as an Arab/Muslim patriarchal violence, represented in the violent pathologies of Palestinian manhood (Hammami (forthcoming)).

The goals set by donor-driven gender activism and global development funding institutions make a possible rapprochement or shared vision between West Bank and Gaza ever more difficult. For instance, combating gender-based violence as the top strategic goal for the years 2017–22 was turned into a big industry that involves many actors within the government and non-government sectors. Women's activism around combating violence and women's rights are delinked from the Palestinian national context, making a shared vision on gender justice between the West Bank and Gaza harder to achieve. Thus, alongside the logic of factional politics, different understandings of gender justice may be seen as a contributory factor to deepening the schism between the West Bank and Gaza, both Palestinian entities living in an illusion of sovereignty.

Conclusion

More than a decade ago (Jad 2008) I had argued that that the dual dynamics of state building after the Oslo process, the adoption of a gender agenda promoted by the global donor community and the NGOisation of women's movements in Palestine led to their demobilisation and isolation from the grass roots of society, acting to disempower and delegitimise civil society and secular actors and their movements. In the years that followed, donor-driven gender activism created a massive infrastructure in defence of women's rights that was initially rejected by Islamists as a Western imposition and later presented as largely irrelevant to the realities of their war-torn society. The schism between the West Bank and Gaza administrations deepened the chasm between the Fatah-led PA and the Hamas-dominated Gaza in matters of gender equality and justice. The contestations over the Palestinian Women's Charter and the question of compliance with international standard setting instruments such as CEDAW meant that the two ministries (in West Bank and Gaza) adopted divergent positions. While the West Bank ministry continued to operate within priorities set by donors (such as gender-based violence), the ministry in Gaza adopted a welfarist approach geared to providing for women's basic needs such as shelter, food, job opportunities and assistance for widows of martyrs and their families. They thus donned the mantle of national resistance, reverting to images of women as heroic mothers and sisters-in-arms, albeit in traditional dress and an Islamic idiom this time. Ironically, however, not only did the women cadres of Hamas struggle to find an alternative language for an articulation of women's rights, but could not entirely turn the clock back on the benchmark documents and frameworks generated by West Banks activists, not least since they were interested

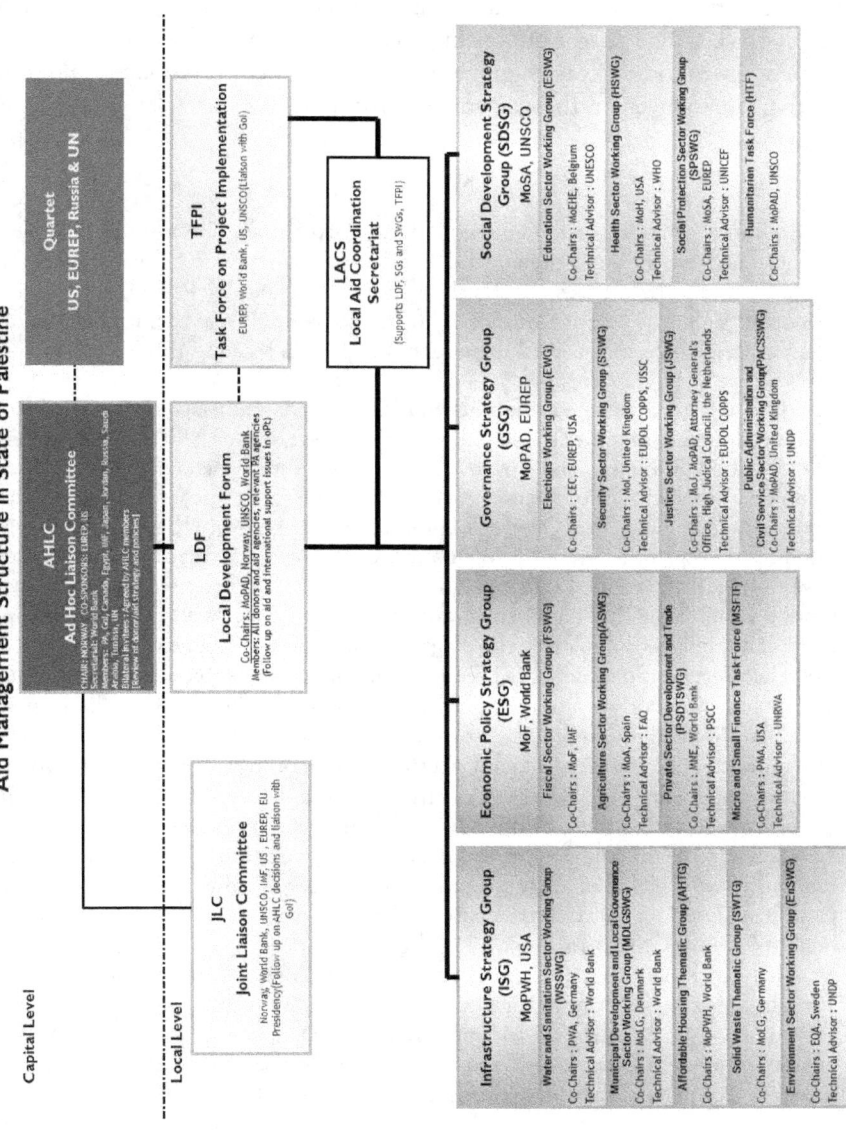

Figure 7.1 Aid Management Structure in State of Palestine. Source: http://www.lacs.ps/ (accessed on 2 January 2018).

in securing political legitimisation and channelling some direly needed donor funding to the distressed Gazans. Thus, Islamist women instrumentalised donor-driven gender activism to gain political traction and financial assistance, whilst working to subvert its basic premises among their own constituencies. These dynamics have added to the mounting weakness of the Palestinian women's movement, a weakness greatly aggravated by the system of governance endorsed by international players in the Occupied Territories.

Notes

1. The al-Aqsa intifada is the name commonly used to describe a series of violent clashes between the Palestinians and Israel in the timeframe between 2000 and 2004. Triggered by the visit of the then Prime Minister Ariel Sharon to al-Aqsa Mosque (Temple Mount) in late September 2000, viewed as an intentional attempt by Israel to infringe on the Muslim presence on al-Aqsa Mosque, this led to a violent riot and the re-invasion, by Israel, of all West Bank cities.
2. The Quartet is a foursome of nations and international and supranational entities involved in mediating the Israeli–Palestinian peace process. The Quartet comprises the UN, the US, the EU and Russia. The group was established in Madrid in 2002, recalling the Madrid Conference of 1991, as a result of the escalating conflict in the Middle East. The Quartet's current special envoy is Kito de Boer, who assumed the position after the resignation of Tony Blair in 2015. The Quartet developed a sophisticated structure in which Israel is represented in the ad hoc Liaison Committee that has oversight of strategy and policies and the channelling of all donor aids to the PA (see the diagram of its structure in Figure 7.1).
3. The Hamas government in Gaza used to get funding from the government of Qatar and some Islamic organisations in Turkey, and some funding for its militant wing from Iran. With the tightening of the closure and siege, Qatar reduced some of its funding and it became more difficult to bring direct funding to Gaza (Haroun 2018).
4. Islamist women are those who support the Islamic movement of Hamas or Islamic Jihad and who want to live by the rules of Islamic sharia (rulings).
5. The concept of bringing gender issues into the mainstream of society was clearly established as a global strategy for promoting gender equality in the Platform for Action adopted at the United Nations Fourth World Conference on Women, held in Beijing (China) in 1995. It highlighted the necessity to ensure that gender equality is a primary goal in all area(s) of social and economic development.
6. Mariam Saleh, the first minister of the Ministry of Women's Affairs in the tenth government (29 March 2006 to 15 February 2007), spoke to leaders of women's organisations on 5 November 2006 (*Al-Quds* newspaper 2006). Amal Siam, her successor in the national unity government (the eleventh government), which was formed on 17 March 2007 and ended with Hamas' takeover of the Gaza Strip on 14 June 2007, also called for a meeting with women's organisations and unions, but only a few responded (*Al-Hayat al-Jadidah* newspaper 2007).
7. The Ifta Council is a recognised religious authority which gives Islamic religious rulings, a scholarly opinion on a matter of Islamic law.

8. The concept of complementarity is based, in general, on the notion of a biological destiny for men and women that makes them unequal but complementary, locking women into roles of motherhood and domesticity; men's roles are to fend for their families and be in the public sphere.
9. The position is actually ambiguous. There are those who reject the idea of women holding high state office or in the judiciary. However, views differ between the moderate current (Muslim Brotherhood) and some of the most stringent fundamentalist (Salafi) trends.
10. A new group of national activists such as *nabd* (pulse) was created in 2015, including men and women that were critical of donor-driven women's rights activism and were hostile to the NGOisation of all popular national movements in the Occupied Territories. They work to bring back to the fore the core issues of the Palestinian national struggle (Hamayel 2018, interview).
11. See, for example, the National Plan for Combating Violence Against Women (2011–19), the National Coalition for Combating Violence, the National Plan for the Security Council Resolution 1325 and the National Action Plan for the Implementation of the UNSCR 1325: Women, Peace and Security (2017–19); the Strategic National Frame for 1325 (2015); and the Intersectoral Plan 2017–22 (Partners in Construction).
12. There are three areas in terms of the PA's authority: Area A (17.2 per cent of the West Bank), where the PA has sole civil jurisdiction and security control while Israel retains authority over movement in and out of the area; Area B (23.8 per cent), where the PA has civil authority and responsibility for public order, while Israel maintains security presence and overriding security responsibility; Area C (59 per cent), where the PA has restricted civil authorities in the fields of education and welfare. Most civil authorities and all security authorities have remained within the hands of the IDF (Diakonia Easy Guide to Humanitarian Law in the oPt, <http://www.diakonia.se/sa/node.asp?node=1125> (last accessed 4 December 2008) (UNDP 2012: 21)
13. Hammami refers to numerous attempts by the Institute of Women's Studies at Birzeit University and its individual research affiliates to produce counter-knowledge to Palestine's VAW 'common sense', especially the consistent attempts by Penny Johnson: Penny Johnson (2008), 'Violence all around us: dilemmas of global and local agendas addressing violence against Palestinian women, an initial intervention', *Cultural Dynamics*, 20: 2, pp. 119–31; Penny Johnson (2010), 'Violence, gender-based violence and protection: a dangerous decade', in *A Dangerous Decade: the Second Gender Profile of the West Bank and Gaza* (2000–2010), Birzeit: Birzeit University, pp. 93–104, available at <https://fada.birzeit.edu/> (last accessed 2 February 2018); Penny Johnson (2010), 'Displacing Palestine: Palestinian householding in an era of asymmetrical war', *Politics and Gender*, 6: 2, pp. 295–304. See also Palestinian Non-Governmental Organization Against Domestic Violence Against Women (Al Muntada) (2007), 'Crimes of women's killing in Palestine in the period 2004–2006', March, available at <http://www.sawa.ps/Upload/Reports/CrimesofWomensKillinginPalestine_arabic.pdf> (last accessed 2 February 2018); and the analytical report on the 2005 PCBS survey undertaken for the Bureau by the Institute of Women's Studies Birzeit University (2006), 'Domestic violence in the

Palestinian Territory, analytical study', December, available at <http://www.pcbs.gov.ps/Downloads/book1340.pdf> (last accessed 2 February 2018).

Bibliography

Almayadeen.net (2018) 'Momathel al monazmat al khayria fi ghaza: al qita' mantiqa manqoba insaniyan' (Representative of Charitable Organisations in Gaza: the Strip is a human disaster area), *Almayadeen.net*, 25 January, <http://www.almayadeen.net/news/politics/855017/> (last accessed 26 January 2018).

Badran, Margot (1995), *Feminists, Islam, and Nation: Gender and the Making of Modern Egypt*, Princeton: Princeton University Press.

Chatterjee, Partha (1990), 'The nationalist resolution of the women's questions', in K. Sangari and S. Vaid (eds), *Recasting Women: Essays in Indian Colonial History*, New Brunswick, NJ: Rutgers University Press: pp. 238–48.

—— (1993), *The Nation and Its Fragments: Colonial and Postcolonial Histories*, Princeton: Princeton University Press.

Eisenstein, Zillah (1989), *The Female Body and the Law*, Berkeley: University of California Press.

Haddad, Tawfiq (2010), 'The future of the Palestinian movement', *International Socialist Review*, 73, September <https://isreview.org/issue/73/future-palestinian-movement> (last accessed 30 November 2017).

Hammami, Rema (2019), 'Follow the numbers: global governmentality and the Violence Against Women agenda in Occupied Palestine', in J. Halley, P. Kotiswaran, R. Rebouché and H. Shamir (eds), *Governance Feminism: Notes from the Field*, Minneapolis: University of Minnesota Press, pp. 479–560.

Hanafi, Sari (ed.) (2008), *Crossing Borders, Shifting Boundaries: Palestinian Dilemmas*, Cairo: American University in Cairo Press.

Hanafi, Sari and Linda Tabar (2005), *The Emergence of the Palestinian Globalized Elite: Donors, International Organizations and Local NGOs*, Washington, DC: Institute of Palestine Studies.

Haroun, Amira (2009), 'The Palestinian Women's Bill of Rights', workshop, Gaza, on 5 June 2009, <http://www.mowa.gov.ps/news_details.php?id=10> (last accessed on 12 August 2011).

Al-Hayat al-Jadidah, 20 May 2007.

Hilal, Jamil and Mushtaq H. Khan (2004), 'State formation under the PNA', in M. H. Khan, G. Giacaman and I. Amundsen (eds), *State Formation in Palestine: Viability and Governance during a Social Transformation*, London: Routledge, pp. 64–119.

Hussein, Khadija (2010), 'Rereading the Palestinian Women's Bill of Rights', Women's Affairs Committee, Ramallah, unpublished report.

Jad, Islah (2005), 'Islamist women of Hamas: a new women's movement?', in F. Nouraie-Simone (ed.), *On Shifting Ground: Muslim Women in a Global Era*, New York: Feminist Press, pp. 256–96.

—— (2008) 'The demobilization of women's movement: the case of Palestine', in S. Batliwala (ed.), *Changing Their World: Concepts and Practices of Women's*

Movements, Toronto, Mexico City, Cape Town: Association for Women's Rights in Development (AWID), pp. 53–4.
—— (2011), 'The post-Oslo Palestine and gendering Palestinian citizenship', *Ethnicities*, 11: 3, September, pp. 360–73.
Jayawardena, Kumari (1986), *Feminism and Nationalism in the Third World*, 2nd edition, New Delhi: Kali for Women.
Kandiyoti, Deniz (1991a), 'Identity and its discontents: women and the nation', *Millenium Journal of International Studies*, 20: 3, pp. 429–43.
—— (1991b), *Women, Islam and the State*, London: Macmillan.
MDG (2013), 'MDG Achievement Fund: final narrative report, Occupied Palestinian Territories. Joint programme title: gender equality – social, political and economic in the oPt', *MDG-F Secretariat*, March, <http://www.mdgfund.org/sites/default/files/Palestinian%20Territory%20-%20Gender%20-%20Final%20Narrative%20Report.pdf> (last accessed 2 January 2018).
MIFTAH (2006), 'Women in Peace and Negotiation, Women Political Forum', third meeting minutes taken by the author on 26 February 2006, Ramallah: MIFTAH office.
Ministry of Women's Affairs (2004), 'Strategic vision and a plan of action', March, Ramallah: Ministry of Women's Affairs.
—— (2017–22), 'Partners in construction: intersectoral national strategic plan to enhance gender justice, equality and empowerment', Ramallah: Ministry of Women's Affairs.
—— (2018), 'Gaza: goals', <http://www.mowa.gov.ps/mowa1/gov/index.php> (last accessed 20 January 2018).
Mohanty, Chandra T. (1991), 'Introduction: cartographies of struggle: Third World women and the politics of feminism', in C. Mohanty, A. Russo and L. Torres (eds), *Third World Women and the Politics of Feminism*, Indianapolis: Indiana University Press, pp. 1–50.
Molyneux, Maxine (1998), 'Analysing women's movements', in C. Jackson and R. Pearson (eds), *Feminist Visions of Development: Gender Analysis and Policy*, London: Routledge, pp. 65–88.
—— (2001), *Women's Movements in International Perspective – Latin America and Beyond*, Basingstoke and New York: Palgrave Macmillan.
Oxfam (2017), 'Backbone document for the gender justice programming in OPTI (Occupied Palestinian Territories and Israel)', plan in progress (permission required for quotation).
PCBS (Palestinian Central Bureau of Statestics) (2015), 'Main finding of the impact of Israeli Aggression in 2014 on socio-economic conditions of households in the Gaza Strip survey', Press Release, Ramallah, Palestine.
Palestinian National Report (2009), 'Beijing + 15', ESCWA, Beirut (unpublished report).
Al-Quds (2006), No. 13192: 1, Jerusalem.
Al Sabti, Randa (2009), 'The most important pillars and themes of Women's Bill of Rights', The Palestinian Women's Bill of Rights' workshop, Gaza, on 5 June 2009, <http://www.mowa.gov.ps/news_details.php?id=10> (last accessed 12 August 2011).

Schulz, Helena Lindholm (1999), *The Reconstruction of Palestinian Nationalism, between Revolution and Statehood*, Manchester: Manchester University Press.

Sharkey, Heather J. (2003), *Living with Colonialism: Nationalism and Culture in the Anglo-Egyptian Sudan*, Berkeley: University of California Press.

UNDP (2012), 'A review of Palestinian legislation from a women's rights perspective', Jerusalem: United Nations Development Programme.

Yeatman, Anna (1990), *Bureaucrats, Technocrats, Femocrats: Essays on the Contemporary Australian State*, Sydney: Allen and Unwin.

INTERVIEWS

Hamayel, Yassmine (activist in *nabd* (pulse) movement in Ramallah), on 21 April 2018 (3–4 p.m.).

Haroun, Amira (Deputy Adjutant Women's Affairs Ministry – Gaza), phone interview on 28 January 2018 (7–8 p.m.).

Al-Saqa, Majida (Deputy Director of Culture and Free Thought Centre – Gaza), phone interview on 29 January 2018 (8–9.39 p.m.).

Chapter 8

Iraq: Gendering Violence, Sectarianism and Authoritarianism

Nadje Al-Ali

Introduction

In March 2017, the Iraqi parliament and media experienced a huge uproar after a female MP called for the promotion of polygamy in order to support and help the high number of widows, divorcees and single women as a result of war and conflict. Jamila Al-Obaidi, a Sunni member of the Iraqi parliament from the National Coalition, convened a press conference, encouraging women to denounce the culture of monogamy. Aside from demanding the lifting of legal restrictions making polygamy difficult, she recommended 'financial incentives to encourage the men and help them to marry more than one woman, and to double these incentives for those who marry a widow or a divorcee'.[1]

Opinions amongst MPs, journalists and the general public were extremely polarised in reaction to Al-Obaidi's statement. Many Sunni and Shia female MPs expressed their outrage at Al-Obaidi's suggestions, which, in their view, was demeaning to women, with one angry MP even slapping her and throwing a shoe at her – the ultimate form of humiliation in Iraqi culture. However, some journalists, writers and religious figures praised Al-Obaidi and stressed the religious roots of her argumentation. While this particular debate lacked the sectarian undertones of many other heated discussions and conflicts in contemporary Iraq, it illustrates both the centrality of gender issues in contestations about the 'new Iraq' as well as the limitations of numerical representation in terms of the women's political participation (McKernan 2017). Al-Obaidi's case, as with several others previously, showed clearly that women parliamentarians are not necessarily promoting women's equality and rights.

This was not the first time in post-invasion Iraq that gender issues took centre stage in political and media debates. In fact, questions around women's legal rights, their political representation as well as gender-based and domestic violence have constituted symbolic markers of difference between the old Ba'th regime and new forms of governance in central and southern Iraq on the one hand, and the Kurdish Regional Government (KRG) in northern Iraq on the other. At the same time, contestations around gender have also been at the heart of ethnic and sectarian tensions and conflict.

In this chapter I will briefly explore the historical background to the more recent post-invasion developments, before arguing that increases in gender-based violence, contestations about women's legal rights, as well as wider gender norms and relations, are central to understanding and shaping sectarian and authoritarian governance in post-invasion Iraq. Finally, my chapter will show that Iraqi women's rights mobilisation has not only attempted to challenge the shrinking of political and social spaces for women, as well as the different forms of violence they have been exposed to, but this mobilisation has also been at the forefront of the struggle against sectarianism and political authoritarianism.

Shifting Gender Regime under the Ba'th Party

Despite indisputable political repression in the 1970s, the first decade of the Ba'th regime (1968–79) was characterised by an economic boom and rapid development, which were a result of the rise of oil prices and the government's developmental policies. State-induced policies aimed to eradicate illiteracy, educate women and incorporate them into the labour force (Al-Ali 2007: 127). In 1974, a government decree stipulated that all university graduates – men or women – would be employed automatically. The policies of encouraging women to enter waged work cannot be explained in terms of egalitarian or even feminist principles, however, even though several women I talked to over the years did comment positively on the early Ba'thi policies of the social inclusion of women. This resonates with Suad Joseph's earlier assertion (1991) in *Women, Islam and The State* that the Iraqi state was motivated by the same development goals as other states in the region.

The specific motivations and ideology of the Ba'th regime with respect to women's roles and positions is beyond the scope of this chapter. What can be said is that human power was scarce. Instead of looking for labour outside its national boundaries, as many of the oil-producing Gulf countries did at the time, the Iraqi government tapped into the country's own human resources. In time, working outside the home became not only acceptable for women but prestigious and the norm. Another factor to be taken into account was the state's attempt to indoctrinate its citizens – whether male or female. A great number of party members were recruited through their work places. Obviously, it was much easier to reach out to and recruit women when they were part of the so-called public sphere and reachable outside the confines of their homes (Al-Ali 2007: 132–3).

How far this access to education and the labour market resulted in an improved status for women is a more complex question. Conservative and patriarchal values did not automatically change because women started working. Furthermore, there were great differences between rural and urban women as well as between women from different class, ethnic and religious backgrounds. Kurdish women in the north and Shia women in the south of Iraq and in rural areas tended to be excluded from the state's modernist developmental policies, and were often targeted as part of the state's repression, not only of political opposition but also of the Kurdish and Shia populations more broadly. However, literacy programmes, organised by the General Federation of Iraqi Women, appeared to have been implemented throughout Iraq and amongst all ethnic and religious communities (Al-Ali 2007: 136–7).

Saddam Hussein, who became president in 1979, used techniques of power utilised by previous Iraqi regimes – exclusion of rivals, promoting communal mistrust, developing patronage networks, and the use of violence (Tripp 2000: 194). He privileged his extended clan, whilst also developing communal and tribal relations as mechanisms of patronage and coercion (Tripp 2000: 194). During his dictatorship, Kurdish nationalists and Shia political Islamists were particular targets of regime repression and atrocities (Al-Ali and Pratt 2014), but his internal political repression and his strategy of using armed warfare to deal with conflict affected the entire population. As Suad Joseph (1991) has argued convincingly, the Ba'th regime systematically attempted to sideline tribal and religious authorities and alliances in favour of greater central state control. While the government attempted to establish a monopoly over social control, as well as trying to become the main vehicle for socialisation and education, it encouraged the rise of nuclear families as units of consumption.

During the years of the Iran–Iraq war (1980–8), women's increased participation in the public sphere to replace male soldiers coincided with the further militarisation of society and a glorification of certain types of masculinity, that is the fighter, the defender of the nation and the martyr. Women were simultaneously encouraged by the state to replace male workers and civil servants who were fighting at the front, and to 'produce' more Iraqi citizens and future soldiers. The glorification of a militarised masculinity coincided with the glorification of the Iraqi mother. Women's sexuality, and more specifically, reproduction, became a greater focus of the regime that not only outlawed abortion and contraception, but also engaged in Arabisation policies, which involved encouraging Iraqi Arab men to marry Kurdish women. While the country was at war with Iran, the Iraqi women's movement was reduced to the General Federation of Iraqi

Women (GFIW), which had become a mouthpiece for Ba'thi ideology and a vehicle for indoctrination.

Only two 'peaceful' years were followed by the invasion of Kuwait (August 1990) and the Gulf War (January–March 1991). The devastating gendered impact of the economic sanctions system has been illustrated effectively by Yasmin Al-Jawaheri (2008). In the context of the weakening of political and economic control by the Ba'th regime, policies of inclusion and encouragement in terms of women's education and labour force participation shifted to the emergence of new forms of patriarchal control and the increase of social conservatism. To counter the weakening of his authority, Saddam Hussein instrumentalised gender norms to bargain with tribal and religious authorities. In other words, the regime ceded control back to tribal and family formations into whose territory the state had encroached in the previous two decades. At the same time, Saddam Hussein aligned himself with the idea of the 'Muslim *ummah*', resisting 'western Satan', tapping into both the increase in religiosity amongst the Iraqi population as well as transnational Islamist tendencies. Aside from the effects of greater patriarchal control on women's mobility, dress codes, behaviour and relations with men, Iraqi women were particularly affected by poverty and the radical decline of Iraq's infrastructure, including its education and healthcare systems (Al-Ali 2007; Al-Jawaheri 2008).

The breakdown of the welfare state had a disproportionate effect on women, who had been its main beneficiaries. Women were pushed back into their homes and into the traditional roles of being mothers and housewives. From being the highest in the region, estimated to be above 23 per cent prior to 1991, women's employment rate fell to only 10 per cent in 1997, as reported by the UNDP in 2000. Monthly salaries in the public sector, which, since the Iran–Iraq war, had increasingly been staffed by women, dropped dramatically and did not keep pace with high inflation rates and the cost of living. Many women reported that they simply could not afford to work anymore. The state withdrew its free services, including childcare and transportation (Al-Ali 2007: 185–91).

Between the first decade of the Ba'th regime in the 1970s and the sanctions period (1990–2003), Iraq's gender regime shifted from a secular-oriented modernist and developmental authoritarian dictatorship which promoted women's education, labour force participation and women's participation in public life, to a conservative gender regime that placated and collaborated with religious and tribal forces at a time when the state's grip on power was weakened. The regime used notions of custom, tradition and culture around gender norms and relations as bargaining chips with different constituencies, including families.

Emergence of a 'New Iraq'

Since the invasion of 2003, Iraq has experienced unprecedented levels of violence and a series of political crises, as well as extreme manifestations of sectarianism that is shaping not only political but also everyday lives. Unresolved tensions and conflict between the KRG and the Iraqi central government over the distribution of oil revenues, disputed territories and, more recently since the referendum in 2017, the independence of Iraqi Kurdistan, have continued alongside the systematic political marginalisation of Iraq's Arab Sunni community, which used to be dominant prior to the fall of Saddam Hussein. Intra-Shia tensions and in-fighting complicate the apparent predominance of Shia Islamist political parties and militia in central and southern Iraq. Despite the stated aim by the coalition forces to demilitarise Iraq after the toppling of Saddam Hussein, the country is extremely militarised, with a mushrooming of both state and non-state armed groups (Dodge 2012). Rather than democracy and human rights, all regions of Iraq have experienced the re-emergence and consolidation of political authoritarianism, including political repression, intimidation, arrests and targeted assassinations.

Initially, women were promoted as the 'heroines' of the reconstruction of post-invasion Iraq. Yet the degree to which this rhetorical support was translated into actual support for women's involvement in reconstruction was brought into question by the US' pursuit of its 'national strategic interests' (Al-Ali and Pratt 2009). US support for its local political allies and proxies operated to encourage the fragmentation of the state and political authority (Herring and Rangwala 2006) in ways that have undermined women's participation and women's rights. It became obvious in the Iraqi context, even if not as explicitly as in the Afghan case, that the promotion of women's participation in peace-building and reconstruction had to be understood in the context of larger international processes of imperialism and global capitalism.[2] In the political process, the US has empowered sectarian and communal political forces and these, in turn, have further fuelled the violence. In the reconstruction process, the US has given multi-billion-dollar contracts to US companies rather than to Iraqi companies, failed to provide sufficient oversight of reconstruction funds and reallocated a significant portion of those to 'security' (that is, the security of US personnel and contractors). This has all been to the detriment of rebuilding the Iraqi state, infrastructure and basic services (Al-Ali and Pratt 2009).

Explanations of the failure of the post-invasion political transition have frequently been divided between flawed implementation versus flawed design. The timing of the elections and the constitution-drafting process have been described as premature and/or too hurried, thereby undermining possibilities for reconciliation and confidence-building amongst Iraq's different communities

(Al-Ali and Pratt 2009). Meanwhile, several authors have illustrated that the US attempted to shape the transition process according to its strategic interests: initially marginalising the Sunni population, which it regarded as the source of the anti-US insurgency (International Crisis Group 2004); and later, bringing unelected Sunni representatives into the process in an attempt to curb the insurgency (International Crisis Group 2005). However, it would be too simplistic to frame the failures, conflicts and chaos of post-invasion Iraq on the US and the UK alone, as various regional, national and local actors used and contributed to the ongoing conflict, violence and lawlessness that has plagued Iraq since 2003.

The main Iraqi political leaders, including those belonging to political parties and militia have all been complicit in increasing corruption and paralysis of decision-making. Most political parties do not represent different political ideologies or ideas, but rather factional interests of an ethnic or sectarian nature (Al-Ali and Pratt 2009). Attempts at power sharing within the cabinet, through the allocation of ministerial posts to different parties/ethno-sectarian groups in proportion to seats in parliament (called the *muhasasa* system), has become an opportunity for asset-grabbing and zero-sum politics, rather than cooperation (Dodge 2014). This has greatly delayed the formation of governments following different rounds of elections, presenting obstacles to effective decision-making. Perhaps even more worryingly, there have been clear trends towards authoritarian politics and a new dictatorship since Prime Minister Nouri al-Malaki was in power (from 2006 to 2014) (Dodge 2012).

The failure to reconstruct political institutions capable of reconciling Iraq's different political, ethnic and religious groupings has weakened both the central government as well as the KRG; it has also increased corruption within state institutions, and fed into ethnic and sectarian violence, thereby creating a favourable environment for the emergence of the so-called Islamic State (IS) (or *daesh*) (Al-Ali and Pratt 2009). In central and southern Iraq, a powerful Shia Islamist alliance has systematically marginalised Sunni political players and communities, while intra-Shia tensions have largely revolved around allegiance to neighbouring Iran as opposed to more Iraqi nationalist positions. Prime Minister Haidar al-Abadi, generally perceived to be a more moderate political figure than his predecessor Nouri al-Malaki, was expected to appease Sunni communities, while also responding to calls for reform, better infrastructure and an end to corruption on behalf of a growing protest movement. However, al-Abadi's politics and alliances have not broken the sectarian Shia Islamist stranglehold on Iraq or decreased corruption and lack of transparency. Meanwhile, the Iraqi nationalist Shia Sadrist movement, linked to the Iraqi Shia cleric Muqtada al-Sadr, has become a major player both in terms of anti-sectarian politics as well as the youth-led protest movement against corruption.

In the Kurdish Region of Iraq (KRI), it has become apparent that the KRG has miscalculated badly and lost both the prospect of independence from Iraq as well as political legitimacy vis-à-vis its own population. While the KRG experienced a period of economic boom, increased autonomy and political strength in the first decade after the fall of the Ba'th regime in 2003, it increasingly reverted to patronage, corruption and political repression as a modus operandi of governance. The political elite, mainly represented in the two main political parties, that is the Kurdistan Democratic Party (KDP) and the Patriotic Union of Kurdistan Party (PUK), has historically relied on patronage and propaganda to create dependencies and loyalty. The KRG, particularly the KDP in Erbil, has used a well-developed security apparatus for surveillance and control of political opposition as well as refugees, especially Arabs from central and southern Iraq and Kurds from Syria. However, a severe economic crisis since 2014, triggered by a budget dispute with the central government linked to alleged illegitimate oil sales, has severely weakened the KRG's ability to create docile dependent citizens. The economic crisis has been exacerbated by a crisis of political legitimacy due to the former president Massoud Barzani's attempt at holding on to power,[3] and his badly conceived efforts to consolidate authority through the independence referendum in 2017. In the aftermath of the referendum, in which the overwhelming majority of voters supported independence, the Iraqi government reacted with both political and military pressure, and eventually escalated by retaking the oil rich city of Kirkuk, which had been under Kurdish control since 2014.

Both the tensions between the KRG and the central government and sectarian tensions in central and southern Iraq continue to shape political dynamics and developments in Iraq. Although IS is being defeated militarily with the help of US troops, Kurdish Peshmerga, and Kurdish fighters linked to the Kurdistan Workers Party (PKK), the Iraqi government's ongoing sectarian policies might lead to a reconfiguration of radical Sunni Islamists and the transformation of IS into a different organisation, mirroring the currently existing radical Shia Islamist groups and ideologies.

Institutionalising Sectarianism: Contestations of the Personal Status Code

In the post-invasion context, there has been a great push towards conservative social norms and sectarian Islamist politics. Contestations around gender norms and relations have been at the centre of political power struggles. One early example of the growing impact of Islamist tendencies was the attempt, very early on after the invasion, in December 2003, to scrap the Personal Status Code (PSC), also referred to as family laws. The existing PSC was to be changed in favour of sharia-based jurisdiction by the Iraqi Governing Council under then chair Abdel Aziz al-Hakim, head of the Shia Islamic Supreme Council of Iraq (formerly known as the Supreme Council for the Islamic Revolution in Iraq).

There had been a unified family law in Iraq since the formulation of a new constitution in 1959, following the revolution against the monarchy and British meddling in 1958. The PSC (Law No. 188), enshrined in the 1959 Constitution was based on a relatively liberal reading of Islamic law. It codified all laws and regulations related to marriage, divorce, child custody and inheritance. This set of laws combined Sunni and Shia regulations and applied to all Iraqis, contributing to a sense of national unity. It facilitated mixed marriages between Sunni and Shia Iraqis, as well as between Arabs and Kurds. Amendments to the family laws were made under the Ba'th regime in 1978. The amended PSC widened the conditions under which a woman could seek divorce, outlawed forced marriages, required the permission of a judge for a man to have a second wife, and prescribed punishment for marriages contracted outside the court.

Although unsuccessful in 2003, the initial attempt to change the law and the discussion around it revealed a shift in the Iraqi gender regime and the dangers lying ahead. The debate about the personal status laws in particular and Islamic law in general emerged again in the context of debates about a new constitution in 2005. While not the only source of legislation, Islam was designated as the official religion and a basic source of legislation. Neither the previous transitional administrative law (TAL) nor the constitution explicitly mention women's rights in the context of marriage, divorce, child custody and inheritance. Instead, article 41 states that 'Iraqis are free in their adherence to their personal status according to their own religion, sect, belief and choice, and that will be organized by law' (Al-Ali and Pratt 2009: 134).

In other words, article 41 of the new Iraqi constitution stipulates that the existing family laws that had applied equally to all members of society are to be replaced by family laws pertaining to specific religious and ethnic communities. This could potentially empower conservative religious leaders to define laws according to their particular interpretation of their beliefs. It provides no safeguards against extremely regressive and discriminatory interpretations of Islamic law. Crucially, article 41 not only contributes to the erosion of women's existing rights but has also contributed to an increase of sectarianism in Iraq. It has made mixed marriages virtually impossible and has threatened already existing ones. Most significantly, it fosters a sense of communalism as opposed to unified citizenship.

The debate around the PSC became even more heated after Justice Minister Hassan al-Shimmari, formerly head of the Shia Islamic Virtue Party (Hizb al-Fadhila al-Islami), a rival to the Sadrist movement, introduced a draft law to the Council of Ministers in October 2013. The draft law came to be known as the Ja'fari Personal Status Law, based on an interpretation of the Ja'fari School of Shia religious jurisprudence. Despite widespread opposition not only from civil society activists, journalists and even Shia senior clerics, the Shia Islamist controlled Council of Ministers approved a draft law in February 2014. The draft law included provisions that:

> prohibit Muslim men from marrying non-Muslims, legalizes marital rape by stating that a husband is entitled to have sex with his wife regardless of her consent, and prevents women from leaving the house without permission from their husbands. The law would automatically grant custody over any child age two or older to the father in divorce cases, lower the marriage age to nine for girls and fifteen for boys, and even allow girls younger than nine to be married with a parent's approval. (Human Rights Watch 2014)

Most controversially, the draft law considered, in line with Ja'fari jurisprudence, nine as the age of maturity (*sin al-balagha*). In other words, the draft law, once passed, would have legalised marriages of nine-year-old girls. As Zahra Ali (2017a) has convincingly argued:

> The Ja'fari law represents a rupture with the PSC (Personal Status Code). On the one hand, it questions what is considered by Iraqis as a historical gain in terms of legal rights such as the minimum legal age of marriage fixed at 18 years old for both sexes, and the limit imposed on polygamy and unions contracted outside the civil court. On the other hand, it also constitutes a rupture with the unifying and non-sectarian nature of the PSC that gathers both Sunni and Shia jurisprudence and thus is applied to both sects and renders possible intersect marriages.

The draft law was vehemently opposed by many constituents of the Iraqi public and was not passed by parliament in 2014. It was clear that al-Shimmari and the al-Fadhila party had tried to pass the law as a way to seek popular support among the Shia population in the run-up to parliamentary elections at the end of April that year. It might not be a coincidence that on 1 November 2017, shortly after the date for presidential elections were announced as May 2018, two parliamentary commissions started seeking once again to introduce a sectarian personal status code along the lines of the previous suggested Ja'fari law.

Ali (2017a) has argued that the attempt to sectarianise the PSC is rooted in sectarian politics as opposed to sectarian societal values. Iraqi women's rights activists, as well as many leading civil society activists, have been consistently trying to challenge the imposition of a law they view as regressive and dangerous. Sunni Islamist clergy and politicians, as well as several Shia clerics, have also voiced their opposition to the continuation of the previously unified set of laws. However, while Ali makes the case that only the conservative Shia Islamist parties that came to power after 2003 push for the sectarianisation of the PSC, I would argue that there might also be support among some segments of the Shia population who are voting for these sectarian political parties. In my view, it is unlikely that Shia Islamist politicians would pursue this conservative and sectarian law without the expectation that it will mobilise political support amongst some segments of the Shia population. However, it is important to recognise that the Shia population is clearly very much divided in terms of their political allegiances and commitment to Iraq as a national entity as opposed to a Shia federal state, as well as their specific relationship to Islam and Islamism. At the same time, Shia populations have diverse visions about the kind of gender regime Iraq should adopt, and also varied attitudes towards the different forms of gender-based violence experienced by Iraqi women.

The Iraqi Continuum of Violence

Gender-based violence has received more media and policy attention since the atrocities against Yazidi women and girls committed by IS during and in the aftermath of the capture of the city of Sinjar (Shengal in Kurdish) in the Niniveh province in the summer of 2014. Yet, since the invasion of Iraq in 2003, increased social conservatism, the glorification of militarised masculinities, lack of security and a growing sectarianism have all contributed to the increase in pervasive forms of gender-based violence above and beyond IS-related atrocities. Without wanting to diminish the human rights violations and specific forms of gender-based and sexual violence committed by and during the Ba'th regime (1968–2003), Iraqi women have experienced unprecedented levels of violence and insecurity in post-invasion Iraq. As I have argued previously, there has been a systematic turning of blind eyes where women's rights and gender-based violence are concerned, on the part of both the international community, particularly the coalition forces involved in the invasion and occupation, and the successive Iraqi governments and political parties (Al-Ali 2016; Al-Ali and Pratt 2009).

Women have been particularly vulnerable in the context of chaos, lawlessness, prevalence of endemic violence and the manipulation of gender norms by Islamist parties and militias. The monitoring of women's dress codes, control of their mobility and sexuality has been an important tool for Shia and Sunni militias alike to assert authority and control over communities and neighbourhoods. So-called honour-based crimes, or 'moral crimes', have been rampant, as have been instances of domestic violence, forced marriages, forced prostitution, child marriages and trafficking. The situation has worsened over the years with the growth of internally displaced people (IDPs), estimated at about three million, with large numbers living in camps or inadequate shelter arrangements. Due to the lack of gender-segregated showers and toilet facilities, adequate lighting, door locks, privacy for families and access to health and legal services, internally displaced women and girls are particularly vulnerable (IOM 2017).

The central Iraqi government has generally been extremely slow, ineffective and unwilling to respond to the escalating and wide-ranging forms of gender-based violence that mainly women, but also some men, have been experiencing. Men who do not fit the hegemonic and increasingly conservative and militarised norms of masculinity and heteronormativity, have also been at the receiving end of harassment, violence and even killings. Some attempts at reform were made, such as the introduction of the anti trafficking law in 2012, for example, or the 'National Strategy on Combating Violence Against Women' approved by the Council of Ministers in 2013. However, there has been no political will to properly review and reform the existing discriminatory legislation, and to protect women from the numerous forms of violence, particularly rampant domestic violence.

Meanwhile, the KRG has been far more proactive in reacting to pressure by female MPs and women's rights activists, seeking state protection for the widespread gender-based violence that has also been prevalent in the Kurdish Region of Iraq (KRI). Following the establishment of an inter-ministerial Commission on Violence Against Women in 2007, the regional government adopted a law to 'combat domestic violence' in 2011, based on a quite progressive understanding of domestic violence as 'any act, speech or threat that may harm an individual of the household physically, sexually and psychologically and deprives his/her freedom and liberties' (Ali 2017b; Kaya 2016). Later in 2013, all three Kurdish governorates established High Committees of Combatting Violence Against Women and Families.

Despite these legal reforms, women in the KRI experience high levels of gender-based violence, particularly in terms of honour-based violence and female genital cutting. Domestic violence is rampant as well but remains under-reported and unprosecuted (Kaya 2016). Moreover, it is apparent that the KRG has made instrumental use of gender issues to present itself as more democratic and progressive than the Shia Islamist and Arab-controlled central Iraqi government, especially vis-à-vis the international donor and political community. Although women activists in KRI were far more successful than their counterparts in central and southern Iraq in influencing government legislation on gender issues, in practice it emerged that the KRG is interested in neither involving women in the executive nor in actually implementing legislation that is supposed to protect women from gender-based violence. Government officials argue that their priority has to be security and stability as opposed to women's rights, stating 'the KRG has only limited economic and institutional capacity to implement and monitor new laws and regulations to improve the position of women' (Kaya 2016). Family or tribal mediation continue to be the preferred means of dealing with violence, instead of seeking police intervention and the judgements of courts. Moreover, neither the police nor the judiciary is well trained to deal with gender-sensitive issues and often reproduce conservative and misogynistic gender norms and family values.

In central and southern Iraq, as well as in the KRI, the impact of heightened and long-lasting militarisation of society, in conjunction with the continued and often growing significance of tribal affiliations, ethnic conflict, and widespread sectarian and religious extremism, have all contributed to a striking continuum of violence. The privileging of militarised masculinities, whether in acute conflict situations or at home, has developed side by side with the privileging of conservative gender norms and relations that stress women's honour need for protection and control. Despite differences in legislation, neither the various governments in Baghdad nor the KRG have shown actual political will and interest in tackling gender-based violence.

Women's rights and gender norms were used as bargaining chips both vis-à-vis the international community to show a facade of egalitarianism and vis-à-vis conservative tribal and religious authorities that were placated with more stringent controls and regulation.

Women's Political Participation

Despite the initial rhetoric linked to women's inclusion and liberation (Al-Ali and Pratt 2009), Iraqi women have had very limited political influence and decision-making power. Partly, this is a direct consequence of the re-emergence of political authoritarianism, particularly under former Prime Minister al-Maliki of the Shia Islamist Dawa party. During his reign (2006–14), all political actors experienced systematic sidelining, a lack of rule of law and widespread political violence and repression. However, women became particularly marginalised in a context where they were increasingly perceived as incapable to lead and strategise, where social attitudes had shifted towards more conservative gender norms, and where power networks were thoroughly masculinised as a result of armed attacks and political intimidation.

Many women who made it into the Council of Representatives were given access to meet the stipulated quota of 25 per cent, which is a constitutional requirement. Of the 25 per cent, several women parliamentarians have been the wives, sisters or daughters of male politicians eager to fill the required seats with loyal followers without having to engage with wider issues of gender equality and women's genuine political representation rights. In some instances, male politicians have even put pressure on their female relatives to run for office.

Prior to provincial elections in 2009, for example, Fadhila Hanoosh Khalif, the wife of Sheikh Hamid al-Hais, who heads one of the largest tribal-based political parties in Iraq's desert Anbar province, was famously quoted as saying: 'I don't want to be a candidate. He forced it on me . . . I don't even know what number I am on the list. Ask him' (Hauslohner 2009).

Many Iraqi women's rights activists I spoke to over the last years bemoan the phenomenon of female parliamentarians often being more interested in expressing partisan views – frequently Islamist and sectarian – instead of furthering the gender interests of Iraqi women. It is important to stress that the situation in the KRG area is slightly different for female parliamentarians and politicians, given that they have been allowed to play a more active role in shaping legislation and policy. In the KRI, the quota for women's political participation is 30 per cent and, as stated above, the KRG has amended existing legislation and issued new laws to address problems of gender inequality and gender-based violence (Kaya 2016). Many Kurdish women's rights activists, however, also complained to me about tokenism and lack of proper consultation, in addition to the small number of women in decision-making positions (Al-Ali and Pratt 2011). They also pointed to the tendency to revert to traditional means of mediation and reconciliation based on families and tribes as opposed to the pursuit of legal means in cases of conflict, discrimination against women or widespread gender-based violence.

In addition to the frequently tokenistic use of the gender quota, women have remained under-represented at all levels of government and political life, including in important committees and commissions. This has been particularly acute in relation to the central government, although Kurdish women' rights activists I talked to also criticised the limited participation of women in decision-making processes and ministerial posts. There were six female-headed ministries in 2005–6, but no woman was appointed to a senior post in the forty-four-member cabinet after the 2010 elections (Al-Ali 2013). Only two ministries of state were offered to women, one without portfolio lost her position as part of Prime Minister al-Maliki's downsizing, leaving only one female minister, Ibtihal al-Zaidi, who was appointed minister of state for women's affairs. She herself stated that her ministry 'has no jurisdiction over the directorate of women's welfare or increasing funds allocated to widows'. In fact, she argued 'the ministry is no more than an executive-consultation bureau with a limited budget and no jurisdiction on implementing resolutions or activities'. Her predecessor, Nawal al-Samaraie, resigned due to lack of jurisdiction and an insufficient budget (NCCI 2011; *Reuters* 2011; Schmidt and Ghazi 2011). Aside from the lack of adequate resources, it was clear that al-Zaidi was not promoting gender-based equality:

'I am against the equality between men and woman,' she said. 'If women are equal to men they are going to lose a lot. Up to now I am with the power of the man in society. If I go out of my house, I have to tell my husband where I am going. This does not mean diluting the role of woman in society but, on the contrary, it will bring more power to the woman as a mother who looks after their kids and brings up their children'. (Abdulla 2012)

In August 2015, Prime Minister Haider al-Abadi issued a decree announcing the elimination of several deputies and combining some ministries in reaction to public pressure and outrage at government corruption and inefficiency. Bayan Nuri, the minister of state for women's affairs, and one of the few Kurdish members of government, lost her position as the State Ministry for Women's Affairs was going to be combined with the Ministry of Human Rights and Ministry of Provincial Affairs (Rudaw 2015).

Aside from the obvious lack of political will to properly address gender inequalities in political decision-making, the ongoing insecurity, armed conflict, sectarianism and growing social conservatism have posed severe obstacles to women's participation in government and political life. In terms of social and cultural attitudes, it is apparent that there is only a small segment of the population that would rally behind policies to address gender-based inequalities. It is worth noting that even under the regime of Saddam Hussein, at times of political and economic crisis when the political centre weakened, as in the 1990s following the invasion of Kuwait, the control of women was used as a bargaining chip to appease various subnational entities, such as tribal and religious leaders.

Yet, despite the systematic marginalisation and sidelining of Iraqi women in the official political institutions and processes, they have not merely stood by but have mobilised at the level of formal civil society organisations, social and political movements, as well as more informal community and interest groups. While some organisations clearly came about as a result of donor-assisted efforts, others emerged more organically with links to both returning women activists after the invasion and local political mobilisation and humanitarian efforts.

The women involved in the numerous organisations tend to be urban-based, middle-class and of diverse ethnic and religious backgrounds. While many organisations were founded by women of elite background, some groups have a broad membership and have branches throughout the country. The Iraqi Women's Network (al-Shabaka al-Mar'a al-Iraqiya), for example, consists of over eighty women's organisations, which are spread throughout Iraq. The activities of these organisations revolve around humanitarian and practical projects, such as income generation, legal advice, free healthcare and counselling, as well as political advocacy and lobbying. Women's rights activists have worked across political divides in terms of their political party ties or lack thereof, their ethnic and religious backgrounds and, to some extent, have also worked across secular and religious positions.

Mobilisation around women's rights has mushroomed over the past decade, despite the many challenges and threats to women's rights activists. Women-led NGOs, as well as more informal community associations, have been campaigning about women's legal rights, especially with reference to the unresolved dispute over the PSC (article 41), and criminal laws that do not offer sufficient protection against gender-based violence, particularly 'honour-based crimes'. Women's rights activists have also been mobilising against domestic violence, trafficking and honour-based crimes, providing shelters and advice to victims. Given the dire humanitarian situation, most organisations have also been involved in welfare and charity work, providing income-generating activities as well as training for women. Very few activists, however, make a link between increased privatisation and neo-liberal economic policies on the one hand, and the increase in women's unemployment and the feminisation of poverty, on the other.

Iraqi women's rights activists have been at the forefront of a growing political movement for democracy and human rights that, in line with wider political movements and processes in the region, has been asking for greater transparency and an end to corruption and political authoritarianism. They have been central to the movement demanding a *dawla medanya* (civil state), adamantly denouncing the instrumentalisation of religion in politics (Ali 2017b). Many Iraqi women's rights activists have realised that their struggle for greater gender equality and social justice cannot be separated from the struggle against an emerging new dictatorship, the remilitarisation of society, corruption and nepotism. Most recently, Iraqi women's rights activists linked to the Iraqi Women's Network, the Organization for Women's Freedom in Iraq and many prominent intellectuals and civil society activists have organised demonstrations, protests and a number of events to oppose the sectarianisation of women and family issues through the proposed amendment of the Personal Status Law, previously referred to as the Ja'fari Law.

Mobilisation of Kurdish Women

Meanwhile, Kurdish women's rights activists were initially not concerned with the mobilisations around the Personal Status Code launched by predominantly, but not exclusively, Arab women activists in Baghdad, choosing instead to focus on securing women's rights in the Iraqi Kurdistan Constitution. The fact that the majority of Kurdish politicians work within a secular framework and reject political Islam represents an important element of distinction between the women's movements in the KRI and in central and southern Iraq where Islamist political parties and movements play a more significant role. However, during my research with Iraqi Kurdish women's rights activists it became obvious that some regretted their lack of involvement in wider national mobilisation around the Iraqi constitution. Prior to the more recent move towards independence, they bemoaned the fact that the laws linked to the Iraqi as opposed to the Kurdish regional constitution applied when trying to seek a new passport: according to Iraqi law women are required to have the permission of a male guardian (*mahram*) when requesting or renewing passports. However, in the context of increased tensions and conflict between the KRG and the central government, the majority of Kurdish women's rights activists were not interested in pursuing joint campaigns and advocacy linked to the Iraqi constitution. A small minority of Kurdish women's rights activists are, however, still pursuing a feminist politics across the ethnic and political divide between the KRI and central and southern Iraq.

Historically, the Kurdish women's movement in KRI, unlike the Iraqi women's movement more broadly, started to mushroom before the invasion of Iraq in 2003, in the post-1991 period, when KRI became a semi-autonomous region. While women's organisations started to emerge in the 1990s, they were initially fiercely challenged and fought against by the male political establishment. It is only since 2003 that they have received support from the two main rival political parties: the Kurdistan Democratic Party (KDP) and the Patriotic Union of Kurdistan (PUK). Several Kurdish women's rights activists I talked to over the years, complained about the lack of independent women's rights activism and the dependence on and interference of the main Kurdish political parties. Like women's organisations in central and southern Iraq, Kurdish women's organisations have benefitted from foreign funding and international interventions, which have contributed to the NGOisation of the Kurdish women's movement. Across both the Kurdish and wider Iraqi women's movement, the influence of donor-inspired neo-liberal agendas focusing on women's empowerment, preferably through entrepreneurship, and women's leadership, cannot be overemphasised. However, while women's activists in central and southern Iraq are, by and large, part of a wider political movement that is not only mobilising for gender-based rights but also protesting authoritarianism, sectarianism and corruption, the Kurdish women's movement is tied much more closely to the dominant political parties. The few activists and organisations that have been consistently critical of the Kurdish political elite might have toned down their criticism given recent political developments with the KRI under attack and threat by the Iraqi government and regional powers.

Concluding Reflections

Iraq is an example par excellence of the intimate links between the politics of gender and changing political regimes at local, regional, national and international levels. Iraqi women, their bodies and sexuality, as well as wider gender norms and relations, have been at the centre of political contestations and power struggles in post-invasion Iraq. The increase in authoritarian and more sectarian governance structures and patterns has gone hand in hand with more socially conservative, repressive and coercive gender politics.

There is no doubt that the invasion and occupation led to multiple political crises, fragmentation of the state, radicalisation and increased sectarianism, which, in turn, contributed to more conservative gender norms and increased gender-based violence (Al-Ali and Pratt 2009). Yet, I would argue that we cannot analyse the ongoing political and humanitarian crises in Iraq and their devastating gendered consequences simply with reference to US and UK policies and interventions. This would not only be simplistic and reductionist but would ignore historical factors and continuities, and also conceal the complexities of the interplay of local, regional and international actors and complicities. As discussed above, this has become apparent, for example, in the context of increasing corruption and paralysis of decision-making in which all political parties have been complicit. This has also been evident in the contestations around the personal status code, which have been driven by sectarian Shia Islamist political elites.

Local constituencies and forces need to be recognised as important drivers of the politics of gender and governance structures, characterised by violence and authoritarian politics: Iraqi politicians, militia, tribal leaders, religious authorities, the business elite, criminal gangs and families have all been complicit in, if not directly responsible, for the normalisation of gender-based violence and the shift towards an incredibly conservative and restrictive gender regime. We also have to add to the mix regional players, like Saudi Arabia, Qatar, Iran and Turkey, who have attempted to consolidate ethnic and religious identities and political blocs in order to further their own geopolitical interests and establish power bases.

While the various institutions, social actors and practices that define the political field across Iraq and the Kurdish Region of Iraq have partly been designed or established by the occupying powers and have developed in the context of occupation and the ongoing international influence in Iraq, they have also had a dynamic of their own. Moreover, Iraqi and Kurdish politicians, militants, tribal and religious leaders have actively created their own institutions, policies and practices that are more intended to serve authoritarian, and sectarian, networks of patronage rather than national agendas or universal notions of citizenship. Finally, it is important to recognise the interactive nature of the political developments we have seen unfolding since 2003: while the occupying powers set up sectarian structures of representation in the name of democracy, political parties and other subnational groups have subverted any possible democracy project by entrenching sectarian interests and patronage networks that further fragment the polity and make any notion of common citizenship more difficult to contemplate. Yet amongst some elements of the Iraqi population inside Iraq, including sections of the Iraqi women's movement, as well as many Iraqis in the diaspora, the longing for unitary citizenship remains.

Notes

1. Available at <Youtube.com/watch?v=I5BD0XLzOL0>, posted 13 March 2017 (last accessed 1 August 2018).
2. Nicola Pratt and I have engaged in an in-depth study of the gap between the rhetoric on women's liberation and the actual policies on Iraq (Al-Ali and Pratt 2009).
3. Massoud Brazani was president of the Kurdish Region of Iraq from 2005 to 2017. His tenure expired in 2015 and his refusal to step down caused much controversy and protest.

Bibliography

Abdulla, Mufid (2012), 'Outrage as Iraqi women's affairs minister opposes equality for women', *Kurdistan Tribune*, 14 February, <http://kurdistantribune.com/outrage-iraqi-womens-affairs-minister-opposes-equality-for-women/> (last accessed 1 August 2018).

Al-Ali, Nadje (2007), *Iraqi Women: Untold Stories from 1948 to the Present*, London and New York: Zed Books.

—— (2013), 'Iraq: gendering authoritarianism', *Open Democracy*, 15 July, <https://www.opendemocracy.net/5050/nadje-al-ali/iraq-gendering-authoritarianism> (last accessed 1 August 2018).

—— (2016), 'Sexual violence in Iraq: challenges for transnational feminist politics', *European Journal of Women's Studies*, March, pp. 1–18.

Al-Ali, Nadje and Nicola Pratt (2009), *What kind of Liberation? Women and the Occupation of Iraq*, Berkeley: University of California Press.

—— (2011), 'Between nationalism and women's rights: the Kurdish women's movement in Iraq', *Middle East Journal of Culture and Communication*, 4, pp. 339–55.

—— (2014), 'Iraq's triple challenge: state, nation, and democracy', in P. Burnell, V. Randall and L. Rakner (eds), *Politics in the Developing World*, Oxford: Oxford University Press, pp. 406–16.

Ali, Zahra (2017a), 'Iraqi feminists mobilise against sectarian laws', *Open Democracy*, 15 June, <https://www.opendemocracy.net/north-africa-west-asia/zahra-ali/iraqi-feminists-mobilise-against-sectarian-laws> (last accessed 1 August 2018).

—— (2017b), 'Struggles and challenges for feminists in post-invasion Iraq', *The Region*, 7 August, <https://theregion.org/article/11094-struggles-and-challenges-for-feminists-in-post-invasion-iraq> (last accessed 1 August 2018).

Dodge, Toby (2012), 'The resistible rise of Nuri al-Maliki', *Open Democracy*, 22 March, <https://www.opendemocracy.net/toby-dodge/resistible-rise-of-nuri-al-maliki> (last accessed 1 August 2018).

—— (2014), 'Can Iraq Be Saved?' *Survival*, 56: 5, pp. 7–20.

Efrati, Noga (2012), *Women in Iraq: Past Meets Present*, New York: Columbia University Press.

Fischer-Tahir, Andrea (2010), Competition, cooperation and resistance: women in the political field in Iraq, *International Affairs*, 86: 6, November, pp. 1381–94.

Hauslohner, Abigail (2009), 'How Iraq fills the quota for female politicians', *Time*, 12 January, <http://content.time.com/time/world/article/0,8599,1870765,00.html> (last accessed 1 August 2018).

Herring, Eric and Glenn Rangwala (2006), *Iraq in Fragments: the Occupation and its Legacy*, London: Hurst & Co.

Human Rights Watch (2014), 'Iraq: don't legalize marriage for 9-year-olds', 11 March, <https://www.hrw.org/news/2014/03/11/iraq-dont-legalize-marriage-9-year-olds> (last accessed 1 August 2018).

International Crisis Group (2004), *Iraq's Transition: on a Knife Edge*, Amman and Brussels: International Crisis Group.

—— (2005), *Unmaking Iraq: a Constitutional Process Gone Awry*, Amman and Brussels: International Crisis Group.

—— (2006), *In their own words: Reading the Iraqi insurgency*, Amman and Brussels: International Crisis Group.

IOM (2017), 'IOM-DTM workshop strengthens humanitarian response to gender-based violence for IDPs in Iraq', 6 September, <https://www.iom.int/news/iom-dtm-workshop-strengthens-humanitarian-response-gender-based-violence-idps-iraq> (last accessed 1 August 2018).

Al-Jawaheri, Yasmin Husein (2008), *Iraqi Women: the Gender Impact of International Sanctions*, London and New York: I. B. Tauris.

Joseph, Suad (1991), 'Elite strategies: Iraq and Lebanon, in D. Kandiyoti (ed.), *Women, Islam and the State*, Philadelphia: Temple University Press, pp. 176–200.

Kaya, Zeynep (2016), 'Women in post-conflict Kurdistan', *Open Democracy*, 26 February, <https://www.opendemocracy.net/westminster/zeynep-n-kaya/women-in-post-conflict-iraqi-kurdistan> (last accessed 1 August 2018).

McKernan, Bethan (2017), 'Female Iraqi MP proposes law that encourages men to marry multiple women for financial benefits', *The Independent*, 13 March, <https://www.independent.co.uk/news/world/middle-east/iraq-marriage-women-ploygamy-mp-legislation-jamila-al-ebeidi-a7627071.html> (last accessed 1 August 2018).

NCCI (2011), *Iraq's Female Face*, Op-Ed, 15 November, <https://www.ncciraq.org/en/?option=com_content&view=article&id=31&lang=en> (last accessed 1 August 2018).

Reuters (2011), 'Nuri al-Maliki, Iraq prime minister, trims size of cabinet, 30 July, <https://www.huffingtonpost.com/2011/07/30/nuri-al-maliki-iraq-prime_n_914034.html;> (last accessed 1 August 2018).

Rudaw (2015), 'Iraqi ministries to be eliminated as premier advances reforms', 16 November, <http://www.rudaw.net/english/middleeast/iraq/160820156> (last accessed 1 August 2018).

Schmidt, Michael S. and Yasir Ghazi (2011), 'Iraqi women feel shunted despite election quota', *New York Times*, 12 March, <https://www.nytimes.com/2011/03/13/world/middleeast/13baghdad.html> (last accessed 1 August 2018)

Tripp, Charles (2000), *A History of Iraq*, Cambridge: Cambridge University Press.

Chapter 9

Defiance not Subservience: New Directions in the Pakistani Women's Movement

Afiya Shehrbano Zia

Introduction

In her 1991 contribution to *Women, Islam and the State*, titled 'The convenience of subservience', Ayesha Jalal offered one of the earliest critiques of the women's rights movements of Pakistan. Since the founding of Pakistan in 1947, she argued, women's groups opted for 'submission' as the 'path of least resistance', particularly during the two military-led regimes of General Ayub Khan (1958–69) and General Muhammed Zia-ul-Haq (1977–88). Jalal suggests that these historical compromises entwined gender, national and class interests, and cemented the Islamic social order that dominated thereafter. Nearly three decades and yet another period of military rule (General Pervez Musharraf 1999–2008) later, women's relationships with the state, religion and social development in Pakistan continue to be defined mainly by confrontation and sometimes by concessions and compromises. Moreover, in the intervening years we have witnessed both the rise of women's political agency and new forms of defiance that contest established sexual norms, poised to subvert rather than accommodate the Islamic gendered order.

Under General Khan's regime, women's rights were defined by welfare activism and there was no challenge to the military rule. By the time of General Zia-ul-Haq's regime of Islamisation, a new generation of rights-based feminist activists directly challenged state-led theocracy and military repression (Mumtaz and Shaheed 1987). This was also a period that witnessed the expansion of liberal framings of women's issues towards more radical feminist political expressions (Saigol 2016). A key debate took place over the strategic value of pursuing women's rights through progressive interpretations of Islam, as against the argument that a secular resistance was imperative against the rising orthodoxy of the state, and that Islamic laws must be repealed to guarantee equal status and rights for women and minorities (Zia 2009).

In the democratic interregnum of 1988–99, the struggle for women's rights became a more organised and better funded enterprise with the proliferation of non-governmental organisations (NGOs) in Pakistan. The very vocabulary of the rights movement shifted under the influence of the neo-liberal global regime. References to patriarchy, feminist politics and equal rights were superseded by the more neutral concepts of gender equity, good governance and economic empowerment. Furthermore, the argument for adopting secular strategies rather than opting for a faith-based orientation was challenged when some NGOs decided to bid for funds for programmes that instrumentalised Islam as a source of personal piety and empowerment for women. To achieve empowerment, they argued, religion simply needs to be cleansed of the 'polluting' effects of culture, tradition and custom, and kept separate from the state and politics. Arguably, this bifurcation of feminist interests undermined secular strategic resistance against the Islamisation of state and society (Zia 2009).

By the time of the 9/11 attacks in the US, and the ensuing War on Terror that propelled Pakistan into becoming a frontline ally of the US, championing women's rights became a convenient theme for the self-proclaimed 'liberal' military ruler, General Musharraf, who had just overthrown a democratic government in 1999. He had sought and won the support of liberal forces including several NGOs (with some notable exceptions) and some members of women's groups as part of his purported effort to replace the corrupt and conservative elected government with his own regime of 'enlightened moderation' (Zia 2015).

This chapter traces how after years of top-down Islamisation policies targeting the family and gender relations, the state under Musharraf combined an anti-extremism and development discourse with the enhancement of women's rights. Cutting across diverse locations from metropolises to tribal areas, gender and development projects encouraged women's direct participation in politics and lobbying for national legislation, policies and the broader rights-based narrative. Yet, the unshifting core of conservatism in Pakistan remains concentrated around the control of female sexuality. In this context, the exercise of sexual autonomy on the part of many women is no longer just limited to 'runaway', 'free-will' marriages that may trigger reprisals from family members, or which result in honour-based murders of assertive women. This chapter highlights a new assertiveness in women's demands for autonomy and control over their bodies and sexuality in the post-2001 era, suggesting that the 'convenience of subservience' has given way to a bolder subversion of the Islamic gender order.

Gender and Governance under 'Liberal' Military Rule

The coup that was staged by General Musharraf in 1999 made it clear that military rule can never be discounted in Pakistan. The liberal elites were relieved not to have another faith-based moral crusader in uniform (Zaidi 2015; Zia 2015) and the 'enlightened moderation' theme of his rule become the *raison d'être* for remaining at the helm of state affairs rather than calling for elections and reverting to civilian governance.

One of the most important policy change Musharraf made was the constitutional amendment that enabled a substantial increase in seats reserved for women at all levels of the legislature. Under his leadership, prominent women's rights activists were included in his cabinet and appointed to key government posts and influenced policy (Zia 2015). Undoubtedly, women served as the leading symbols of Musharraf's 'enlightened moderation'. Significantly, there was no concerted pro-democracy protest against his rule by opportunist supporters across the political spectrum, including the right-wing Islamists who participated in his government. While the lobby and pressure group of the Women's Action Forum that had been active under Zia-ul-Haq's rule also opposed Musharraf's regime, several individual members took the opportunity to participate in government-led processes and programmes that promoted women's causes and attempted to reform discriminatory laws. During his decade-long rule, the only concerted challenge prior to the Lawyers' Movement (2007–9) was the one offered by the radical Islamist movement of the Jamia Hafsa women during the Lal Masjid uprising in 2007[1] (Afzal-Khan 2008; Zia 2015). Jalal's thesis about the support of women's groups to military rulers seemed poised for vindication even into the new millennium.

Despite the malaise of co-optation by a military regime, these key women appointees deserve credit for leveraging visible results and progress for women's rights in policy and practical terms. Several commissions were established, women's rights policies were adopted, and women were appointed at senior state levels, such as governor of the State Bank, and in the Armed Forces.[2] Even more significant than international commitments, domestic laws, such as the law on honour killings, were strengthened (2004, 2016) and the Women's Protection Act of 2006 effectively stymied the discriminatory Zina (adultery) Laws of 1979[3] in a manner that no previous government had been able to do. Women's rights became part of the official state narrative. Parliamentary debates between Islamists and liberal political representatives reflected the national contestations on women's issues at the time and make for rich reading (Mirza and Wagha 2007; Zia 2015). The notion of gender-responsive governance as a means of mitigating gender inequality, in compliance with the UN resolutions on peace and human security priorities, became part of Musharraf's purported commitment to counter-terrorism policies for Pakistan.

On the other hand, in the province of Khyber Pukhtunkhwa, a coalition of religious parties, the Muttahida Majlis Amal (MMA), won the 2002 elections in a post-9/11 fervour after they were allowed to canvas in return for recognising the legitimacy of Musharraf as a uniformed president (Zia 2015). This Islamist coalition launched a systematic 'anti-obscenity' drive to purge all public spaces of female imagery, including the removal of mannequins from shop windows and depictions on billboards and hoardings. Women's shelters were shut down and participants in sporting activities were harassed and attacked (Brohi 2006). Islamist women leaders and activists were complicit in such campaigns that included denying women their right to vote in local government elections.

There were other incongruities in the 'enlightened moderation' regime, such as the treatment of rape/honour crime survivor, Mukhtaran Mai, whose case made international headlines. General Musharraf alleged her case had been blown out of proportion and exemplified how Pakistani women cry 'rape' every time they want to gain international sympathy and claim visa/asylum rights to countries such as Canada. He later banned her from travelling to the US to prevent tarnishing Pakistan's image abroad (Al Jazeera 2005). A poor rural woman, Mai went on to fight for justice taking her case right up to the Supreme Court and become a global symbol of resistance against honour-based crimes (Mai 2007). Another prominent case was that of Nilofer Bakhtiar, the minister for tourism in Musharraf's government. In 2007 she was forced to resign after clerics passed a fatwa (religious edict) against her when newspapers carried a photograph of her 'inappropriate' act of hugging the male instructor after a parachuting stint in France as part of a media call. She was neither defended nor supported by her party nor the president of the 'enlightened moderation' regime (Zia 2015).

The inherent contradictions that marked the relationship between religious authorities, military leadership and progressive women's movements continued into the new millennium. However, the events of 9/11, the ensuing War on Terror and resulting propaganda on the need to rescue 'oppressed Muslim women' opened two new challenges within feminist discourses. The first was an academic intervention by the late Pakistani émigré, US-based scholar, Saba Mahmood, who denounced the colonial feminist rescue of the Muslim woman as a counter-insurgency justification (Hirschkind and Mahmood 2002). Such scholarship urged the recognition of the non-liberal, pietistic aspirations of Muslim women and the rewards of the search for virtue rather than autonomy, which has been one of the main planks of feminist platforms (Mahmood 2005). The second was the concerted effort to reframe a new praxis in social development programmes for women emphasising religious sensitivity in Muslim contexts. Post-9/11 scholarship delved into exploring, rescuing and, in some cases, reinventing the agency of veiled Muslim women, even if it signified compromising the principle of equality (Abu-Lughod 2002; Bano 2012; Jamal 2005; Iqtidar 2011; Mahmood 2005). These shifts marked a new chapter in gender politics and opened further contestations on the questions of democracy, secular resistance and universal human rights in Pakistan.

Instrumentalising Islam in Gender-responsive Governance

In the 1980s, several women's research and advocacy groups, such as Women Living under Muslim Laws,[4] critically engaged with Islamic frameworks to pursue a gender equality agenda. However, these activists were in solidarity with movements that resisted the increasing theocratisation of the Pakistani state and struggled to retain its original secular constitution. This secular orientation was not limited to urban-based, Western-educated women's groups but included rural women's nationalist–political organisations, such as Sindhiani Tehreeq.

After 9/11, well-funded research interest on Pakistan, including work on gender, began focusing exclusively on the study of religious identities, the rehabilitation of Muslim masculinities, the reform of madrasas (Islamic seminaries) and encouraging women's religious leadership. These were supported and underpinned by several academic works that emerged during this period. Some examples include the suggestion that it is the Islamists of Pakistan rather than secularists who can serve as authentic agents of an appropriate (redefined) secularisation (Iqtidar 2011); that Islamist women are rational believers who can benignly use Islam to achieve social justice and development in Pakistan (Bano 2012); that Islamic legal regimes are viable alternatives to the unworkable 'occidental secularization' (Aziz 2005); and that moral rewards can emerge from Islamic readings of all financial and political legal cases, especially for the 'poor and disenfranchised people of Pakistan' (Cheema and Akbar 2010). These proposals challenge the viability of universal, liberal and indigenous secular feminist possibilities in Muslim-majority countries as culturally inappropriate and imperialist impositions.

Many of these collaborative projects were led by foreign consultants, local journalists-cum-informants, and newly minted 'experts' on Islam, terrorism, jihad, security and conflict studies. A large number of Pakistani experts/academics went on to work in think tanks with the UK and US governments, while others moved to a Western academia that was keen to learn about 'Muslims'. Political economist, Akbar Zaidi argued that '"class" has become a category that has lost relevance for the social sciences in Pakistan and that 'the country has been forced into an analytical Islamic framework as if no other sense of existence or identity existed' (Zaidi 2014: 50).

This turn to faith-based projects in development may be seen as an example of 'donor-driven Islam' in Pakistan. They focus on women's sense of religious empowerment as an indicator of developmental progress. The specific and tangible gendered implications of how these initiatives reinforce conservativism and stereotypical gendered relations and divisions of labour are ignored (Zia 2011, 2018). It is assumed these projects will not be a throwback to the decade of Islamisation (1979–88), even though they limit focus on piety, faith-based empowerment and heavenly rewards but not on political or material rights (Zia 2011, 2013).

One of the examples of such expensive endeavours in Pakistan was the Religions and Development Research Programme spearheaded by the British government's development agency, DFID.[5] Similarly, various US government departments have funded countless madrasa reform projects (USAID 2010) and gender-related projects, such as Behind the Veil (USAID 2008). Many NGOs in Pakistan are now required by donors to include faith and religious sensitivity in their projects, paying no heed to the lessons of the faith-based women's rights projects of the 1990s, which achieved no legal advances or social policy successes.

The overwhelming interest of the US government and other donors' insistence on the inclusion of faith-based approaches and the participation of religious clergy (which I label 'Rent-a-Maulvi' projects) are all part of the dubious attempt to counter religious militancy by replacing the universalist rights-based framework adhered to by rights activists in Pakistan with an 'appropriate' faith-based approach for Muslim-majority contexts (Zia 2011). They also cement the connection between neo-liberal development and Islam, by entrenching capitalist development as a moral cause with a humanitarian base underpinned by an Islamic ethos that is mindful of 'Muslim' gender relations. Zaim traces the birth of a new type of entrepreneur, the 'Homo Islamicus' in Turkey (Zaim 1994, cited in Moudourus 2014). This concept may also be applied to the case of gender and development efforts in Muslim contexts as a legitimate moral effort to harmonise Islam with capitalist development and to offset critiques of the oppression of Muslim women by including them in entrepreneurial and social reform projects without disrupting the patriarchal cultural or religious gendered order.

The allegation by several post-secular analysts (Aziz 2005; Cheema and Akbar 2010; Iqtidar 2011) that Musharraf enforced a muscular and top-down 'liberal-secularism' was, in fact, an attempt to counter extremist ideologies through 'moderate' interpretations of Islam. To further this objective, progressive jurisconsults, such as scholar, Javed Ghamdi, who supported women's rights and a peaceful 'moderate' version of Islam, were employed. While the success of this effort is contestable, the sheer expansion of liberal and women's freedoms did come at the cost of muted criticism and practically no opposition to the military regime itself. At this point, it seemed as if Jalal's analysis of the compromised relations between progressive women's rights groups, Islamic politics and the military regimes was proving to be prescient once again.

Women's rights movements of Pakistan seem to be most motivated to offer direct radical resistance to conservative governments, but their activism tends to become muted under liberal regimes that attempt to co-opt them (Zia 2014a). However, as will be seen below, after a decade of turbulent but uninterrupted civilian-led democratic rule this too seemed to be changing. The post-Musharraf state has started appreciating the real value of women's empowerment as a commodity that will help both to cast the regime in a progressive light, benefit overall development and counter extremist politics. Gender-aware governance practices – problematic and contested as they may be – are starting to play a significant role in women's new citizen-subjectivity.

Defiance not Subservience

Jalal's core observations in 1991 had centred around her thesis that subservience was a socially rewarding path for women from the middle and upper strata who tended to set the agenda for women's rights at the state level. She argued that these activists were 'not quite the hapless and unsuspecting victims of "Islamic" chauvinism which certain secular critics and especially "the feminists" among them would like to believe' (Jalal 1991: 78).

Jalal's critique regarding the class composition and priorities of the women's movement has been superseded by the expansion of women's rights activism across classes and generations in the new millennium. The demands for women's rights are not limited to elite women but echoed by working women's organisations and small collectives of feminist groups in urban centres and small towns.[6] Currently, a variety of feminist collectives and online chat groups/networks, and university women's groups monitor sexist offences and initiate legal challenges against harassment. Women activists from various NGOs are invited to assist in drafting and lobbying for legislation and policies for women's rights. Leaving the efficacy of these efforts aside, the process of mobilising, articulating goals and lobbying with legislative assemblies is impressively led by middle- and lower-middle class NGO workers and activists. Many rural and tribal women are consciously and directly involved and active in the political mainstream. The inspiration for many of these initiatives are linked in variable ways to the non-funded and voluntary-based Women's Action Forum (WAF), the nationwide political lobby that struggled against the military regime in the 1980s and which hosts branches in various cities. Many of the new feminist campaigns today comprise original WAF members as well as new entrants from varied class backgrounds.

Secondly, Jalal's claim that upper- and middle-class women activists and public office holders are not targets of Islamic bigotry has, sadly, been refuted. In the fallout of the decade of the War on Terror (2002–14) that reverberated across Pakistan, a series of murderous attacks on women officials and human rights activists have taken place. It was not only the former prime minister, Benazir Bhutto, who had been the target of several murder attempts by religious militants and was eventually assassinated at a public meeting in 2007.[7] Even prior to her assassination and for years to follow, women from the upper middle classes, such as the minister, Zille Huma,[8] political candidate, Zahra Shahid[9] and prominent activists, such as Parveen Rehman,[10] Fareeda Afridi[11] and Sabeen Mahmud[12] have all been murdered for their political views by those associated with religious organisations or with faith-based motivations. Over the past two decades, women lawyers and human rights activists have been under constant threat for defending the rights of women and minorities and require around the clock security.

The legacies of three military dictatorships continue to affect the relationship between women's movements and the state, activism and religion. These will be discussed below with a focus on the new forms and expressions of defiance from women across classes and in light of the impact of gender-responsive policies and the unexpected challenges that these have thrown up for the state and religious conservative quarters.

STATE AXIS AND GENDER PRAXIS

The Constitution of Pakistan[13] gives an equal status to women and the government of Pakistan is signatory to almost all international conventions. Additionally, the National Commission for the Status of Women (NCSW) and the National Commission for Human Rights (NCHR) are functioning bodies with provincial representation. The women heading these bodies since 2000 have been well-respected women's rights activists and professionals. Each of the five Pakistani provinces have fairly comprehensive and independent gender policies which are drafted with the technical assistance of local UN offices. While there is no measurable evidence that these policies have been adequately implemented, some national initiatives, such as the cash transfer to the poorest of women under the Benazir Income Support Programme (BISP) have shown impressive and tangible results across the nation (Cheema et al. 2015).

It is on the legislative front that representatives have been most active and have passed some key pro-women laws and amendments. Some of these include: the Anti-Honour Killing Laws (Criminal Amendment Bill), 2015; the Anti Rape Laws (Criminal Amendment Bill), 2015; the Acid Control and Acid Crime Prevention Act, 2011; and the Protection against Harassment of Women at the Workplace Act, 2010.[14] The Sindh Provincial Assembly has been bolder and passed the Amendment of the Child Marriage Restraint Act of 1929 (2013), which raises the age of marriage for girls to eighteen, despite strong contestation by religious lobbies who consider puberty to be the permissible age according to Islam.

One of the common critiques of the spurt of donor-funded NGOs in the 1990s was their domination by an upper/middle-class elite of Western-educated left-leaning women activists. Today, however, the non-governmental sector has not just mushroomed in size, diversity of composition and geographical spread, but the broad range of projects and membership that defines this sector is indicative of a clear crack in the 'class ceiling'. Furthermore, a high number of men have entered what used to be considered a 'soft' sector of gender and development and even head some women's rights NGOs and projects with, as yet, unexamined consequences. Debates over NGO politics still remain tense and split over the precarious balance between feminist political transformation and the compromises of working for women's and minority rights within the neo-liberal social development sector.

Some Pakistani analysts believe that the turn in the tide is coming from the shifts in women's roles in society as a result of globalisation, communications and connectivity. They cite empirical and observational evidence to confirm women's increasing mobility, economic and educational empowerment, marital choices based on free will, and access to information and connectivity provided by the media (Hasan 2016; Zaidi 2015).

Another set of analysts focus on structural factors and point out that the role and responsiveness of the state is far more critical, as it can facilitate or impede such progress more effectively than any other player (Zia 2016). The reforms under General Musharraf, and particularly the reform of the Islamic Law of Zina (adultery) in 2006 was not just a historic victory for women's rights but also offered a symbolic opportunity towards reclaiming the secular possibilities of gendered relations in the Islamic Republic of Pakistan. Increasingly, feminists, human rights activists and secularists are no longer dismissed as 'traitors' by the state, even though Islamists of various stripes feel threatened and express their fear of these developments in zealous and, often, violent ways (Zia 2014b). A series of brutal terrorist attacks on women, religious minorities and children has made violence by religious groups more reprehensible even amongst the more conservative commentators.

The judicial culture of the state, which used to accept the informal laws of dispute settlement for rural, tribal peripheries as non-state issues, is now being redefined by an active judiciary. Violence against women in the private domain and in public is defined as a punishable offence that requires justice. Inefficiencies in implementation aside, the vocabulary of law enforcers has changed considerably under pressure from the state.

Even though there is no firm indication of uniform success of their implementation yet, state apparatuses are receiving directives from the civilian governments that followed the Musharraf era to adopt more gender-sensitive policies. The Election Commission of Pakistan has set up a gender unit and appointed a gender specialist. Her role has had a critical impact on the pursuit of cases where women were prevented from voting. Also, women in the ombudsman's offices are gaining a voice in state structures. Women parliamentarians are vocal and active in the legislative processes (Awan 2016; FAFEN 2013). Whereas women were barely present in the legislatures of the past, Pakistan has now had a woman speaker of the parliament (and acting president) and, in the provinces of Khyber Pukhtunkhwa and Baluchistan, have elected women as deputy speaker and speaker for their assemblies. Although male bureaucrats do not overtly resist the incorporation of gender-sensitive policies in their offices, they remain apathetic or display genuine incompetence when it comes to implementation or giving institutional permanence to these policies.

The Pakistani state's political axis has realigned with a new gender praxis and the woman question has become a pivotal one. This shift is due to a combination of pressures from a strong women's movement, international financial conditionalities, such as those set by the Generalised Scheme of Preference Plus (GSP Plus),[15] and indefensible brutalities committed by the Taliban creating consensus on the need to protect women's rights. By targeting women as beneficiaries of the cash transfer through the BISP, the state sends the message out to the men in their families that it sees these women as de facto heads of households. Countering the opinion of the Council of Islamic Ideology on child marriage, the Sindh government has begun arresting the *nikahkhwans* (marriage registrars) for contracting underage marriages. Courts have started awarding jail sentences to perpetrators of domestic violence. Child marriages have decreased or at least, law enforcement is vigilant on this question; girls' school enrolment has increased, male attitudes towards many traditions has changed, such as, girls' education but also, wilful marriages across ethnicities (Hasan 2016). However, this is not uniform and as women remain repositories of culture and religious morality, the backlash against women as they rupture patriarchal orders tends to be expressed more violently (Zaidi 2015). Certainly, women will keep paying with their lives for every inch of freedom, mobility and rights that they struggle for, but governance and state institutions are becoming responsive to the injustices meted out to women, minorities and the marginalised, especially by non-state actors.

The Inconvenience of Sexual Impropriety

General Ayub Khan's benevolent dictatorship modelled its 'modern' gender policy around the progressive Muslim Family Law Ordinance of 1961, while

General Zia-ul-Haq's Islamisation policy instrumentalised the Zina Laws of 1979 in order to regulate women's sexualities and ensure a stable Islamic gendered order in the country. By the time that the 'liberal' General Pervez Musharraf amended this Zina Law in 2006, and thus, overturned Zia-ul-Haq's policy of *chador* and *chardewari* (veiling and domesticity), other trends that were even more subversive of hegemonic discourses on sexuality and gender were already emerging.

In particular, the Khwajasara (also known as *hijras*), a gender-variant group with a long history in the Indian subcontinent, has been the subject of recent academic and political interest (Hamzić 2016). The sexual politics articulated by such groups disrupt imposed identity categories and put pressure on the Islamic Republic of Pakistan to engage with the previously evaded issue of sexual identities in relation to citizenship and its associated rights. Various transgender alliances in Pakistan have lobbied and won basic civil rights including the recognition on national identity cards as a third gender, the right to vote as third gender, and also to contest elections as transgender candidates (Transgender Person (Protection of Rights) Bill 2017). Inheritance rights and affirmative action for the Khwajasaras are now recognised by the higher courts. Some clerical authorities recognise the right of transgendered persons to marry, inherit property, and have an Islamic burial if they settle into a clear sex category. Despite legal recognition by the state and clerics, this does not mean that the Khawajasara community are guaranteed safety of life or that their sexual freedoms have become normative (Khan 2014). Their gender status denies them access to mosques for communal prayers unless they dress as men and, while there is no official ban for pilgrimage to Saudi Arabia as there is on homosexual men, they are regularly denied visas. Transgender activists are harassed and even murdered just like the women activists mentioned above or, indeed, where the motivation is said to be one of honour.

Rights activists acknowledge the ease of same-sex relations and lifestyle for the LGBTQ community in Pakistan and their ability to socialise, organise, date and even live together as couples, but usually only secretly.[16] Sexual encounters between same-sex partners are easily accessible, especially in urban centres and, like Iran, private gay parties in Pakistan have been thriving for a number of years.[17] While transgender identities can be accommodated through Islamic legal manoeuvres, and cross-dressing is tolerable, there is no constitutional space or legal tolerance for LGBTQ or women's sexual freedoms or rights. Furthermore, while there is some paternalistic tolerance for the transgender, homosexual and cross-dressing communities as biological misfits, there is no acceptance of or latitude for heterosexual women who exercise sexual liberties or flaunt their sexuality in terms of dress, behaviour, or in defiance of stereotypes and norms expected of well-behaved Muslim women.

In the post-9/11 period, Muslim women's agency as pious subjects (Mahmood 2005) has received celebratory attention in the field of women's studies, Islamic studies and the development sector, but Muslim women's sexual desires and their expressions have been treated more cautiously, suspiciously or not at all. Privileging their virtue and piety drew attention to a limited set of bodily practices but, otherwise, treated Muslim women as disembodied subjects rather than sexual beings who could also be at the receiving end of violence. Meanwhile, sexually assertive women, gay, lesbian, intersex or transgender individuals may be tolerated in the Islamic Republic of Pakistan, but sexual diversity still needs to be controlled to preserve socio-sexual stability.

The vulnerabilities of those who challenge patriarchal models of sexuality may be observed in the case of honour-crime victim, Fouzia Azeem, famed as Qandeel Baloch. In comparison to cases of transgender rights she received far more ambiguous sympathy (Boone 2017; Dad 2016; Zia 2017). Celebrity and victim of a high-profile honour killing in 2016, Qandeel Baloch represented a generational shift in the approach to women's rights issues in Pakistan. In a short span of time, this young woman of middle-class background acquired a celebrity pseudonym, a mobile phone and, under an expanding media, became a new-generation professional – something called a 'social media celebrity' (Bari and Khan 2017). She caught the attention and earned the wrath of audiences because she asserted and flaunted her sexuality with defiance and abandon. She pushed the boundaries of dominant norms and expectations and, unlike several younger women activists, Qandeel claimed to be a 'modern feminist' with little anxiety.[18] Her murder by her brother revealed that, paradoxically for sexually agentive women, she had many male supporters who argued that regardless of her lifestyle there was no justification for her murder. Despite Qandeel's mocking of a religious cleric on TV in 2016 – an incident believed to have triggered the final 'shame' that led her brother to murder her for 'honour' (Boone 2017) – she was not accused of being a traitor or an 'imperialist feminist' who exposed Muslim male misogyny (Toor 2012).

Qandeel's millennial supporters argued that she turned heteropatriarchy on its head by using the master's tools (sexual objectification) and by taking control of her sexuality for her own purposes. She also challenged the religious orthodoxy that was critical of her inappropriate social media postings. However, digital rights activist Nighat Dad notes the backlash of abuse on social media when she supported and sympathised with Qandeel and, in response, several men bid her the same fate of death (Dad 2016). Dad finds that Qandeel's Twitter feed reveals a time where she had celebrated 'Malala Day' to honour the young Pakistani Nobel Prize winner and education advocate who survived an assassination attempt by Taliban militants in 2014. Dad notes that one user responded by wishing that Qandeel too would get 'shot in the head like Malala' so people could 'celebrate #QandeelDay' (Dad 2016).

The legacy of Qandeel Baloch is not simply that she flung the doors of debate around Pakistani female sexuality wide open but that she demonstrably exposed the uncomfortable connection between sex, and the sham of piety and honour.[19] Women's expression of sexuality has different connotations under a hegemonic Islamic gendered order that is shaped by culture and religion. Such expressions of defiance are not simple individual cases of sex positivity, but they unsettle the implicit code in Muslim contexts that defines women's sexuality as a permanent potential force of *fitna* (chaos through seduction or sexual subversion/sedition of the religious order) if not controlled by marriage or related men (Mernissi 1975).

The influential classes may rightfully claim that their political struggles resulted in the 2016 law, Amendment to Offences in the Name/Pretext of Honour Act. However, societal taboos against women's sexual liberties cannot be expunged by legal action and gender sensitivity training alone. It is women like Qandeel Baloch who expand the arbitrary and gender-discriminatory boundaries of acceptable sexual conduct and redefine feminine agency. More defiant and 'inconvenient' women like her would need to survive and be supported to change the narrative around sexual independence and gender equality.

Reforming the Zina Laws ended the conversion of the victim of a sex-crime into a criminal herself and it is now difficult to accuse and indict a woman of adultery. But the law still makes the state responsible for regulating and controlling sexuality. Heads of households act as extensions of the state and wield legal authority as guardians and execute punishment in their homes especially when they consider the state is not doing a good enough job. Sexual defiance is a form of resistance against the last three decades of targeted and overt state and male patriarchal and legal control over women's choice in dress code, marriage, reproductive matters and consensual as well as non-consensual sex, using Islamic justifications. Women survivors of rape used to be vulnerable to accusations of *zina* (sex outside of marriage) if the violation could not be proven or was not witnessed by four honest, upright Muslim men. Qandeel Baloch's sexual impropriety was not simply about entertainment or forging a career but was a testing of the post-*zina* context and a pushing of the envelope on what constitutes the boundaries of appropriate sexual choice and the role of religious and cultural authorities in prescribing these limits.

Opportunities and Limits under Gender-responsive Governance

The Pakistani state is not fixed along any single power axis and multiple power centres (geographical and identitarian) compete over the regulation of gender within its metropolises, tribal belts and agrarian economies. Gender, as an unstable category in itself, is a useful tool of governance and political leverage across such a diverse body politic. The conventional notions of women's empowerment in the 1960s had been limited to voting rights, access to welfare, right to divorce, and to work and participate in public office. Today, the demand and entry of women in non-traditional occupations finds them in state offices, as airplane pilots, Oscar award-winning documentary makers, film actors, sportswomen competing in international arenas and as Nobel prize winners. The state has shifted from its earlier paternalistic and even misogynistic partnership with local male-headed communities towards a more rights-based approach, and women's expectations, demands and practices are boldly aligning themselves with new policies. The state finally dares to penetrate the private realm of the *chardewari* (four walls of the home) and offers protection via the Domestic Violence Act or amendments to the Child-restraint Marriage Act and restricts community-based justice on women's issues. It even adjudicates harshly on murders of health workers who go door-to-door providing vaccines to children.[20] This weakens the traditional hold on power of male-headed communities and men as proxies of the state.

At the same time, constitutional state bodies such as the Council of Islamic Ideology (CII) have objected to the term 'gender equality' as an 'absurd' notion.[21] While many of the new policies are pro-women, they do not challenge the heteropatriarchal norms that define the Islamic gendered order and which insist on gender segregation and dissuade women's mobility such that women's participation in the labour force remains one of the lowest in the world.[22] These disjunctures between different state apparatuses demonstrates how the state may use women-friendly governance policies instrumentally and tactically but without dismantling or radically confronting the socio-economic, cultural or religious obstacles to gender equality. Such a cautious and arbitrary approach may defend women's and minorities' rights but draws the line at supporting women's sexual rights or awarding them comprehensive autonomous citizenship.

Nonetheless, gender policies are now enacted through a state-sponsored infrastructure of 'community-based social mobilisers', 'village organisers' and 'gender focus persons' that includes and connects various classes of professional activists to the metropolises and who communicate through a common vocabulary of development. This gender-responsive governance has remained primarily focused on development goals such as, the Millennium Development Goals (MDGs) and Sustainable Development Goals (SDGs). When women's empowerment extends beyond livelihood and basic needs and translates into sexual agency, this clearly threatens heteronormativity, the Islamic gendered order, and even the interests of a donor community unwilling to confront the cultural/religious order. The state itself is unsure about how to respond to this challenge as are many members of women's groups who identify as feminists.

Through newly amended laws and gender-aware policies, the Pakistani state has distanced itself from its earlier collusion with patriarchal traditions, but its role remains confined to criminalising rather than preventing these practices. Meanwhile, the moral panic over sexual impropriety is evident in the judicial banning of Valentine's Day and censorship of social media for blasphemous and pornographic content. Islamists have concentrated their energies toward preempting the annual celebration of Valentine's Day, preventing gender mixing in universities and public spaces, and continuing to oppose any legislation that challenges male control over female sexuality, including the domestic violence bill.

Conclusion

In Pakistan, 'gender' has become a viable indicator of progressive policy and one that is compatible with both liberal development and Islamic agendas and norms. However, the place of sex and sexual expression even after the reform of the Zina Laws is limited to conservative Islamic frames. Transgender rights are permissible if they adhere to settling on either side of the gender binary. Women sexual provocateurs carry the potential to resist the prescribed gendered order in Pakistan. Considered to be *fitna*-causing seductresses, their resistance to sexual boundaries encourages a new subject citizenry that breaks social and religious controls and acts as a driver of autonomy for women. There is a likelihood that sexuality may simply become co-opted as part of the gender development schema and become aligned with health, culture and the broader development paradigms. Women's right to education, mobility and politicking are less contested sites according to state laws, government policies and even within male-dominated communities. However, women's sexual defiance is more potent and threatening to the gender order. This is because there is no alternative frame for dealing with women who refuse to be dispossessed of their sexual freedoms or behave as disciplined sexual subjects in the Islamic Republic of Pakistan. If women's sexual transgression resists the limitations of the acceptable confines of Islam, neo-liberalism, and the male gaze, then that will refute the 'convenience of subservience' thesis.

If this defiance is not tamed under NGO projects or restricted within neo-liberal empowerment themes, then it is likely to become an additional and more unsettling and challenging political driver against the perpetuation of patriarchal politics in Pakistan. In the absence of a *zina* law as a lever of control available to the state, clerics and men, the only method of controlling women's sexualities is through moral shaming or killing, as was the case for Qandeel Baloch. Honour-based killings of women who defy sexual codes continue unabated and the growth of social media has become a forum where genders mix more easily and expressively than in conventional public spaces. As sexual expression stands poised to spill into a form of political challenge to the Islamic gendered order, Pakistani feminists will have to devise a strategy to protect and channel women's sexual freedoms and autonomy. Yet, everything remains in the balance with a new incumbent after the 2018 elections appearing to be driven by populism and very receptive to Islamic politics and which give the accolade to gender-regressive measures.

Notes

1. In 2007, the young women of the Jamia Hafsa (JH) madrasa initiated a series of vigilante activities in Islamabad and illegally occupied the premises adjoining the mosque of the Lal Masjid. This was in protest against the government's threat to demolish and reclaim the mosque because it was suspected to have become a hotbed for terrorist indoctrination. The JH women wore complete black veils, carried bamboo sticks and kidnapped a woman from the neighbourhood whom they accused of running a prostitution enterprise. They only let her free once she 'repented'.
2. Some examples include: the National Commission on the Status of Women in 2000; a National Policy for Development and Empowerment of Women in 2002; the National Health Policy 2001; unprecedented quotas for women; the Human Trafficking Ordinance 2002; the Gender Reform Action Plan; the Women's Political Participation Project; the Beijing Plus Ten process.
3. The Islamic law that criminalised adultery was part of the Hudood Ordinances promulgated by the president of Pakistan, General Zia-ul-Haq in 1979. It was amended in 2006 under General Musharraf's regime and contested by Islamists in the Federal Shariat Court. The amended form remains law under the Women's Protection Act, which has introduced reforms such as distinguishing rape from adultery and which was previously blurred under the Islamic law/Hudood Ordinances.
4. Available at <http://www.wluml.org/> (last accessed 27 February 2019).
5. A projects record (2005–10) can be found on the website of the University of Birmingham, available at <http://www.birmingham.ac.uk/schools/government-society/departments/international-development/rad/index.aspx> (last accessed 27 February 2019).
6. Some examples include: the nationwide Lady Health Workers' Programme; the Women Councillors' Network; nurses' organisations; the Okara Peasant Women's movement in Punjab; the public tea-stall-occupying Girls at Dhabas in Karachi; the literary women's circle, Khana Badosh in Hyderabad, Sindh; We The Humans women's group in Baluchistan; Khwendo Kor in Khyber Pukhtunkhwa; and Taqrha Qabaili Khwenday (Tribal Sisterhood Organisation) in the Federally Administered Tribal Areas.
7. 'Garhi Khuda Bux awaits another Bhutto: Benazir felled by assassin's bullets; 21 others killed in suicide bombing; Asif Zardari, children taking remains to Larkana', *Dawn*, 28 December 2007, available at <https://www.dawn.com/news/282027> (last accessed 27 February 2019).
8. 'Woman minister killed by fanatic', *Dawn*, 21 February 2007, available at <https://www.dawn.com/news/233951> (last accessed 27 February 2019).

9. 'PTI senior leader Zahra Shahid killed on eve of Karachi re-polls', *Dawn*, 19 May 2013, available at <https://www.dawn.com/news/1012155> (last accessed 27 February 2019).
10. 'Pakistan mourns murdered aid worker Parveen Rehman', BBC News, 14 March 2013, available at <http://www.bbc.com/news/world-asia-21783304> (last accessed 27 February 2019).
11. Anissa Haddadi (2012), 'Pakistani women's rights activist Fareeda "Kokikhel" Afridi shot dead in Peshawar', *International Business Times*, 5 July, available at <http://www.ibtimes.co.uk/woman-activist-fareeda-kokikhel-shot-dead-peshawar-359823> (last accessed 27 February 2019).
12. 'Director T2F Sabeen Mahmud shot dead in Karachi', *Dawn*, 24 April 2015, available at <https://www.dawn.com/news/1177956> (last accessed 27 February 2019).
13. The Constitution of the Islamic Republic of Pakistan (last updated in 2012), National Assembly of Pakistan. Available at <http://na.gov.pk/uploads/documents/1333523681_951.pdf> (last accessed 27 February 2019).
14. Other examples include: the Prevention of Anti-Women Practices Act, 2011; the Criminal Law Amendment Act, 2010; the Protection of Women (Criminal Laws Amendment) Act, 2006; the Women in Distress and Detention Fund Act, 2010.
15. The GSP Plus status was awarded to Pakistan in 2013 allowing almost 20 per cent of Pakistani exports to enter the EU market at zero tariff and 70 per cent at preferential rates for developing countries in order to contribute to their growth. Eligibility requires compliance with criteria such as, combating child labour, respecting internationally recognised worker rights, providing adequate and effective intellectual property protection.
16. 'Gay Pakistanis, still in shadows, seek acceptance', *The New York Times*, 3 November 2012, available at <https://www.nytimes.com/2012/11/04/world/asia/gays-in-pakistan-move-cautiously-to-gain-acceptance.html?pagewanted=all&_r=0> (last accessed 27 February 2019).
17. Walsh, Declan (2006), 'Pakistan society looks other way as gay men party', *The Guardian*, 14 March, available at < https://www.theguardian.com/world/2006/mar/14/pakistan.gayrights> (last accessed 27 February 2019).
18. '10 powerful quotes by Qandeel Baloch', *The Express Tribune*, 16 July 2016, available at <https://tribune.com.pk/story/1143032/10-inspiring-quotes-qandeel-baloch/> (last accessed 27 February 2019).
19. For a sample of the varied responses, discussions and debates on Qandeel Baloch's case, see 'The threats and abuse outspoken Pakistani women receive', BBC News, 19 July 2016, available at <http://www.bbc.com/news/world-asia-36824514> (last accessed 27 February 2019). The government of Pakistan's Provincial Commission on the Status of Women released a press statement condemning the honour killing: 'Deadly attack: Qandeel Baloch's murder condemned', *The Express Tribune*, 17 July 2016, available at <https://tribune.com.pk/story/1143289/deadly-attack-qandeel-balochs-murder-condemned/> (last accessed 27 February 2019). The case was reviewed in international popular magazines too; see Hamra Zubair (2016), 'How comparing Qandeel Baloch to Kim Kardashian West exposed a crisis of feminism in Pakistan', *Vogue*, 1 August, available at <https://www.vogue.com/article/qandeel-baloch-crisis-of-feminism-in-pakistan> (last accessed 27 February 2019).

20. 'Murderer of polio worker sentenced to death', *The News International*, 7 December 2017, available at <https://www.thenews.com.pk/print/252970-murderer-of-polio-worker-sentenced-to-death> (last accessed 27 February 2019).
21. In 2008, the CII objected to the use of the term 'gender equality' by the government body, the National Commission on the Status of Women. It considered it a 'vague', 'un-Islamic' and 'absurd' term and an impractical concept given the distinct differences in 'anatomy and mental capacities' between men and women. See '"Gender equality" vague, "Un-islamic" Term, Says CII', *Dawn*, 17 December 2008, available at <http://www.dawn.com/news/334648/gender-equality-vague-un-islamic-term-says-cii> (last accessed 27 February 2019) cited in Zia 2018.
22. 'Pakistan Labour Force Survey (2014–2015)', Thirty-third Issue, Statistics Division, Federal Bureau of Statistics, Government of Pakistan. Available at <http://www.pbs.gov.pk/content/labour-force-survey-2014-15-annual-report> (last accessed 27 February 2019).

Bibliography

Abu-Lughod, Lila (2002) 'Do Muslim women really need saving? Anthropological reflections on cultural relativism and its others', *American Anthropologist New Series*, 104: 3, pp. 783–90.

Afzal-Khan, Fawzia (2008), 'What lies beneath: dispatch from the front lines of the Burqa Brigade', *Social Identities*, 14: 1, pp. 3–11.

Awan, M. Ali (2016), 'Political participation of women in Pakistan: historical and political dynamics shaping the structure of politics for women', *Frankfurter Forschungszentrum Globaler Islam*, <http://www.ffgi.net/files/dossier/polpart-pakistan-awan.pdf> (last accessed 27 February 2019).

Aziz, Sadaf (2005), 'Beyond petition and redress: mixed legality and consent in marriage in Pakistan', *Bayan*, IV, Lahore: Simorgh Publication, pp. 55–70.

Bari, Tazeen and Saad Khan (Directors) (2017), 'Qandeel', *Guardian Documentaries*, September, <https://www.theguardian.com/world/ng-interactive/2017/sep/22/qandeel-baloch-the-life-death-and-impact-of-pakistans-working-class-icon> (last accessed 27 February 2019).

Bano, Masooda (2012), *The Rational Believer: Choices and Decisions in the Madrasas of Pakistan*, Ithaca: Cornell University Press.

Bhatti, M. Waqar (2013), 'Unicef publishes fatwas in favour of polio vaccination', *The News International*, 14 March, <http://www.thenews.com.pk/Todays-News-4-165123-Unicef-publishes-fatwas%E2%80%8E> (last accessed 27 February 2019).

Bhutto, Fatima (2016), 'Women bear the brunt of Pakistan's obsession with dishonour', *Financial Times*, 22 July, <https://www.ft.com/content/b1216552-4fe8-11e6-8172-e39ecd3b86fc> (last accessed 27 February 2019).

Boone, Jon (2017), '"She feared no one": the life and death of Qandeel Baloch', *The Guardian*, 22 September, <https://www.theguardian.com/world/2017/sep/22/qandeel-baloch-feared-no-one-life-and-death> (last accessed 27 February 2019).

Brohi, Nazish (2006), *The MMA Offensive: Three Years in Power, 2003–2005*, Islamabad: ActionAid International.

Buncombe, Andrew (2013), 'Pakistan's youth favour sharia law and military rule over democratic governance', *The Independent*, 3 April, <http://www.independent.co.uk/news/world/asia/pakistans-youth-favour-sharia-law-and-military-rule-over-democratic-governance-8558165.html> (last accessed 27 February 2019).

Cheema, Iftikhar, Maham Farhat, Simon Hunt, Sarah Javeed, Katharine Keck and Sean O'Leary (2015), 'Benazir income support programme: second impact evaluation report', *Oxford Policy Management*, December, <https://www.opml.co.uk/files/Publications/7328-evaluating-pakistans-flagship-social-protection-programme-bisp/bisp-second-impact-evaluation-report.pdf?noredirect=1> (last accessed 27 February 2019).

Cheema, Moeen H. and Shahzad Akbar (2010), 'Liberal fundamentalism?' *The News International*, 7 January, <https://www.thenews.com.pk/archive/print/215205-liberal-fundamentalism?> (last accessed 27 February 2019).

Dad, Nighat (2016), 'The dishonourable killing of a Pakistani social media celebrity', *Open Democracy*, 15 September, <https://www.opendemocracy.net/5050/nighat-dad/dishonourable-killing-of-pakistani-social-media-celebrity> (last accessed 27 February 2019).

Fair and Free Election Network (FAFEN) (2013), 'Women MPs performance report', 8 March, <http://fafen.org/fafen-women-mps-performance-report-2/> (last accessed 27 February 2019).

Hamzić, Vanja (2016), 'The resistance from an alterspace: Pakistani and Indonesian Muslims beyond the dominant sexual and gender norms', in P. Nynäs and A. Kam-Tuck Yip (eds), *Religion, Gender and Sexuality in Everyday Life*, Abingdon and New York: Routledge (first published 2012, Ashgate Publishing), pp. 17–36.

Hasan, Arif (2016), '"Honor" killings', *Arif Hasan*, 7 August, <http://arifhasan.org/development/social-change-development/honour-killings> (last accessed 27 February 2019).

Hirschkind, Charles and Saba Mahmood (2002), 'Feminism, the Taliban, and politics of counter-insurgency', *Anthropological Quarterly*, 75: 2, pp. 339–54.

Iqtidar, Humeria (2011), *Secularizing Islamists? Jamaat-i-Islami and Jama'at-ud-Da'wa in Urban Pakistan*, Chicago and London: Chicago University Press.

Jalal, Ayesha (1991), 'The convenience of subservience: women and the state of Pakistan', in D. Kandiyoti (ed.), *Women, Islam and the State*, London: Macmillan, pp. 77–114.

Jamal, Amina (2005), 'Feminist "selves" and feminism's "others": feminist representations of Jamaat-e-Islami women in Pakistan', *Feminist Review*, 81, pp. 52–73.

Al Jazeera (2005), 'Pakistan president denies rape remark', 18 September, <http://english.aljazeera.net/archive/2005/09/2008410112050342208.html> (last accessed 27 February 2019).

Kalmbach, Hilary and Masooda Bano (eds) (2011), *Women, Leadership, and Mosques: Changes in Contemporary Islamic Authority*, Leiden: Brill.

Khan, Faris A. (2014), 'Khwaja Sira: "transgender" activism and transnationality in Pakistan', in S. S. Wadley (ed.), *South Asia in the World: an Introduction*, Abingdon and New York: Routledge, pp. 170–84.

Khattak, Saba Gul (2006), 'Inconvenient facts: women's political representation and military regimes in Pakistan', in *Transforming Institutions of Power: Towards Gender-responsive Governance*, Islamabad: n. pub.

Mahmood, Saba (2005), *Politics of Piety: the Islamic Revival and the Feminist Subject*, Princeton: Princeton University Press.

Mai, Mukhtara (2007), *In the Name of Honor: a Memoir*, trans. L. Coversdale, New York: Washington Square Press.

Mernissi, Fatima (1975), *Beyond the Veil: Male–Female Dynamics in a Modern Muslim Society*, Cambridge, MA: Schenkman Publishing Co.

Mirza, Naeem and Wasim Wagha (2007), 'A five-year report on performance of women parliamentarians in the 12th National Assembly (2002–2007)', Aurat Foundation, Pakistan.

Moudouros, Nikos (2014), 'The "harmonization" of Islam with the neoliberal transformation: the case of Turkey', *Globalizations*, 11: 6, pp. 843–57.

Mumtaz, Khawar and Farida Shaheed (1987), *Women of Pakistan: Two Steps Forward, One Step Back*, London: Zed Books.

Pakistan Demographic and Health Survey, 2012–2013 (2013), National Institute of Population Studies, Islamabad, December, <http://www.nips.org.pk> (last accessed 27 February 2019).

Saigol, Rubina (2016), 'Feminism and the women's movement in Pakistan: actors, debates and strategies', *A Country Study (Pakistan)*, Islamabad: Friedrick Ebert Stiftung.

Shehrbano, Afiya (2016), 'The cost of national security', *The News International*, 7 January, <http://www.thenews.com.pk/print/86875-The-cost-of-national-security> (last accessed 27 February 2019).

Toor, Saadia (2012), 'Imperialist feminism redux', *Dialectical Anthropology*, 36: 3–4, pp. 147–60.

USAID (2008), 'Evaluation of the access to contemporary markets for homebound women embroiderers project', report, April, Washington, DC: MSI, <http://pdf.usaid.gov/pdf_docs/PDACL798.pdf> (last accessed 27 February 2019).

—— (2010), 'Religion, conflict and peacebuilding', a report from a roll-out event, 8 March, under the aegis of the US Agency for International Development and including the Bureau for Democracy, Conflict and Humanitarian Assistance, the Office of Conflict Management and Mitigation.

Zaidi, S. Akbar (2014), 'Rethinking Pakistan's political economy: class, state, power and transition', *Economic and Political Weekly*, 1 February, 49: 5.

—— (2015), 'All power to women', *The News International*, 17 June, <https://www.thenews.com.pk/print/46389-all-power-to-women> (last accessed 27 February 2019).

Zaim, Sabahaddin (1994), 'Ekonomik Hayatta Müslüman İnsanın Tutum ve Davranışları', in H. Şencan (ed.), *İş Hayatında İslam İnsanı (Homo İslamicus)*, Istanbul: MÜ SİAD (cited in Moudouros 2014, above), pp. 101–12.

Zia, Afiya S. (2009), 'The reinvention of feminism in Pakistan', *Feminist Review*, 91: 1, pp. 29–46.

—— (2011), 'Donor-driven Islam?' *Open Democracy*, 21 January, <http://www.opendemocracy.net/5050/afiya-shehrbano-/donor-driven-islam> (last accessed 27 February 2019).

—— (2013), 'Faith-based vs rights-based development for Pakistani women', in S. G. Khattak and A. M. Weiss (eds), *Development Challenges Confronting Pakistan*, Sterling, VA: Kumarian Press.

—— (2014a), 'Motivated by dictatorship, muted by democracy: articulating women's rights in Pakistan', in S. Nazneen and M. Sultan (eds), *Voicing Demands: Feminist Activism in Transitional Contexts*, London: Zed Books, pp. 152–86.

—— (2014b), 'Being Malala', *Open Democracy*, 13 October, <https://www.opendemocracy.net/5050/afiya-shehrbano-zia/being-malala> (last accessed 27 February 2019).

—— (2015), 'Faith-based challenges to the women's movement in Pakistan', in H. A. Ghosh (ed.), *Contesting Feminisms: Gender and Islam in Asia*, New York: SUNY Press, pp. 181–206.

—— (2016), 'Women and the changing state', *The Express Tribune*, 24 August, <https://tribune.com.pk/story/1169353/women-changing-state/> (last accessed 27 February 2019).

—— (2017), 'A year after Qandeel Baloch', *The News on Sunday*, 9 July, <http://tns.thenews.com.pk/year-qandeel-baloch/#.Wi7GT4UZIfo> (last accessed 27 February 2019).

—— (2018), *Faith and Feminism in Pakistan: Religious Agency or Secular Autonomy?* Brighton: Sussex Academic Press.

Chapter 10

Muslim Diasporas in Transition: Islam, Gender and New Regimes of Governance

Kathryn Spellman Poots

Introduction

On New Year's Eve 2015, gangs of reportedly North African and Arab asylum seekers and migrants robbed and sexually assaulted hundreds of women as they were celebrating in public spaces in Cologne and other German cities. As moral panic set in, politicians, academics, the media and the wider public furiously debated the German government's liberal stance on refugees, the failure of cultural integration and the challenges Islam posed to the secular West. Whereas some leftists and anti-racist feminists warned against drawing on broader cultural stereotypes of Muslim violence to explain the incident, pointing out that sexualised violence is a serious problem among 'German' men, for the political right and many on the left, the Cologne incident proved that Arab and Muslim men were essentially predatory, misogynist and violent. The incident, which melded into international media commentary on the rise of 'Muslim immigrant' violence across Western European countries,[1] led to a convergent moral panic about the threat that refugees and immigrants pose to 'our' Western culture, 'our' values and, crucially, 'our' white women. Indeed, the mainstream discourses that normally justified the War on Terror as a means to rescue Muslim women shifted to espousing the need to protect white, 'Western' women, as well as sexual minorities, from Muslim men (Zakaria 2017; Bangstad 2011).

The Cologne episode highlights the deepening of divisions and generalised state of anxiety about Muslims in the West. Indeed, in the twenty-eight years since the publication of *Women, Islam and the State* (Kandiyoti 1991), there has been a major shift in Western countries with regard to immigrants of Muslim extraction and the subsequent diasporic generations. Whereas people were initially referred to mostly with reference to their ethnic and national backgrounds, it became increasingly common for 'Muslim' self- and group-identification and notions of 'Islam' and 'Muslim Diaspora' to be regarded as fixed and ahistorical cultural/political units. This is despite the great diversity of people from Muslim backgrounds living in Western countries. What were the local, national and transnational political, social and economic conditions that gave rise to 'culturalised'[2] understandings of the Muslim 'other'? To what extent have paradigmatic shifts in governance and policy-making in Western states contributed to the deepening of the structural and cultural fault lines between ex-colonial subjects and other migrant minorities and majority Europeans? How have 'identity politics' translated into the politics of fear?

This chapter will argue that gender roles, gender relations and sexual politics have been key ingredients in defining a so-called 'Muslim Diaspora'. Focusing on gender politics in both pre- and post-9/11 War on Terror periods that followed the 9/11 terrorist attacks on the US, I will examine the rising prominence of 'Muslim' self- and group-identification in relation to the integration of 'Islam' and Muslim practices into Western states. My focus will involve consideration of the rise and deterritoralisation of political Islam, the monitoring of Muslim diasporic communities in the context of increasing 'securitisation' policies and the more recent rise of anti-Islam rhetoric in the post-Brexit and Trump era. The recent influx of refugees and asylum seekers as a result of conflicts in Syria, Iraq and Yemen have also encouraged a 'fortress' mentality in receiving countries. The chapter will show how constructions of the 'Muslim man' and 'Muslim woman' have consistently been used by both anti-Muslim hate groups and Islamist groups to define antagonistic group identities and protect dominant gender ideologies.

A brief look at my ethnographic data on Shia Muslim networks in the UK will be presented to illustrate the divergent ways in which diasporic women are navigating these dynamics at the grass roots. Muslim women in the diaspora have long created and employed a wide range of tools, platforms and strategies to challenge gender ideologies and inequalities in their host and home countries, albeit from diverse socio-economic and political standpoints (Joly and Wadia 2017; Al-Ali 2007; Mojab and Gorman 2007; Salih 2010). Transnational feminist networks, for instance, have created new spaces for women to organise and reinforce advocacy work and campaigns across borders and other social barriers.[3] The effectiveness of women's transnational mobilisation, however, depends on its capability to involve women at the grass roots and to understand the changing factors that affect daily lives.

Demographic Background

There are approximately twenty million Muslims in the EU (including the UK).[4] Although there has been a long history of Muslim presence in the West, migration from Muslim-majority societies has greatly increased since the 1950s. In brief, decolonisation brought North and West Africans mainly to France, South Asians to Britain, and Indonesians to the Netherlands. The appeal for mainly male labourers in the post-war boom brought Turkish and Kurdish guest workers to Germany, additional South Asians to the UK and North Africans to France. Family reunification became a major factor in the 1970s. More recently, political upheaval, wars and civil strife brought male and female refugees and asylum seekers mainly from Middle Eastern countries – Iran, Iraq, Afghanistan, Lebanon and Palestine – and East Africa and Eastern Europe. Most recently, there has been a large influx of asylum seekers from Syria, and smaller numbers from Iraq, Afghanistan and Yemen.[5] Other types of migrants, such as students, businessmen and women and skilled workers, also make up European Muslim populations, as do European converts to Islam. The US census does not ask a question on faith, but the Pew Research Center estimated in 2011 that 3.3 million Muslims live in the US (1 per cent of the population), from seventy-seven different countries (Pew Research Center 2011). According to Canada's 2011 National Survey, there were 1,053,945 Muslims in Canada making up about 3.2 per cent of the population, mainly from Pakistani, Indian, Iranian and Egyptian descent. Finally, the Australian 2016 Census recorded 604,200 people from Muslim countries, or 2.6 per cent of the total Australian population.[6]

The Making of the 'Muslim Diaspora'

Past sociological research[7] has shown the analytical limitations in the conceptualisation of pan-religious groupings (as well as pan-ethnic and national groupings) as such categories mask other important socio-economic, religious, gendered and political identifications (Gilliat-Ray 2010; Zubaida 2007; Spellman Poots 2018). A Muslim diasporic category, for instance, glosses over and homogenises the wide range of theological schools of thought, Sufi Orders, reformist movements and religious practices within Muslim communities, and conceals the many different ways that women and men orient themselves to their faith or Muslim backgrounds. Whereas some diasporic Muslims are conservative, others have liberal orientations or feel indifferent to their religious upbringing – and these positions might all be experienced during one person's lifetime (Gilliat-Ray 2010; Modood 2005; Spellman 2004). Furthermore, combining diverse Muslims into a 'Muslim Diaspora' overlooks generational change and how younger generations might question their identities or re-examine the religion they have inherited.

The social and political experiences of Muslims are greatly influenced by a combination of overlapping factors in the migration and settlement process. These include shifting immigration and citizenship models and policies – from welcoming migrant labour to xenophobic retrenchment–citizenship models, from assimilation and multiculturalism to exclusion and securitisation.[8] Other factors to be considered are austerity measures and other general policies concerning education, health, housing or employment. Further, ongoing wars, conflicts and economic sanctions as well the historic, often post-colonial relations between the country of descent and adopted country, continue to create unequal conditions for navigating migration and settlement. Transnational dimensions, such as digital communication links and inexpensive travel that enable immigrant groups and their descendants to maintain varying degrees of social, religious, economic and political connections with people and places in other territories, must also be part of our analysis.

Pre-9/11: Accommodating Islam

A survey of sociological research in the post-World War II period reveals three interrelated explanations for the ascendancy of 'Muslim' self- and group-identification in Western countries: the politics of recognising 'Islam' in state structures, the 'Muslim awakening' and the rise of Islamic transnational movements and virtual communities, and Western responses to Muslim politics and Islamic movements. The following section will draw on a few cases to illustrate how contestations about Muslim women, and what they symbolise, as well as shifting gender norms and relations, have been key political components in shaping immigration and citizenship experiences for Muslims living in Western societies both pre- and post-9/11.

Institutionalising 'Islam' and the neo-liberal turn

In the years following the post-World War II migration movements to Western Europe, immigrants of Muslim extraction joined together to make political demands for the official recognition of Islam and its ritual practices (such as religious holidays, dress codes and halal food) in state institutions and the public domain. This led to the emergence and mobilisation of 'Muslim' umbrella groups – united in a single faith/cultural identity across Muslim sects – to counter racism and lobby for the accommodation of Muslims within national frameworks. The public debates and policy measures that followed varied greatly in different countries depending on their respective histories, pre-existing political and legal frameworks, and commitment to secularism. For instance, the pragmatic multicultural framework in the UK (Lewis 2007; Grillo 2004), the political culture of assimilation and *laicité*[9] in France (Bowen 2004; Cesari 1998), the multi-establishment federal system in Germany (Malik 2013), and the 'principled pluralism' in the Netherlands (de Koning 2010; Sunier 2012) resulted in different types of campaigns and political strategies.

What all countries had in common was the unrepresentative nature of Muslim leadership and authority. Which Muslims, from what backgrounds, should represent an assumed 'Muslim community' in local and state/public domains? Whose Islamic theological school and gender norms should serve as exemplars for all? Despite variations from country to country, it was often older, self-appointed, male community brokers, from religiously conservative backgrounds, who jockeyed to fill the gate-keeper positions (Gilliat-Ray 2010; Ferrari 2005). As a result, matters that pertained to women and the family – such as marriage, divorce, inheritance and other legal rights, as well as vexed issues such as domestic violence, forced marriage, female genital mutilation (FGM), honour-based crimes and other forms of gender-based violence – were grossly neglected. These matters were subsequently taken up by women mainly in informal community networks and emerging grass-roots organisations (Brah 1996; Spellman 2004; Salih 2003). This is ironic considering that Islamic modes of dress and the question of violence against women (often collapsed into one category) were at the core of public debates over Muslim immigration and integration. Nevertheless, female activist groups encountered opposition. For example [they] 'faced dual resistance, both from conservative male community leaders, and from a state apparatus that often endorsed these community leaders and therefore resisted the funding of women's activism' (Gilliat-Ray 2010: 217). The community leaders not only controlled the funding but were also empowered to choose what issues were placed on the state's agenda.

In France, the process of institutionalising Islam and regulating Muslim practices took a different course, mainly due to its evolving tradition of *laicité*. Modelled on the hierarchical pattern of the Catholic Church, the French Republic created its first consultative 'Islamic' body with an appointed leader in 1989. With a clear agenda, French politicians hoped to design a 'distinctively "liberal" French Islam, with its Way or sharia *"bien tempérée a la française"* (seasoned the French way)' (Caeiro 2005: 71). It tended to marginalise 'bad' (illiberal) Muslims and promote 'good' Muslims (for these terms see Mamdani (2004)) by co-opting suitable men and women members who would help create 'a transparent, open, modern and liberal Islam compatible with the laws of the Republic' (Nicolas Sarkozy quoted in *Le Monde*, 8 April 2003, Caeiro 2005: 78).

Consequently, an array of Muslim groupings and their local (mostly male) leaders who didn't fit the 'good' Muslim mould, and who in many cases had already established grass-roots centres to deal with community concerns, criticized the French government for creating a body that was 'unrepresentative' and 'undemocratic'. As stated by Caeiro: 'By privileging the Islamic component of immigrant identity, the state was accused of practicing a "reverse [religious] communitarianism" and of pursuing electoral gains, as well as playing into the hands of Islamist movements active in the French suburbs' (Caeiro 2005: 80). Secular elites of Muslim heritage also resented the official institutionalisation of 'Islam'. Throughout the 1990s, the nature of the representation of Muslims in state regulations was fought over by successive ministers of interior, sundry Muslim leaders, feminists and other French actors (Caeiro 2005: 72).

These battles were expressed through the well-known, highly publicised debates over women's dress, and the perennial question as to whether Muslim women should be allowed to wear headscarves within public schools and other public domains.[10] Thus, it was well before the 9/11 attacks that women's dress – often framed in terms of a defence of the rights of Muslim women against a patriarchal order versus the right of women to exercise their freedom to choose – emerged as a central trope in shaping the boundaries of citizenship, legislation and new forms of nationalism in France (Gaspard and Khosrokhavar 1995).

It is worth adding a caveat here on the role of neo-liberal policies in the process of 'culturalising' citizenship and defining the parameters of women's organisations and activism. Returning to women's activism in the UK, for instance, women's advocacy organisations found themselves caught up in the crossfire of Tony Blair's policy shift from 'multi-culturalism' to 'multi-faithism' (Patel 2008). New Labour's neo-liberal policies, which aimed to 'manage' and 'monitor' diversity from above, actively encouraged civil society groups to organise exclusively around religious identities. In the process, as observed by the chair of the women's advocacy organisation, the Southall Black Sisters, 'the complex web of social, political and cultural processes were reduced by both state and community leaders into purely religious values, while concepts of human rights, equality and discrimination were turned on their head' (Patel 2008).[11] Thus, many secular anti-racist women's advocacy organisations, with missions to counter all forms of inequality based on ethnicity, gender, religion and caste between and within communities, were pruned, limited in scope and in some cases shut down (Patel 2008).

Along similar lines, New Labour policies defunded state education while providing new sources of public funding to Muslim schools. Whereas some Islamic schools struck a balance between the national curriculum and religious education, others imported Wahhabi textbooks and curricula from Saudi Arabia, which propagated rigid patriarchal views on the family, gender roles and sexuality, as well as racist comments about Jews and Christians (Gilliat-Ray 2010). Moreover, sharia councils (like other faith-based tribunals) were allowed to operate in the UK and a few other Western countries. As in the case of faith-based schools, the councils raised serious concerns about gender discrimination, and provoked highly charged and divisive public and political debates on the implications of sharia law in relation to Western legal norms (Bowen 2016). Whether for or against sharia councils, feminists acknowledge that neo-liberal funding cuts in legal aid have spurred the growth of religious-based legal councils (Bowen 2007; Grillo 2015).

There is a growing body of research on the relationship between austerity measures, the 'culturalisation' of immigration and citizenship policies, and their impact on women's status (Guenif-Souilamas 2017; Lentin 2015). As pointed out by Jonsson and Willen: 'Under austerity, paths to citizenship and rights of residency that used to be distributed according to principles of equality have in effect become tools of segregation and demographic selection' (Jonsson and Willen 2017: 12). The massive post-World War II housing projects in France – known as *banlieues* – are a case in point. Despite economic inequalities and collective withdrawal from French society, Maghrebis and their 'Islamic' culture have often been named as the main culprits for the high crime rates, Islamic extremism and gender-based violence (both real and imagined) in these 'no go' areas (Jonsson and Willen 2017: 12).[12]

The above snapshots of the effects of policy shifts in the UK and France highlight the complexity of forces at play in the creation of the category 'Muslim' as a self- and group- identity marker. The rise and mobilisation of male political/cultural brokers subsumed in a single identity across Muslim denominations to counter discrimination and accommodate religious obligations – combined with the implementation of neo-liberal policies – has consolidated 'Muslim' enclaves and faith-based definitions of identity. These examples show the various ways in which gender relations and women's rights have been appropriated, reinterpreted and represented within these enclaves, and have effectively masked the ways that women have been marking their own political trajectories and setting their own agendas. The troubled political, social and economic conditions in the Middle East and South Asia, the 'Muslim awakening' and the rise of Islamic transnational movements acted to strengthen these structural and social conditions.

'Muslim Awakening' and the Rise of Islamic Transnational Movements

The global 'Muslim awakening' is understood to have emerged from several different contexts. Key influences were the 1979 Iranian Revolution and its popular appeal in the Islamic world and the (competing) dominance of Saudi Arabia and the regional and international influence of Salafism. The wider geopolitical factors, including the legacy of US Cold War policies, including the support of *mujahedin* against the Soviet occupation of the invasion of Afghanistan, nurtured Islamist ideas and militant jihadi movements in Afghanistan, other Middle Eastern countries and the global arena. These jihadi movements led to the eventual formation of al-Qaida, the prime mover behind the 9/11 attacks.[13] Contributing to these geopolitical movements was the emergence of home-grown (mostly non-militant) transnational Islamic social movements in response to failing nationalist and developmental projects, and disastrous western military interventions in the Middle East and South Asia.

There is a vast body of scholarship showing how Islamic movements have travelled geographically across borders, and historically, across time, evoking earlier movements and golden ages (Kepel 2006; Mandaville 2001). Zubaida points out:

> The liberties and communication facilities of the West have provided a fertile medium for the development and spread of ideas and movements, ranging from Sufi mysticism to Islamic feminism to exclusivist communalism, many active in associational life, and crucially, with their own web-sites. (Zubaida 2003: 48)

For example, Saudi-style Salafi/Wahhabi orthodoxy, advanced through the distribution of free Qur'ans, pamphlets, Internet sites and the building of new mosques and centres, has dominated 'Muslim Diasporic' space on and offline (Cesari 2009). Although only a very small percentage of Muslims living in the West adopt literalist Salafism, 'the Wahhabi dress codes – white tunic, head covering, beards for men, *niqab* for women – nonetheless often becomes the standard image of what a good Muslim ought to be' (Cesari 2009: 75). Reformed Salafi intellectuals and popular preachers, on the other hand, exerted considerable influence among younger generations of Muslims in the West, arguing the compatibility of their Muslim faith with life in the West.

Moreover, there are many cases where diasporic communities in Western countries have incorporated the influences of Islamic politics in their countries of origin. The most prominent Shia jurists (*marja*) (based mainly in Iran and Iraq), for example, have international headquarters and representatives in London, as well as interactive websites for adherents to query jurisprudential rulings on religious matters (Spellman Poots 2018). Another case in point is Recep Tayyip Erdoğan's 'new diaspora policy', including his recent controversial attempt to mobilise Turkish imams, mosques and diasporas in Europe to support his constitutional changes (Aydun 2014: 5).

With heightened religious awareness, practice and visibility of Islamic dress came a renewed emphasis on gender roles. In this line of thinking, 'good' Muslim women are pure and submissive, whereas 'bad' Muslim women are impure and of loose morals, like 'Western' women. Strong symbolic boundaries and moral guidelines have helped conservative Muslims to assert their gender codes and mark the difference between 'us' and 'them'. This pervasive piety movement, often conceptualised as an anti-liberal form of agency (Mahmood 2006), has led to controversies about Islamic 'difference' and how embodied ethical practices should be received and framed in Western secular countries (Mahmood 2006).

Transnational concerns about war and violence in Afghanistan, Palestine, Bosnia, Iraq and Chechnya also became symbols of Muslim unity and stimulated a shared perception that Muslims and Islam are under attack and require defence (Werbner 2002). Werbner shows that women, too, quite early on in the 1980s mobilised in response to these atrocities (Werbner 2002). As pointed out in Inge's research on the development of literalist Salafism among women in the UK, the Rushdie Affair (1989), the Gulf War (1990–1) and the Bosnian War (1992–5) were integral to creating the conditions for the emergence of 'new forms of Muslim religiosity and its expression in Islamic activist groups' (Inge 2016: 26). Naber's work on the Muslim global justice movement in the US also demonstrated how violence against Muslims, including the US-led economic sanctions on Iraq and the Israeli occupation of Palestine, greatly contributed to building a distinctly Muslim consciousness among Muslim women activists.

These groups in turn fed into wider shared consciousness of Muslim youth cultures who connect music (particularly hip hop), black internationalism and political activism. As Aidi writes: 'Whether through actual migration or virtually – through the Internet and social media – Muslim youth are reaching across the Atlantic to draw on the black freedom movement and the Islam of the African-descent communities of the New World' (Aidi 2014: xvi). Transnational Sufi Orders have also been important arenas for diasporic Muslims (Aidi 2004: 70–85). Ironically, hip hop music and Sufi music have both been used by Western governments to counter Islamist movements and mobilise 'moderate' forms of Islam (Aidi 2004; Corbett 2016).

Following the 'Muslim awakening', reactionary 'othering' of Muslim practices started to become more prevalent in dominant discourses in Western countries throughout the 1980s and 1990s. The political and social integration of Muslims raised alarm bells for a range of different constituencies on the compatibility of 'Islam' or 'being Muslim' with Western liberal states and societies.[14] Perceptions that Muslims posed a threat to Western values, such as women's equality, free speech and LGBTQ rights, were at the heart of public discussion and violent episodes. The 'Muslim awakening', in all its manifestations, has entrenched the view that Islam stands in opposition to secular modernity. This was greatly exacerbated after the shock of the 9/11 attacks in the US, masterminded by al-Qaida. Henceforth, Muslims across gender and generations were viewed as potential threats to national security.

Post-9/11: Securitising the 'Muslim Diaspora'

The atrocities in New York and Washington in 2001, the Madrid train bombings in 2004 and the London 2005 (7/7) bombings, alongside the murder of filmmaker Theo van Gogh in the Netherlands, the Danish cartoon crisis, and the ongoing controversy over integration issues such as Islamic dress and mosque architecture, have all enormously aggravated the already complex social and political conditions for Muslims living in the West. The dominant public discourses on Muslims have reached new crisis levels in recent years with the threat of home-grown terrorists, the rise of IS, and the continued string of abhorrent terrorist attacks on Western soil, including the Charlie Hebdo shootings and concerted attacks in Paris in 2015, the Manchester Arena bomb in 2017 and the recent pedestrian attacks in Nice, Barcelona, Berlin, New York and London. What Islam is, and what being a Muslim implies, are at the very core of bitter academic and public debates on immigration and integration in Western countries. Public hostility and hysteria regarding Muslims are so prominent that it is increasingly difficult for Muslim immigrants and their offspring to escape the 'securitisation' and 'culturalisation' of Islam in the West.

The 9/11 attacks and their aftershock created an unprecedented conjuncture for American immigrant Muslim populations in the US.[15] This is not to suggest that racial profiling and negative media representations of 'the Arab' and 'the Iranian' – usually as culturally backward, potential terrorists, rich, and uncivilised in the case of men, and exotic, submissive and subordinated for women – were not prevalent before 9/11. They were seen, however, as an Orientalised 'other,' rather than a threat to the social and cultural fabric of American society. This changed after 9/11, when Muslims and Arabs moved from being 'invisible citizens to visible subjects' in political and public domains (Jamal and Naber 2007). This shift has become more pronounced in recent years with the rise of populism and Donald Trump's rise to power (Brubaker 2017).[16]

Post-9/11 Security Measures and Gender Profiling

A new culture of unprecedented security measures took shape in the aftermath of 9/11. The US Patriots Act (Providing Appropriate Tools Required to Intercept and Obstruct Terrorism), passed within six weeks of the attack, greatly extended the powers of federal law enforcement agencies to gather intelligence and scrutinise anyone suspected of terrorism (Jamal and Naber 2007: 1). The spotlight was mainly trained on young 'Arab'-looking men and identifiably

Muslim women. Germany, for example (the student home of 9/11 'Hamburg cell' leader, Muhammad Atta and two other group members), made it a requirement for all male students and graduates from Muslim backgrounds between ages of eighteen and forty-four to undergo mandatory screenings in the months following 9/11 (Cesari and McLoughlin 2005: 39–51). Legitimate concerns about acts of terrorism combined with societal moral panic over the need to locate additional 'sleepers' (a term from bacteriology, invoking the image of a dormant disease that needs to be removed for the sake of public health) led to an estimated eight million individuals being profiled, scanned and questioned by state officials (Niehaus and Achelpöhler 2004: 504 in Cesari 2005: 42). Ewing's research on the stigmatisation of Turkish Muslim men in Berlin, for instance, unearthed continuous portrayals of the violent oppressors pitted against 'ideal' German men, who live virtuously according to the principles laid out in the post-Nazi gender egalitarian constitution. In this line of thinking (as illustrated in the Cologne episode), female German Muslim citizens and 'white' women need to be saved from Muslim men.

Veiled women were also targeted in the wake of 9/11. For instance, Naber's research found veiled women, on the one hand,

> reduced to 'daughters of Osama', and transformed into the 'property' and 'the harmonious extension' of the enemy of the nation within, or symbols that connect to the 'real actors' or 'terrorists' but who do not stand on their own (and lack agency). (Jamal and Naber 2007: 32)

On the other hand, veiled women [continued] to be cast as oppressed and innocent victims who need salvation from their men and their religion.[17] Paradoxically, Muslim women were also recruited to assist Western governments in implementing strategies to tackle radicalisation in local communities. The UK's Prevent Programme, for instance, 'empowered' Muslim women to head off extremism amongst Muslim youth. These programmes have been heavily scrutinised in academic and public discourses for collapsing immigrants and potential terrorists into one category (Gupta 2017: 176–88). By encouraging women to 'spy' on their families they have also generated a lack of trust within and between community members and the officials (Kundnani 2009). Furthermore, it has divided women's activism, as the government opted to fund Muslim women's groups at the expense of other faiths and secular women's groups. This has, in turn, hampered feminist organisations that work on gender-based violence and forms of activism that promote race and gender equality, economic empowerment and welfare initiatives.

The War on Terror, Anxious Politics and the Culturalisation of the Other

Rescue narratives

Much has been written about the instrumentalisation of women's oppression narratives to prop up both foreign and domestic interventions and pursuits (Abu Lughod 2015). As stated by Rafia Zakaria:

> Few things helped to fuel war and Islamophobia more successfully in those days than the stories of women being killed by the men who'd fathered them or married them or were related to them and whose murderous acts went unpunished in a society that sanctioned them. (Zakaria 2017)

The most cited and debated example was of course the Bush administration's promotion of the War on Terror as 'a fight for the rights and dignity of women in Afghanistan' (see Torunn Winplemann, Chapter 6). Rescue narratives were (and continue to be) a source of heated debate among and between politicians and feminists. As appalling as the conditions faced by Afghan women were under the Taliban regime, many anti-racist and post-colonial feminists viewed Bush's rescue campaign as condescending and the continuation of the West's long history of empire politics and colonial 'civilising' missions (Cook et al. 2008). Other feminists, however, argued that military intervention was a viable strategy to counter the fundamentalism and to save 'the Muslimwoman'[18] from male domination (Cook et al. 2008).

The rise of anti-Islam and pro-imperialist viewpoints (particularly put forth by personalities such as Ayaan Hirsi Ali and Brigite Gabriel and non-profit organisations like the Clarion Fund[19]) have become enormously influential in popular and political discourses.[20] As we will see below, their take on the *niqab* and dress codes, sharia councils and, in a different vein, FGM, grooming and gang rapes, honour killings and forced marriage have been influential in informing and shaping Western media outlets, political debates and policy.

Gendering 'Muslim' policies

The continuation of the War on Terror and its devastating effects, and the 2008 financial crisis, which coincided with numerous terrorist attacks on Western soil, spurred a further backlash against lax multicultural policies, in the name of a new realism (de Koning and Modest 2016: 99). New regimes of governance,[21] fuelled by the anxiety surrounding cultural contamination by the Muslim 'other' and the concomitant threat posed by terrorism, 'conjured up restrictive and exclusionary models of national identity and belonging, which regulates and disciplines the presence of those defined as 'other' (de Koning and Modest 2016: 99). These approaches have included the institutionalisation of tough policies to curtail migration from Muslim-majority societies, as well as the creation of mechanisms to monitor and screen immigration and integration processes in order to minimise 'Muslimness' and Islamist leanings.

The turbulent political conditions prompted several Western states to redefine citizenship rights and regulate the cultural values that mark national borders. For example, the UK, France, the Netherlands, Germany and Belgium (among other countries) have new or revised citizenship tests and courses that require outsiders to have a comprehensive civic and cultural knowledge of receiving countries. Dubbed in many countries colloquially as 'Muslim' tests, the questions try to distinguish the 'good Muslim' from the 'bad', especially in relation to gender and sexuality norms. With a focus on women's bodies, sexuality and gender relations, the tests ask for views on a range of topics, including female dress, forced marriage, striking a woman, whether a woman should be allowed in public without a male relative, homosexuality and gay rights, and women's rights in general (Joppke and Torpey 2013). The exam in the Netherlands, for example, asks applicants to comment on images of gay men kissing and topless women sunbathing.[22] According to Cesari, 'those who fail the tests are forced to leave the country (Austria), have fines imposed on them or suffer cuts in their social assistance payments (the Netherlands), or find their residency rights removed or limited (France)' (Cesari and McLoughlin 2005: 49). There has been extensive political and academic debate, as well as legal proceedings, about the constitutionality of these measures and other laws and bans based on religion, culture and demographic forecasts (Joppke and Torpey 2013). In any case, they indicate how culture and gender norms and relations have become normalised and overt indicators in marking national boundaries of belonging and exclusion (Yuval-Davis 1993).

The State of Terror, the Rise of Populism and Blatant Culture Wars

Creating a vicious circle, IS-inspired jihadis and so-called 'lone rangers' have deliberately fuelled conflict and exacerbated the troubled climate by targeting Western liberal lifestyles and social spaces, as witnessed in the deadly attacks in Orlando, San Bernardino, Nice, Paris, Brussels, Munich, London, Manchester and New York. The success of IS in recruiting Western-born women to serve in Syria, Iraq and Libya, as well as the deployment of Western women suicide bombers on Western soil, has further justified policy changes and the wider discursive climate that associates the Muslim woman's body to global terrorism and inherent danger. The 'culture wars' are further inflamed by the transatlantic network of anti-Muslim activists, such as Pamela Geller, Robert Spencer, Frank Gaffney, Brigitte Gabriel and Elisabeth Sabaditsch-Wolff, who spread deeply prejudicial anti-Muslim views via (often bot-induced) twitter accounts, websites and rallies in order influence political discourse and feed the growing 'Islamophobia industry' (Lean 2017).[23]

Converging populisms, most clearly exemplified by the shocks of Brexit in the UK and Donald Trump's electoral victory in the US, and the rise of right-wing populist parties in France, Germany, Austria and in central Europe, have further locked Muslims into a single identity space, and labelled them as 'enemies' of the West. Trump's chaotic regime of rule, exercised through executive orders, anti-Muslim tweets, and the dismantling of customary due process in governance, further feeds the 'culture war' with his deeply suspicious quotes about Muslims and a vision that America is under siege by Islamic terrorism (Brubaker 2017). Abetted by anxious politics and pervasive moral panics, Muslim stereotypes continue to be used as key sites for governance apparatuses to regulate borders and monitor foreign nationals (Attiah 2017).

The mass hysteria surrounding an imagined threat presented by sharia law in the US is a pertinent case in point. Anti-Muslim activists such as David Yerushalmi, Frank Gaffney and Brigitte Gabriel, among others, have raised over $205 million to stir anti-Muslim sentiment and influence lawmakers to implement anti-sharia bills in state legislature (Council on American–Islamic Relations 2016: v). Despite the fact that American Muslims have shown no interest in implementing sharia law in the US, 'from 2010 to 2016, 194 anti-Sharia bills have been introduced in 39 states – of these 18 have been enacted into law' (Elsheikh 2017). The bills, framed to protect women and children from honour killings, underage marriages and FGM, were promoted in the 'March Against Sharia' which took place in twenty-eight cities around the US in June 2017. Although the protestors were outnumbered by counter-protestors, the streets were filled with media grabbing posters that read: 'Islam is the real rape culture'; 'Sharia violates women'; 'Sharia enslaves women: No to FGM' and 'No more Muslims'.

Inside the 'Muslim Diaspora': Navigating the Challenges

What I found is that whenever women are defining themselves, whenever they are coming forward as themselves and writing their own stories, we have religious leaders and self-appointed community leaders who condemn us, who want to define us and want to contain whatever we're saying into whatever fits them. On the other hand, we have racists who want us just to remain in the posture of being victims . . . We have to speak for ourselves. We refuse to be defined by everyone else. The challenges that we're up against are too difficult and too severe. We have too much to lose as women to remain silent. We have to take this into our own hands. (Deeyah Khan, Activist, filmmaker and founder of Sisterhood online magazine, BBC interview, 6 January 2016)

In an era of blatant Islamophobia and rising male-centred authoritarianism, women's advocacy and activist practices face new challenges in exploring the best avenues to push their agendas forward, both locally and transnationally. The gender-informed scholarship on diasporas has emphasised the role of deterritorialised national identities, transnational solidarity networks, international law and declarations in campaigns to challenge gender subordination and violence across locations (Mojab and Gorman 2007; Al-Ali 2007). Transnational feminism has also been a key frame that takes into account the interesecting ways in which oppression is embedded and employed in nationally based legislation as well as transborder politics and conflicts (Mohanty 2006; Abu Lughod 2013; Al-Ali 2007; Salih 2010). Feminist interpretations and rereadings of the Qu'ran and other Islamic sources have also been an emergent strategy used by diasporic women activists (Ali 2006; Barlas 2004; Wadud 2006).

However, there is a need for a renewed sensitivity to local contexts within studies of transnationalism, including for instance, greater attention to shifting communal boundaries and specific political, material and social dynamics within diasporic communities. This is particularly important at a time when feminist agendas shape and are shaped by governmental, NGO and funder driven (often faith-based) community projects.

For example, my own ethnographic data on Twelver Shia Muslims in the UK, obtained between 2012 and 2015, showed how the politicised discursive terrains have deepened communal divisions and impacted gender politics within diasporic Muslim communities (Spellman Poots 2018). Although many Shia remain embedded in ethnic or national diasporas, such as Iraqi, Pakistani, Iranian and East African communities, devoted Shia Muslims, particularly the younger generations, have also been building new multinational Shia institutional, performative and online platforms.[24] My ethnography revealed an increasing salience of a wider cross-ethnic Shia communal identity, in addition to diasporic British Muslim identification. The deepening of sectarian fault lines, particularly between Shia and Sunni (Salafi) groupings, have had transformative consequences on the way they relate to community and public life. For instance, the British Shia position themselves in the public realm as 'good' law-abiding British Shia Muslim citizens, who are the targets and victims of 'bad' Salafis and jihadi Muslims (Spellman Poots 2018).

Many Shia women opted to activate cross-ethnic Shia women's networks and associations, instead of engaging with wider (generally Sunni) Muslim women's or secular advocacy groups. Like their Sunni counterparts, my interlocutors also fashioned an ethical and puritanical lifestyle and contested patriarchal authority by using arguments based on Islamic sources (Mahmood 2005; Naber 2012). They activated forms of resistance by reworking Shia rituals and narratives to speak out against social injustices, such as gender inequality, the violence of IS against women and Shia, and environmental concerns. For example, at the annual ritualised street procession in Hyde Park to commemorate the martyrdom of the Imam Hussain (the quintessential ritual for the Shia to highlight social and political injustices) thousands of young women carried anti-IS banners, and other banners that stated: 'We are equal to men', 'No to terrorism, No to injustice and No to racism' and 'Muslims united against terrorism' (Spellman Poots 2013). While they were appropriating public space and negotiating the boundaries of minority citizenship, they were also distancing themselves from Salafi-styled separatism, jihadi radicalisation and mainstream stereotypes of Muslim's women subordination.

Other reactions have included a mushrooming of local and transnational Shia-endorsed humanitarian projects, charity networks and media to fight a wide range of local and global injustices (Spellman Poots 2018). It is at these popular events that young Shia, of mixed ethnicities and gender, discuss Islamophobia and the challenges of being Muslim in a secular society, as well as intra-community issues such as gender segregation, sectarianism, dress and *hijab*, and temporary marriage. Ethnic customs, such as arranged versus love marriages, funeral and burials (especially whether women can attend a burial), and women's travel restrictions are compared, contrasted and used as bargaining chips for navigating micropolitics at home. Additionally, women often draw upon Islamic sources and Shia rituals to challenge male interpretations and negotiate entrenched patriarchal structures. This is not to say, however, that working within Shia communal boundaries comes without a cost. Several scholars have written about the ways in which Muslim women and their behaviour represents 'the community' at large (Khan 2000; Werbner 2007; Naber 2012). My interlocutors often complain about double standards, backbiting and value judgements within the Shia community, particularly about dress, behaviour and rules of segregation. A girl's reputation and social status are often topics of discussion, and the perils of gossip a constant worry. Men judging women and women judging each other, on proper *hijab*, flirtatious social media exchanges, and outspoken behaviour with men are often sources of tension. Furthermore, some described an invisible yet powerful policing of social behaviour and relationships between young men and women. This illustrates both the possibilities and limitations for women of using the repertoire of meaning and symbols that circulate in the Shia community.

Conclusion

Throughout this chapter I attempted to demonstrate the centrality of gender to the construction of the notion of a 'Muslim Diaspora', and its continued significance in demarcating the boundaries of diasporic citizenship in the charged atmosphere of the post-9/11 national security policies. By looking inside the 'Muslim Diaspora' the chapter also indicated how wider political and geopolitical fields have deepened communal divisions and impacted gender politics within Muslim communities. Women's mobilisation in the diaspora must contend with the multiple dynamics of Islamophobia, male-dominated Muslim identity politics and the challenges posed by male-centred gender regimes and power bases in the home countries.

Although women continue to be deployed as symbols of culture and traditions, there is an acute awareness of the social and political hurdles that Muslim women and men face living in Western societies. They are cognisant of the unequal relations of power and contradictions within family, community and wider societal norms, and the different ways they are positioned in each domain. With the rise in authoritarianism and the generalised state of anxiety about Muslims in the West, they know that it is essential to dismantle and demystify homogenised gendered representations of Muslims and the 'Muslim Diaspora' and assert a more nuanced vision of their diversity and individualities. In our current politicised climate of #MeToo and wider social movements there is a new consciousness, especially among Muslim youth, to subvert pervasive stereotypes and counter discrimination against Muslims. Through local, national and transnational feminist activism, legal battles, scholarship and the arts, citizens from Muslim backgrounds are determined to resist new regimes of governance and their Islamophobic policies. Ultimately, with the salience of negativity surrounding Islam, it is all the more vital to amplify local struggles and the creative ways that women and men are transcending notions of the gendered Muslim 'other'.

Notes

1. For Norway, see Bangstad (2011); Australia, Humphrey (2007); UK, Oborne (2018) and Grattan (2015); the Netherlands, Pakes (2012); Italy, Cousin and Vitale (2012); France, Guénif-Souilamas (2017); US, Lean (2017) and Morgan and Poynting (2012).
2. A term used to explain the process whereby immigrant cultures are identified through their religion and in particular through Islam. A timeless and fixed notion of an illiberal 'Islamic culture' is presented as incompatible to 'Western culture'.
3. Examples of women's organisations include, among many others, Women and Memory Forum, Women against Fundamentalism, Musawah, Al-Masoom, Women Living Under Muslim Laws and Nana Beurs.

4. France and Germany have the largest Muslim populations among EU member countries. As of 2010, there were roughly 4.8 million Muslims in Germany (5.8 per cent of the country's population) and 4.7 million Muslims in France (7.5 per cent). In England and Wales, the 2011 census indicated that the Muslim population rose from 1.5 million to almost three million between 2001 and 2011. This increases the proportion of Muslims in the UK from 2 per cent of the population to 5 per cent. An estimated one million Muslims live in the Netherlands and 2.2 million in Italy. The other Western European countries that have under 500,000 Muslims, such as Sweden, Belgium and Austria, are worth mentioning as the percentage in relation to their populations makes them significant minorities. It is also important to highlight the estimated one million Kurds living in Western European countries, as they are often listed in official statistics according to their nationality and not their ethnicity (Pew Research 2017).
5. Germany is currently processing the most Syrian refugee cases (800,000) followed by Sweden (100,000), Austria (30,000), the Netherlands (30,000) and Hungary (20,000).
6. Even though the chapter refers to the US, Canada and Australia, it mainly focuses on Western European countries, especially countries with the largest Muslims populations.
7. Various notions of 'Muslim Diaspora' have become prevalent in academic and mainstream publications. For instance, the editors in a special issue on 'Conceptualising Muslim Diaspora' in the *Journal of Muslims in Europe* in 2016, noted that: 'such a blithe use of the label [Muslim Diaspora] makes two major hazardous assumptions. First, it implicitly states an ontic category of self-description; and second, it supposes the existence of a scholarly consensus on the appropriateness of its use. Yet neither of these assumptions is accurate.' Nevertheless, they conceded that it can be analytically helpful if it is 'theoretically embedded and methodologically reflected' (Albrecht et al. 2016: 1–2).
8. For a discussion on shifting models of immigration in Western countries, see Bradshaw and Tabachnick (2017).
9. A strict separation between the church and the state. Drawing from the 1905 law, the notion of *laïcité* emerged as a constitutional principle in 1946 and was restated in 1958.
10. The transition from Islam in France to French Islam, within and among Muslims groupings, members of parliament, feminists and the wider French public, was channelled through three high-profile rounds of the well-known *l'affaire du foulard* (the scarf affair) that arose in 1989, concerning the wearing of the veil in French public schools, and constituted as illegal in 2004.
11. Available at <https://www.newstatesman.com/uk-politics/2008/08/religious-state-secular> (last accessed 12 June 2017).
12. A pejorative term for slums dominated by Arabs, blacks and Muslims, *banlieues* have been a major source of public anxiety and heated political debates since the 1970s (Kepel 2006). The studies on these abject suburbs have shown the connection between the neo-liberal move to cut public funding for youth spaces, sports and culture activities (what the French call *encadrement*) and the increase of social alienation and deprivation in these neighbourhoods (Cesari and McLoughlin 2005;

Kepel 2009; Guenif-Souilamas 2017). See the wide coverage and feminists debates on Fadela Amera (2003–4) and the *Ni Putes Ni Soumises* (*Neither Whore, Nor Submissive*), a state-sponsored campaign against violence and subjugation in French suburbs.

13. The US sponsored the *mujahedin* and foreign Arab fighters, while Saudi Arabia and Pakistan supported the Taliban, who gave al-Qaida a base in Afghanistan.
14. In light of the above, the reactionary 'othering' of Muslim practices and principles started to become more prevalent in 1980s, particularly among some right-wing politicians, the media and popular discourses. The Iran hostage crisis, as well as the publication of and reactions to Salman Rushdie's *Satanic Verses* in the late 1980s, significantly fuelled anti-Muslim sentiment and further objectified Muslims as outsiders. The Rushdie crisis was a turning point for many liberal and leftist intellectuals, historically anti-racist activists, who also began to question the compatibility of Western and Islamic principles.
15. Until recently, Muslims in the US were mostly African Americans and perceived in these racial terms. Socio-economically, Muslim Americans from MENA and South Asia fare better than Muslims in Western Europe. See 'Muslim America: Islamic yet integrated. Why Muslim Americans fare better in America', *The Economist*, 6 September 2014, available at <https://www.economist.com/united-states/2014/09/06/islamic-yet-integrated> (last accessed 24 February 2019).
16. According to CAIR (Council of American/Islamic Relations) there have been four waves of anti-Muslim hate crime in the US since 9/11. The first, immediately after 9/11, was followed by a settled period. The second wave was in 2006, probably due to images of unruly Muslim protests against Danish cartoons depicting the Prophet Muhammad, as well as escalating wars in Iraq and Afghanistan. The third, in 2010, was most likely due to the Park51 controversy in New York, in which the city announced building a Muslim community centre and mosque near Ground Zero. And finally, the most recent and concentrated surge, at the end of 2015, has been linked to Charlie Hebdo attacks in Paris and Donald Trump's campaign promise in 2016 to ban Muslims from entering the US until 'we figure out what's going on', available at: <http://www.cair.com/> (last accessed 11 June 2018).
17. These views dovetail with Korteweg and Yurdakul's large-scale research on the headscarf in France, Turkey, Germany and the Netherlands, as well as Canada, the UK and the US. Focusing on dominant discourses in the respective countries, they found common constructions of the headscarf as a symbol of gender inequality, visceral discomfort and a marker of those who do not belong to the nation (Korteweg and Yurdakul 2014). Their research also stressed the necessity to situate the veil debates in relation to the specificities of various historical, political and discursive trajectories.
18. A term coined by Miriam Cooke conflating a woman oppressed by her religion, her culture and her religion. See Cooke et al. (2008).
19. The Clarion Fund is a group that identifies itself as a non-profit organisation that produces and distributes documentaries on the threat of radical Islam. See Stein and Salime (2015: 378–96).
20. See, for example <https://clarionproject.org/senate-ayaan-asra/> (last accessed 11 March 2018).

21. A term used by Sunier (2012) meaning 'Western countries that amalgamate integration, securitization and the "domestification of Islam"'.
22. Available at: <https://www.nytimes.com/2006/03/16/world/europe/16iht-dutch-5852942.html> (last accessed 2 May 2018).
23. See also Joe Mulhall (2016), available at <https://www.opendemocracy.net/can-europe-make-it/joe-mulhall/anti-muslim-hatred-from-margins-to-mainstream> (last accessed 11 July 2018).
24. This is despite ongoing internal cleavages, such class, region, ethnicity, education levels, different religious leaders (*marjas*) and their rulings, gender differentiations, and so forth.

Bibliography

Abu El Haj, Nadia (2008), 'Edward Said and the political present', *American Ethnologist*, 32: 4, pp. 538–55.
Abu-Lughod, Lila (1991), 'Writing against culture', in R. G. Fox (ed.), *Recapturing Anthropology: Working in the Present*, Santa Fe: School of American Research Press, pp. 137–61.
—— (2002), 'Do Muslim women really need saving? *American Anthropologist*, 104: 3, pp. 783–790.
—— (2013), 'Do Muslim women need saving?' *Academe*, May, pp. 21–4.
—— (2015), *Do Muslim Women Need Saving?*, Cambridge, MA: Harvard University Press.
Ahmad, Aijaz (1992), 'Orientalism and after: ambivalence and cosmopolitan location in the work of Edward Said', *Economic and Political Weekly*, 27: 30, pp. 98–116.
Aidi, Hisham (2014), *Rebel Music Race, Empire and the New Muslim Youth Culture*, New York: Vintage Books.
Akbarzadeh, Shahram and Fethi Mansouri (2010), *Islam and Political Violence: Muslim Diaspora and Radicalism in the West*, London: I. B. Tauris.
Aitchison, Cara, Peter Hopkins and Nei-Po Kwan (eds) (2007), *Geographies of Muslim Identities: Diaspora, Gender and Belonging*, Aldershot: Ashgate Publishing.
Alba, Richard, and Mary Waters (2011), *The Next Generation: Immigrant Youth in Comparative Perspective*, New York: New York University Press.
Albrecht, Sara, Tobial Boos, Veronika Deffner, Matthias Gebauer and Shadi Husseini de Araujo (2016) 'Conceptualising "Muslim Diaspora"', *Journal of Muslims in Europe*, 5: 1, pp. 1–9.
Ali, Kecia (2006), *Sexual Ethics and Islam: Feminist Refelctions on Qur'an, Hadith and Jurisprudence*, Oxford: Oneworld.
Al-Ali, Nadje Sadig (2007), *Iraqi Women: Untold Stories from 1948 to the Present*, London and New York: Zed Books.
Al-Ali, Nadje (2013), 'Iraq: gendering authoritarianism', *Open Democracy*, 15 July, <https://www.opendemocracy.net/5050/nadje-al-ali/iraq-gendering-authoritarianism> (last accessed 11 March 2017).
Alterman, E. (2011), 'The professors, the press, the think tanks – and their problems', *Academe*, May–June, 97: 3, pp. 21–3.

Amera, Fadela and Sylvia Zappi (2003–4), *Ni Putes Ni Soumises*, Paris: La Découverte.

Amman, Birgit (2005), 'Kurds in Germany', in I. Skoggard, C. R. Ember and M. Ember (eds), *Encyclopedia of Diasporas: Immigrant and Refugee Cultures Around the World*, New York: Springer, pp. 1011–19.

Attiah, Karen (2017), 'How Trump's travel ban uses Muslim women as pawns', *The Washington Post*, 16 March.

Aydun, Berna (2014), 'Child sexual abuse in Turkey: an analysis of 1002 cases', *Journal of Forensic Sciences*, 60: 1 pp. 61–5.

Ballard, Roger (1996), 'Islam and the construction of Europe', in W. A. R. Shadid and P. S. van Koningsveld, *Muslims in the Margin: Political Responses to the Presence of Islam in Western Europe*, Kampen: Kok Pharos Publishers, pp. 15–51.

Bangstad, Sindred (2011), 'The morality police are coming! Muslims in Norway's media discourses', *Anthropology Today*, 27: 5, pp. 3–7.

Barlas, Asma (2004), *'Believing women' in Islam: Unreading Patriarchal Interpretations of the Qur'an*, Karachi: SAMA.

Berlet, Chip (2012), 'Violence, demonization, and apocalyptic aggression', *Talk to Action*, 22 August, <http://www.talk2action.org/story/2012/8/22/133522/648> (last accessed 4 February 2017).

Berlet, Chip and Matthew Lyons (2000), *Right-wing populism in America: Too Close for Comfort*, New York: Guilford Press.

Berman, Daphna (2007), *'Obsession' Stokes Passions, Fears and Controversy*, Algeria, n. pub.

Berman, Paul (2004), *Terror and Liberalism*, New York: Norton.

Bowen, John, (2004), 'Beyond migration: Islam as a transnational public space', *Journal of Ethnic and Migration Studies*, 30, pp. 879–94.

—— (2010), *Can Islam be French? Pluralism and Pragmatism in a Secularist State*, Princeton: Princeton University Press.

—— (2013), 'Panorama's exposé of sharia councils didn't tell the full story', *The Guardian*, 26 April, <https://www.theguardian.com/commentisfree/belief/2013/apr/26/panorama-expose-sharia-councils-balance> (last accessed 25 February 2019).

—— (2016), *On British Islam: Religion, Law, and Everyday Practice in Shari'a Councils*, Princeton: Princeton University Press.

Bradshaw, Leah and David Tabachnick (2017), *Citizenship and Multiculturalism in Western Liberal Democracies*, Lanham, MD: Lexington Books.

Brah, Avtar (1996), *Cartographies of Diaspora: Contesting Identities*, London and New York: Routledge.

Brechnin, Jessie (2013), 'A study of the use of sharia law in religious arbitration in the United Kingdom and the concerns that this raises for human rights', *Ecclesiastical Law Journal*, Cambridge, 15: 3, pp. 293–315.

Breckenridge, Carol A. and Peter van der Veer (1993), *Orientalism and the Postcolonial Predicament: Perspectives on South Asia*, Philadelphia: University of Pennsylvania Press.

Brubaker, Rogers (2002), 'Ethnicity without groups', *Archives Européennes de Sociologie*, 43: 2, pp. 163–89.

—— (2006), 'The "diaspora" diaspora', *Ethnic and Racial Studies*, 28, pp. 1–19.

—— (2017), 'Why populism?', *Theory Society*, 46, pp. 357–85.

Brubaker, Rogers and Frederick Cooper (2000), 'Beyond "identity"', *Theory and Society*, 29: 1, pp. 1–47.
Bunzl, M. (2005), 'Between anti-Semitism and Islamophobia: some thoughts on the new Europe', *American Ethnologist*, 33: 4, pp. 499–508.
Caeiro, Alexandre (2005), 'Religious authorities or political actors? The Muslim leaders of the French representative body of Islam', in J. Cesari and S. McLoughlin (eds), *European Muslims and the Secular State*, Aldershot: Ashgate, pp. 71–84.
Castle, Stephen and Kimiko De Freytas-Tamura (2014), 'Britain's rift on schools and Islam grows wider', *New York Times*, 8 June.
Cesari, Jocelyne (1998), *Musulmans et Republicains, Les jeunes, l'islam et la France*, Brussels: Complexe.
—— (2009), 'The securitisation of Islam in Europe', *The Changing Landscape of European Liberty and Security*, The Challenge Observatory, Research Paper No. 15, April.
—— (2013), *Why the West Fears Islam: an Exploration of Muslims in Liberal democracies*, New York: Palgrave Macmillan.
Cesari, Jocelyne and Sean McLoughlin (2005), *European Muslims and the Secular State*, Aldershot: Ashgate Publishing Limited.
Chew, Huibin Amelia (2008), 'What's left? After "imperial feminist hijackings"', in R. L. Riley, C. T. Mohanty and M. B. Pratt, *Feminism and War: Confronting US Imperialism*, London and New York: Zed Books, pp. 75–91.
Cincotta, Thomas (2011), *Manufacturing the Muslim Menace: Private Firms, Public Servants, and the Threat to Rights and Security*, Somerville, MA: Political Research Associates.
Cohen, Robin (2008), *Global Diasporas: An Introduction*, London and New York: Routledge.
Cooke, Miriam, Fawzia Ahmad, Margot Badran, Minoo Moallem and Jazmin Zine (2008), 'Roundtable discussion: religion, gender, and the Muslimwoman', *Journal of Feminist Studies in Religion*, 24: 1, pp. 91–119.
Corbett, Rosemary, R. (2016), *Making Moderate Islam: Sufism, Service and the 'Ground Zero mosque' Controversy*, Stanford, CA: Stanford University Press.
Council on American–Islamic Relations (2016), 'New CAIR, UC Berkeley report reveals funding, negative impact of Islamophobic groups in America' 20 June, <https://www.cair.com/new_cair_uc_berkeley_report_reveals_funding_negative_impact_of_islamophobic_groups_in_america> (last accessed 25 February 2019).
Cousin, Bruno and Tommosa Vitale (2012), 'Italian intellectuals and the promotion of Islamophobia after 9/11, in G. Morgan and S. Poynting (eds), *Global Islamophobia: Muslims and Moral Panic*, Farnham: Ashgate, pp. 47–56.
de Koning, Anouk and Wayne Modest (2016), 'Anxious politics in the European city: an introduction', *Patterns of Prejudice*, 50: 2, pp. 97–108.
de Koning, Martjin (2010), 'The quest for religious purity in New Age, Evangelicalism and Islam: religious renditions of Dutch youth and the Luckmann legacy', *Annual Review of the Sociology of Religion – 2009: Youth and Religion*, 1, pp. 289–306.
—— (2016), '"You need to present a counter-message": the racialisation of Dutch Muslims and anti-Islamophobia initiatives', *Journal of Muslims in Europe*, 5: 2, pp. 170–89.
Dittmar, Linda (2004), 'Fending off the barbarians: Agit-Media and the Middle East', *Cinema Journal*, 43: 4, pp. 108-114.

Dittmer, Jason and Tristan Sturm (2011), *Mapping the End Times: American Evangelical Geopolitics and Apocalyptic Visions*, London: Routledge.
Eade, John (1996), 'Nationalism, community, and the Islamization of space in London', in B. D. Metcalf (ed.), *Making Muslim Space in North America and Europe*, Berkeley: University of California Press, pp. 217–33.
Eickelman, Dale and Jim Piscatori (1996), *Muslim Politics*, Princeton: Princeton University Press.
Elsadda, Hoda (2012), *Gender, Nation and the Arabic Novel, 1882–2008*, New York: Syracuse University Press.
Elsheikh, Elsadig (2017), *Legalizing Other: the United States of Islamophobia*, Berkeley: Haas Institute.
Enstedt, Daniel and Goran Larsson (2013), 'Telling the truth about Islam? Apostasy narratives and representations of Islam,' *CyberOrient*, 7: 1.
Ewing, Katherine (2008), *Being and Belonging: Muslim Communities in the US since 9/11*, New York: Russell Sage Foundation.
Ferrari, Silvio (2005), 'The secularity of the state and the shaping of Muslim representative organizations in Western Europe' in J. Cesari and S. McLoughlin (eds), *European Muslims and the Secular State*, Aldershot: Ashgate, pp. 11–24.
Freedman, Samuel (2011), 'Waging a one-man war on American Muslims,' *The New York Times*, 16 December, <https://www.nytimes.com/2011/12/17/us/on-religion-a-one-man-war-on-american-muslims.html> (last accessed 10 January 2017).
—— (2012), 'If the Sikh temple had been a mosque,' *The New York Times*, 10 August, <https://www.nytimes.com/2012/08/11/us/if-the-sikh-temple-had-been-a-muslim-mosque-on-religion.html> (last accessed 11 June 2018).
Gaspard, Francoise and Farhad Khosrokhavar (1995), *Le foulard et la Republique*, Paris: La Découverte.
Geller, Pamela (2014), 'DC media, more anti-Islamic metro bus ads on the way', *Geller Report*, 15 May, <http://pamelageller.com/2014/05/dc-media-anti-islamic-metro-> (last accessed 15 February 2017).
Geaves, Robert (2007), 'A reassessment of identity strategies amongst South Asian British Muslims', in J. R. Hinnells (ed.), *Religious Reconstruction in the South Asian Diasporas: From One Generation to Another*, Basingstoke: Palgrave Macmillan, pp. 13–28.
Gilliat-Ray, Sophie (2010), *Muslims in Britain*, Cambridge: Cambridge University Press.
Gilroy, Paul (1993), *The Black Atlantic: Modernity and Double Consciousness*, Cambridge, MA: Harvard University Press.
Grandin, Greg (2009), 'Empire's workshop: Latin America, the United States and the rise of the new imperialism', *American Empire Project*, Holt Paperbacks.
Grattan, Alan (2016), 'Jihadi John, and how to make a moral panic', *The Justice Gap*, March 1, <https://www.thejusticegap.com/proof-magazine-jihadi-john-and-how-to-make-a-moral-panic/> (last accessed 26 February 2019)
Grillo, Ralph (2004), 'Development anthropology: encounters in the real world,' *American Anthropologist*, 106: 2, p. 424.
—— (2015), *Muslim Families, Politics and the Law: a Legal Industry in Multicultural Britain*, Farnham: Ashgate.
Guénif-Souilamas, Nacira (2017), 'Restrained equality: a sexualized and gendered colour

line', in S. Jonsson and J. Willén (eds), *Austere Histories in European Societies: Social Exclusion and the Contest of Colonial Memories*, Abingdon: Routledge, pp. 161–81.

Gupta, Rahila (2017), 'Is PREVENT too toxic for feminists?', *Feminist Dissent*, 2, pp. 176–88.

Hall, Stuart (1990), 'Cultural identity and diaspora', *Framework*, 36, pp. 222–37.

—— (2003), 'Cultural identity and diaspora', in J. E. Braziel and A. Mannur (eds), *Theorising Diaspora: a Reader*, Oxford: Blackwell, pp. 233–46.

Haritaworn, Jin (2012), 'Women's rights, gay rights and anti-Muslim racism in Europe', *European Journal of Women's Studies*, 19: 1, pp. 73–8.

Hofstadter, Richard (1964), 'The Paranoid style in American politics', *Harper's Magazine*, pp. 77–86.

Hoodfar, Homa (1997), *Between Marriage and the Market: Intimate Politics and Survival in Cairo*, Comparative Studies on Muslim Societies, Berkeley and Los Angeles: University of California Press.

Humphrey, Michael (2007), 'Culturalising the abject: Islam, law and moral panic in the West', *Australian Journal of Social Issues*, 42:1, pp. 9–25.

Huntington, Samuel P. (1993), *The Clash of Civilizations and the Remaking of World Order*, New York: Simon & Schuster.

Inge, Anabel (2016), *The Making of a Salafi Muslim Woman: Paths to Conversion*, Oxford: Oxford University Press.

Jamal, Amaney and Nadine Naber (2007), *Race and Arab Americans Before and After 9/11: from Invisible Citizens to Visible Subjects*, Syracuse: Syracuse University Press.

Janssen, Esther (2015), *Faith in Public Debate: on Freedom of Expression, Hate Speech and Religion in France & The Netherlands*, School of Human Rights Research, Cambridge: Intersentia.

Jenkins, Everett (1999), *The Muslim Diaspora: a Comprehensive Chronology of the Spread of Islam in Asia, Africa, Europe and the Americas, Vol. 1, 570–1500*, London: McFarland & Company.

Jiwani, Yasmin (2004), 'Gendering terror: representations of the orientalized body in Quebec's post-September 11 English-language press', *Critique: Critical Middle Eastern Studies*, 13: 3, pp. 265–91.

Joly, Daniele and Khursheed Wadia (2017), *Muslim Women and Power: Political and Civic Engagement in West European Societies*, Basingstoke: Palgrave Macmillan.

Jonker, Gerdien (2005), 'From "foreign works" to "sleepers": the churches, the state and Germany's "discovery" of its Muslim population', in J. Cesari and S. McLoughlin (eds), *European Muslims and the Secular State*, Aldershot: Ashgate, pp. 113–28.

Jonsson, Stefan and Julia Willen (2017), *Austere Histories in European Societies: Social Exclusion and the Contest of Colonial Memories*, Abingdon: Routledge.

Joppke, Christian and John Torpey (2013), *Legal Integration of Islam: a Transatlantic Comparison*, Cambridge, MA: Harvard University Press.

Kandiyoti, Deniz (1991), *Women, Islam and the State*, Philadelphia: Temple University Press.

—— (2007), 'Between the hammer and the anvil: post-conflict reconstruction, Islam and women's rights', *Third World Quarterly*, 28: 3, pp. 503–17.

—— (2015), 'The triple whammy: towards the eclipse of women's rights', *Open Democracy*, 19 January, <https://www.opendemocracy.net/5050/deniz-kandiyoti/

triple-whammy-towards-eclipse-of-women's-rights> (last accessed 26 February 2019).
Kepel, Gilles (2004), *The War for Muslim Minds: Islam and the West*, Cambridge, MA: Belknap Press of Harvard University Press.
—— (2006), *The War for Muslim Minds: Islam and the West*, Cambridge, MA: Belknap Press of Harvard University Press.
Khan, Shahnaz (2000), *Crafting a North American Identity*, Gainesville: University Press of Florida.
Klager, Florjan and Klaus Stierstorfer (2015), *Diasporic Constructions of Home and Belonging*, Berlin and Boston: Walter de Gruyter.
Knott, Kim (1997), 'The religion of South Asian communities in Britain', in J. R. Hinnells (ed.), *New Handbook of Living Religions*, Oxford: Blackwell, pp. 756–74.
Knott, Kim and Khokher Sadja (1993), 'Religious and ethnic identity among young Muslim women in Bradford', *New Community*, 19, pp. 593–610.
Korteweg, Anna, and Gökçe Yurdakul (2014), *The Headscarf Debates: Conflicts of National Belonging*, Standford, CA: Stanford University Press.
Kumar, D. (2012), *Islamophobia and the Politics of Empire*, Chicago: Haymarket Books.
Kundnani, Arun (2001), 'From Oldham to Bradford: the violence of the violated', *Race and Class*, 43: pp. 41–60.
—— (2009), 'Spooked: how not to prevent violent extremism', Institute of Race Relations Report.
Lean, Nathan, (2017) *The Islamophobia Industry: How the Right Manufactures Fears of Muslims*, London: Pluto Press.
Lentin, Alana (2015), 'What does race do?', *Ethnic and Racial Studies*, 38: 8, pp. 1401–6.
Leweling, Maj Tara (2005), 'Exploring Muslim Diaspora Communities in Europe through a Social Movement Lens: Some Initial Thoughts', *Strategic Insights*, 4: 5, Monterey: Center for Contemporary Conflict.
Lewis, Bernard (1990), 'The roots of Muslim rage', *The Atlantic*, September, <https://www.theatlantic.com/magazine/archive/1990/09/the-roots-of-muslim-rage/304643/> (last accessed 21 April 2018).
Lewis, Philip (2007), *Young, British and Muslim*, London: Continuum.
Lobe, Jim (2007), 'David Horowitz declares Islamofascism awareness week for October 22–26', *Lobe Log*.
Love, E. (2013), 'Beyond post-9/11', *Contexts*, 12: 1, Winter, pp. 70–2.
Ma'Oz, Moshe and Gabriel Sheffer (2002), 'The Muslim diaspora in the West', in M Ma'Oz and G Sheffer (eds), *Middle Eastern Minorities and Diasporas*, Brighton and Portland: Sussex Academic Press, p. 219.
Mahmood, Saba (2005), *Politics of Piety: the Islamic Revival and the Feminist Subject*, Princeton: Princeton University Press.
—— (2006), *Secularism, Hermeneutics, and Empire: the Politics of Islamic Reformation*, Durham, NC: Duke University Press.
Malik, Jamal (2013), 'Integration of Muslim migrants and the politics of dialogue: the case of modern Germany', *Journal of Muslim Minority Affairs*, 33: 4, pp. 495–506.
Mamdani, Mahmood (2000), *Beyond Rights Talk and Culture Talk*, New York: St Martin's.
—— (2004), *Good Muslim, Bad Muslim: America, the Cold War, and the Roots of Terror*, New York: Three Leaves Press.

Mandaville, Peter (2001), *Transnational Muslim Politics: Reimagining the Umma*, London and New York: Routledge.
Manoukian, Setrag (2011), 'Conceptualizing Iranian anthropology: past and present perspectives', *Journal of the Royal Anthropological Institute*, 17: 3, pp. 669–70.
Modood, Tariq (2005), *Multicultural Politics, Racism, Ethnicity, and Muslims in Britain*, Minneapolis: University of Minnesota Press.
—— (2007), *Multiculturalism, a Civic Idea*, Cambridge, Polity.
—— (2011), 'Capitals, ethnic identity and educational qualifications,' in R. Alba and M. C. Waters, *Next Generation Immigrant Youth in a Comparative Perspective*, New York: New York University Press, pp. 185–206.
Modood, Tariq, Richard Berthoud, J. Lakey, James Nazroo, and Philip Smith (1997), *Ethnic Minorities in Britain: Diversity and Disadvantage – Fourth National Survey of Ethnic Minorities*, London: London Policy Studies Institute.
Moghadam, Valentine (2000), 'Transnational feminist networks: collective action in an era of globalization', *International Sociology*, 15: 1, pp. 57–85.
Moghissi, Haideh (2006), *Muslim Diaspora: Gender, Culture and Identity*, New York: Routledge.
Moghissi, Haideh and Halleh Ghorashi (2010), *Muslim Diaspora in the West: Negotiating Gender, Home and Belonging*, Farnham and Burlington: Ashgate.
Moghissi, Haideh, Saeed Rahnema and Mark J. Goodman (2009), *Diaspora by Design: Muslims in Canada and Beyond*, Toronto: University of Toronto Press.
Mohanty, Aliva (2006), *Development of Rural Women*, Delhi: Yash Publications.
Mojab, Shahrzad and Rachel Gorman (2007), 'Dispersed nationalism: war, diaspora, and Kurdish women's organizing', *Journal of Middle East Women's Studies*, 3: 1, pp. 58–85.
Morgan and George, Scott Poynting (eds) (2012), *Global Islamophobia: Muslims and Moral Panic*, Farnham: Ashgate.
Mustafa, Asma (2015), *Identity and Public Participation among Young British Muslims*, Basingstoke: Palgrave Macmillan.
Naber, Nadine (2008), 'Look, Mohammed the terrorist in coming!': cultural racism, nation-based racism and the intersectionality of oppressions after 9/11', in A. Jamal and N. Naber (eds), *Race and Arab Americans Before and After 9/11*, Syracuse: Syracuse University Press, pp. 276–304.
—— (2012), *Arab America: Gender, Cultural Politics, and Activism*, New York: New York University Press.
Niehaus, Holger and Willhelm Achelpöhler (2004), Data screening as a means of preventing Islamic terrorist attacks on Germany', *German Law Journal*, 5: 5, pp. 495–513.
Nussbaum, M. (2012), *The new religious intolerance*, Cambridge, MA: Harvard University.
Oborne, Peter (2018), 'We do not report fairly on Muslims' *British Journalism Review*, 29:1, pp. 29–34.
Pakes, Franis (2012), 'The panicky debate, Moroccan youth in Netherlands', in G. Morgan and S. Poynting (eds), *Global Islamophobia: Muslims and Moral Panic*, Farnham: Ashgate, pp. 35–46.
Parekh, Bhikhu [2000] (2004), 'The report of the Commission on the Future of Multi-Ethnic Britain', *Runnymede Trust Briefing Paper*, London: The Runnymede Trust.
Pargeter, Alison (2008), *The New Frontiers of Jihad: Radical Islam in Europe*, Philadelphia: University of Pennsylvania Press.

Patel, Pragna (2008), 'Defining secular spaces', *New Statesman*, 4 August, <https://www.newstatesman.com /uk-politics/2008/08/religious-state-secular> (last accessed 3 November 2018).

Petchesky, Rosalind (2003), *Global Prescriptions: Gendering Health and Human Rights*, Chicago: University of Chicago Press.

Pew Research (2011), 'Muslim-Western tensions persist', <http://www.pewresearch.org/wp-content/uploads/sites/2/2011/07/Pew-Global-Attitudes-Muslim-Western-Relations-FINAL-FOR-PRINT-July-21-2011.pdf> (last accessed 8 July 2018).

—— (2017), 'Europe's growing Muslim population', 29 November, <http://www.pewforum.org/2017/11/29/europes-growing-muslim-population/> (last accessed 8 July 2018).

Powell, Michael (2012), 'In police training, a dark film on US Muslims', *The New York Times*, 23 January, <https://www.nytimes.com/2012/01/24/nyregion/in-police-training-a-dark-film-on-us-muslims.html> (last accessed 13 March 2017).

Project for the New American Century (2014), <https://www.bibliotecapleyades.net/sociopolitica/sociopol_PNAC01.htm> (last accessed 10 January 2017).

Al-Qaradawi, Yusuf (2000), *The Lawful and Prohibited in Islam*, London: Dar Al Taqwa.

Rahnema, Saeed (2006), 'Islam in diaspora and challenges to multiculturalism', in Haideh Moghissi (ed.), *Muslim Diaspora: Gender, Culture and Identity*, New York; London: Routledge, pp. 23–38.

Reich, R. B. (2013), 'American bile', *The New York Times*, 22 September.

Roy, Olivier (2007), *Secularism Confronts Islam*, New York: Columbia University Press.

Runnymede Trust (1997), *Islamophobia: a Challenge for Us All*, London: Runneymede Trust, <https://www.runnymedetrust.org/companies/17/74/Islamophobia-A-Challenge-for-Us-All.html> (last accessed 12 March 2017).

Safran, William (1991), 'Diasporas in modern societies: myths of homeland and return', *Diasporas: a Journal of Transnational Studies*, 1:1, Spring, pp. 83–99.

Said, Edward (1979), *Orientalism*, New York: Random House.

Saint-Blancat, Chantal (2008), 'Islam in diaspora: between reterritorialization and extraterritoriality', *International Journal of Urban and Regional Research*, 26: 1, pp. 138–51.

Salih, K.O. (2007), 'Underlying causes of violence in the Middle East', *Digest of Middle East Studies*, 16: 1, pp. 58–98.

Salih, Ruba (2003), *Gender in Transnationalism: Home, Longing, and Belonging Among Moroccan Migrant Women*, London: Routledge.

—— (2010), 'Transnational public spheres from "above" and "below": feminist networks across the Middle East and Europe', *Anthropology of the Middle East*, 5: 1, pp. 53–70.

Samers, Michael E. (2003), 'Diaspora unbound: Muslim identity and the erratic regulation of Islam in France', *International Journal of Population Geography*, 9: 4, pp. 351–64.

Sayyid, S. (2000), 'Beyond Westphalia: nations and diasporas: the case of the Muslim *umma*', in B. Hesse and S. Sayyid (ed.) *Un/settled Multiculturalisms: Diasporas, Entanglements, Transruptions*, London: Zed Books, p. 33.

Schulman, S. (2011), 'Israel and pinkwashing', *The New York Times*, <http://www.nytimes.com/2011/11/23/opinion/pinkwashing-and-israels-use-of-gays-as-a-messaging-tool.html?_r¼0> (last accessed 25 February 2018).

Schumann, Christoph (2007), 'A Muslim 'diaspora' in the United States?', *The Muslim World*, 97: 1, pp. 11–32.
Shadid, W. A. R. and P. S.Van Koningsveld (eds) (1996), *Margin: Politcal Responses to the Presence of Islam in Western Europe*, Kampen: Kok Pharos Publishers.
Shanneik, Yafa, Chris Heinhold and Zahra Ali (2017), 'Mapping Shia Muslim communities in Europe: local and transnational dimensions: an introduction to the special issue', *Journal of Muslims in Europe*, 6: 2, pp. 145–57.
Shatz, A. (2008), 'Short cuts', *London Review of Books*, 30: 19, 9 October, <http://www.lrb.co.uk/v30/n19/shtz01_.html> (last accessed 4 February 2017).
—— (2017), 'How the Tariq Ramadan scandal derailed the #Balancetonporc Movement in France', *The New Yorker*, 29 November.
Sheehi, S. (2011), *Islamophobia: the Ideological Campaign Against Muslims*, Atlanta, GA: Clarity Press.
Spellman, Kathryn (2004), *Religion and Nation: Iranian Local and Transnational Networks in London*, Oxford and New York: Berghahn Books.
Spellman Poots, Kathryn (2012), 'Manifestations of Ashura among young British Shi'is', in B. Dupret, T. Pierrot, P. G. Pinto and K. Spellman Poots (eds), *Ethnographies of Islam*, Edinburgh: Edinburgh University Press, pp. 40–9.
—— (2013), 'Who is Hussain?' *The Middle East in London Magazine*, London: SOAS, 9: 4, pp. 7–8.
—— (2018), 'Second-generation Muslims and the making of British Shi'ism', in M. Bozorgmehr and P. Kasinitz (eds), *Growing Up Muslim in Europe and the United States*, New York: Routledge, pp. 192–208.
Spellman Poots, Kathryn, and Sami Zubaida (2013), 'Middle Eastern religious minorities', *The Middle East in London Magazine*, London: SOAS, 9: 4, p. 4.
Spellman Poots, Kathryn and Reza Gholami (2018), 'Iranian immigrants in Great Britain', in M. M. Mobasher (ed.), *The Iranian Diaspora: Challenges, Negotiations, and Transformations*, Austin: University of Texas Press, pp. 93–124.
Stein, Arlene (2001), *The Stranger Next Door: the Story of a Small Town's Battle over Sex, Faith, and Civil Rights*, Boston, MA: Beacon.
Stein, Arlene and Zakia Salime (2015), 'Manufacturing Islamophobia: rightwing pseudo-documentaries and the paranoid style', *Journal of Communication Inquiry*, 39: 4, pp. 378–96.
Sunier, Thijl (2012), 'Beyond the domestification of Islam in Europe: a reflection on past and future research on Islam in European societies', *Journal of Muslims in Europe*, 1, pp. 189–208.
Vertovec, Steven and Ceri Peach (1997), *Islam in Europe: the Politics of Religion and Community*, Basingstoke: Palgrave Macmillan.
Wadud, Amina (2006), *Inside the Gender Jihad: Women's Reform in Islam*, London: Oneworld Publications.
Waldron, Jeremy (2012), *The Harm in Hate Speech*, Cambridge, MA: Harvard University Press.
Werbner, Pnina (2000), 'Divided loyalties, empowered citizenship? Muslims in Britain', *Citizenship Studies*, 4: 3, pp. 307–24.
—— (2002a), *Imagined Diasporas Among Manchester Muslims: the Public Performance of*

Pakistani Transnational Identity Politics, Oxford: James Currey.
—— (2002b), 'The place which is diaspora: citizenship, religion and gender in the making of chaordic transnationalism', *Journal of Ethnic and Migration Studies*, 28: 1, pp. 119–33.
—— (2003) *Pilgrims of Love: the Anthropology of a Global Sufi Cult*, London and Bloomington: Hurst and Indiana University Press.
—— (2007), 'Veiled interventions in pure space: honour, shame, and embodied struggles among Muslims in Britain and France', *Theory, Culture, and Society*, 24: 2, pp. 161–86.
—— (2009), 'Revisiting the UK Muslim diasporic public sphere at a time of terror: from local (benign) invisible spaces to seditious conspiratorial spaces and the "failure of multiculturalism" discourse', *South Asian Diaspora*, 1: 1, pp. 19–45.
Yuval-Davis, Nira (1993), 'Gender and nation', *Ethnic and Racial Studies*, 16: 4, pp. 621–32.
Zakaria, Rafia (2017), 'Why Donald Trump needs Muslim women', *The Nation*, 11 August.
Zubaida, Sami (2003), 'Islam in Europe', *Critical Quarterly*, 45: 1–2, pp. 44–56.
—— (2007), 'The many faces of multiculturalism', *Open Democracy*, 5 June, <www.opendemocracy.net/faith-europe_islam/many_faces_4677.Jsp> (last accessed 12 June 2018).
—— (2011), *Beyond Islam: a New Understanding of the Middle East*, London: I. B. Tauris.

Epilogue: Locating Gender in Contentious Politics

Deniz Kandiyoti

Looking back on the contents of this volume, I could not help but be struck by the remarkable array of instances of resistance against dominant gender orders. These range from individual acts of rebellion, such as Saudi women fleeing the strictures of the male guardianship system or iconoclastic online activists in Pakistan breaking sexual taboos, to collective dissent through protests on the streets of Istanbul, Cairo or Tehran. Dissent, however, can be extremely costly. In countries like Iraq and Afghanistan, where armed factions continue to be locked in conflict, women's rights activists or simply those who dare to step into the public domain may risk their lives. Furthermore, contentious politics generally unfolds against a background of both state-led and bottom-up reactions against any potential threats to entrenched male privileges or conservative gender regimes. These reactions may be variously couched in the language of national identity, cultural authenticity, moral propriety, social stability, Islamic codes or, more often than not, eclectic juxtapositions of those. What is beyond doubt is that an unprecedented level of societal polarisation pits those who acquiesce to and uphold authoritarian rule and strongman leadership against women and men who recognise aspirations to gender equality as part and parcel of a package of demands for democratic representation, human rights and pluralism. This polarisation defies facile categorisations based on gender since both men and women may find themselves on opposite sides of this divide.

The inroads made by global gender equality regimes and donor-assisted rights platforms have tended to be greatly played up in academic circles (whether in positive or critical terms). To the extent that countries are enmeshed, to varying degrees, in complex relations with global governance apparatuses the effects of these inroads cannot be denied. However, as we have seen throughout this volume, governments routinely make selective and instrumental use of gender platforms in pursuit of domestic and geopolitical goals while rights activists endeavour to make strategic use of any spaces available to them, often with only modest degrees of success. It is therefore endogenous dynamics and idioms we must turn to for a better grasp of contentious politics around gender issues.

Although state practices are gendered everywhere a particularly explicit connection exists in the countries surveyed in this volume, regardless of their regime types, between the language of power and that of patriarchal authority. Power-holders often utilise the idiom of patriarchy to legitimise their regulation of citizens' lives, to suppress dissent and manufacture consent. They generally enlist men to their project of rule by explicitly upholding male prerogatives over the control of women both in law and through daily practices. The trade-off in abdicating authority to autocratic state rule, especially for men of popular classes who are themselves subordinated in the class hierarchy, is to retain control over the domestic and communal domains, a control deemed central to the exercise of masculinity. It is this social contract – and its attendant conceptions of masculinity and femininity – that has long sustained cross-class and cross-party alliances among men that appeared to show unexpected cracks and fissures during the brief moments of euphoria that followed peoples' unrest such as the Arab uprisings of 2011 and the Gezi protests of 2013 in Turkey. These were followed by the rise of political Islam in some instances and renewed bids to restore authoritarian control. Whilst recognising that the shift from one mode of authoritarianism to another or from democratic regimes to autocratic rule are often enabled by the acquiescence or active support of the masses, the glimpses offered by the irruption of contentious politics, however ephemeral, are still worth reflecting on.

My personal moment of awakening was occasioned by a now long-forgotten episode of the Green Movement in Iran when after the contested 2009 presidential elections, Majid Tavakoli, a student leader was arrested after delivering a fiery speech against dictatorship and was alleged by pro-government news agencies to have been caught trying to escape dressed as a woman. A series of photographs showing him wearing a headscarf and *chador* were clearly intended to expose him as a coward, and to humiliate his supporters by association. This invitation to fall into line had an unexpected outcome: men started to post pictures of themselves wearing *hijab* on Facebook under the caption 'We are all Majid'. Their reactions embodied two simultaneous moves: ridiculing the regime's transparent and crude attempts to manipulate public opinion and rebuffing its bid to enlist men into accepting that an association with femininity debases them.

This fleeting episode was to be the harbinger of numerous displays of new political sensibilities and inventive means of subversion during the popular uprisings of 2011 and the events of the summer of 2013 in Turkey. The spectacle of mobilised men and women mocking authority, condemning the repression and violence perpetrated by state and non-state actors and unmasking the patriarchal pretensions of power became iconic. If resistance follows and contests the terms of systems of power, why should it surprise us to find anti-patriarchal contestations (and virulent reactions to them) in contexts where the language of power and patriarchy are most intimately and explicitly intertwined? Where does that leave patriarchy as a concept and as a set of practices?

The suppression of popular protests by power-holders may be routinely gendered and sexualised: male youth, and especially working-class youth, may be criminalised as 'terrorists' or out-of-control thugs, whereas women of all classes may be stigmatised as 'loose women' who become unworthy of protection once they step into the public domain. However, new barriers were breached by reactions to popular uprisings. The public revulsion felt in Egypt when female demonstrators were subjected to forced virginity tests in police custody or when they became targets of organised mass sexual molestation during demonstrations turned the spotlight on the political nature of violence as never before. For a long time, violence against women was primarily apprehended through the lens of domestic violence. Indeed, most abused women tended to know their assailants whose offences were routinely covered up to avoid dishonour and shame while states generally upheld kin prerogatives over the control of women in law or in practice. Participation in public collective action clearly exposes women to new types of retribution and brutality. Equally telling are instances of violence that occur in anonymous public spaces, are perpetrated by strangers, and have a deceptively random and spontaneous character such as the attacks on buses, streets and parks regularly reported in Turkey and which spark outrage when culprits are treated with leniency. Both these manifestations of violence, and societal reactions to them, break the mould of silence and dissimulation that were the hallmarks of patriarchy in its more traditional guise. Gender-based violence has now firmly entered the public domain eliciting storms of protest, debates, demonstrations, petitions, blogs, advocacy and solidarity campaigns. Societal transformations result in systems of rule – whether they claim to derive their legitimacy from Islam or not – no longer being able to contain the expectations of their citizenry, as illustrated in this volume by Iran's shifting accommodations to women's demands or by the cracks in the male guardianship system in Saudi Arabia.

The maintenance of patriarchal power becomes increasingly onerous when women have an apparently irreversible presence in the public domain as workers, public employees, artists, entrepreneurs, consumers and citizens. I proposed the term masculinist restoration (Kandiyoti 2013, 2016) to denote a break with the past and identify a phase when patriarchy is no longer secure and requires higher levels of coercion and the deployment of more varied ideological state apparatuses to ensure its reproduction. In this perspective, new patterns of violence against women can no longer be explained with reference to some assumed routine functioning of patriarchy but point to its threatened demise at a point in time when notions of male dominance and female subordination are no longer securely hegemonic. Whether at street level or at the level of governance the bid to maintain power may be reduced to its crudest coercive means and appeals to orthodoxy in Bourdieu's sense since the taken-for-granted fabric of patriarchal acquiescence is frayed and punctured by daily breaches of the gender order.

My tentative reflections were soon overtaken by the realisation that gender orders were undergoing massive convulsions on a global scale in the wake of a new wave of right-wing populisms and the turn to strongman politics. The misogynistic, homophobic and racist pronouncements and practices of new leaders and their visibly empowered followings have become the stuff of our daily headlines. Seldom have culture wars over the family, sexual mores and gender equality mapped more neatly onto political orientations. For those of us who have long argued for the need to de-Orientalise scholarship on gender in Muslim countries and their diasporas this conjuncture has driven home the message that we must finally locate the politics of gender where it belongs: at the frontlines of struggles for democracy and human rights.

Bibliography

Kandiyoti, Deniz (2013), 'Fear and-fury: women and post-revolutionary violence', *Open Democracy*, 10 January, <http://www.opendemocracy.net/5050/deniz-kandiyoti/fear-and-fury-women-and-post-revolutionary-violence> (last accessed 10 March 2018).

—— (2016), 'The fateful marriage: political violence and violence against women', *Open Democracy*, 25 January, <https://www.opendemocracy.net/5050/deniz-kandiyoti/fateful-marriage-political-violence-and-violence-against-women> (last accessed 10 March 2018).

About the Contributors

Nadje Al-Ali is Robert Family Professor of Middle East Studies at Brown University, having recently left her position as Professor of Gender Studies at SOAS, University of London. Her main research interests and publications revolve around feminist activism in the Middle East; transnational migration and diaspora mobilisation; war, conflict and reconstruction; art; cultural studies; and food. Her publications include *Iraqi Women: Untold Stories from 1948 to the Present* (2007); *What Kind of Liberation? Women and the Occupation of Iraq* (with N. Pratt, 2009) and *Secularism, Gender and the State in the Middle East: the Egyptian Women's Movement* (2000).

Islah Jad is Associate Professor of Political Science at the Women's Studies Institute and Cultural Studies Department at Birzeit University, Palestine. Her research interests include the role of women in politics, as well as Palestinian women and their relationship to Islam and NGOs. She is author of *Palestinian Women's Activism: Nationalism, Secularism, Islamism* (2018) and co-author of the UN Arab Development Report on Women's Empowerment (2006).

Deniz Kandiyoti is Emeritus Professor of Development Studies at SOAS, University of London. She pioneered new research into comparative perspectives on patriarchy and the implications of global governance, Islam and state policies for the politics of gender in Turkey, post-Soviet Central Asia and Afghanistan. Between 2011 and 2015 she monitored the effects of the Arab uprisings (as guest editor for 50.50 *Open Democracy*) analysing new forms of gender-based violence and grass-roots mobilisation. Her publications include *Fragments of Culture: the Everyday of Modern Turkey* (with A. Saktanber,

2002), *Gendering the Middle East* (1996) and *Women, Islam and the State* (1991).

Heba El Kholy is Executive Director of the Lutfia Rabbani Foundation in The Hague, the Netherlands. Previously, she was Director of the United Nations Development Programme (UNDP) Global Governance Policy Centre in Oslo, Norway. She has decades of field experience in development and peace-building and has held senior leadership positions in the United Nations including in the Sudan, Tunisia and Albania. She has published on governance, poverty and gender.

Madawi Al-Rasheed is Visiting Professor at the Middle East Centre, London School of Economics. Previously she was Professor of Social Anthropology at King's College, London. Her recent publications include *A Masculine State: Gender, Politics and Religion in Saudi Arabia* (2013), *Muted Modernists: the Struggle over Divine Politics in Saudi Arabia* (2015) and *Salman's Legacy: the Dilemmas of a New Era* (2018).

Nazanin Shahrokni is Assistant Professor of Sociology at the Maxwell School of Citizenship and Public Affairs at Syracuse University. She has held positions at Lund University, Harvard University, and the American University of Beirut. She is the author of *Women in Place: the Politics of Gender Segregation in Iran* (2019).

Kathryn Spellman Poots is Associate Professor at the Aga Khan University Institute for the Study of Muslim Civilisations and Visiting Associate Professor at Columbia University. Her research interests include Muslims in Europe and North America, the Iranian diaspora, transnational migration and gender studies. Her publications include *The Political Aesthetics of Global Protest: the Arab Spring and Beyond* (with P. Werbner and M. Webb, Edinburgh University Press/AKU-ISMC, 2014), *Ethnographies of Islam: Ritual Performances and Everyday Practices* (with B. Dupret, T. Pierret and P. G. Pinto, Edinburgh University Press/AKU-ISMC, 2012) and *Religion and Nation: Iranian Local and Transnational Networks in London* (2004).

Nadia Taher is a Development Anthropologist with expertise in the politics of development and gender and diversity in policy and planning. More recently she has focused on countries in political transition. She has worked in the Middle East, Africa and Asia. She was Director of the PhD Programme at the Development Planning Unit, University College London.

About the Contributors

Torunn Wimpelmann is a Senior Researcher at Chr. Michelsen Institute in Bergen, Norway. Her work focuses on gender, legal orders and politics in Afghanistan. Wimpelmann has published widely in Central Asian Survey, Women's Studies International Forum, Northern Ireland Legal Quarterly and with Routledge and Oxford University Press, and is the author of *The Pitfalls of Protection, Gender, Violence and Power in Afghanistan* (2017).

Afiya Shehrbano Zia is Adjunct Professor at Habib University, Pakistan. She is author of *Faith and Feminism in Pakistan: Religious Agency or Secular Autonomy?* (2018) and *Sex Crime in the Islamic Context* (1994).

Index

al-Abadi, Haider, 150, 158
Abbas, Mahmoud, 122
Abdalla, Mustafa, 31
Abdullah, Dr. Abdullah, 113, 114
Abdullah, King, 71–2, 74
Açik, Necla, 85
Açiksöz, Salih Can, 89
Adak, Sevgi, 90
'Afghan women question', 113, 114
Afghan Women's Network, 114
Afghanistan
    2004 Constitution, 106, 109, 110
    2014 election, 113
    'civil society women' activists, 107
    conflict, 11
    Decree Number 7, 103–4
    gender politics post-2001, 101–19
    Islamic Republic of, 106, 108–12
    jihadi movements, 193
    military interventions, 2
    Ministry of Foreign Affairs, 106
    Ministry of Women's Affairs (MOWA), 106–7, 111, 114
    Muslim solidarity, 8, 194
    National Action Plan for Women Peace and Security, 114, 117n
    National Council of Religious Scholars, 113
    national unity government, 112–15
    NGOs, 6
    rescue narratives, 197
    sexual harassment, 113–14
    shelters, 111
    Supreme Court, 106, 110, 117n
    women's rights infrastructure, 105–8
Afridi, Fareeda, 172
Agence France-Presse, 53
Ahmadinejad, Mahmoud, 51–2, 53
Aidi, Hisham, 194
Al-Ali, Nadje, 12
Ali, Ayaan Hirsi, 197
Ali, Dina, 62–3, 77n
Ali, Zahra, 153–4
Alimohammadi, Fereshteh, 52
al-Qaida, 74, 104–5, 193, 195
alternative dispute resolution (ADR), 6
Amanullah Kahn, 103, 113
Amnesty Law, 105
al-Amoudi, Maysa, 73
Arab League, 29
Arab Spring, 123
Arab uprisings 2011, 73, 74, 91, 94
Arab Women's Organization, 29, 34n
Arafat, Yasser, 122, 125
Arat, Yeşim, 93
Arjomand, Said Amir, 47
Asad, Talal, 7
al-Aqsa intifada, 122, 140n
asylum seekers, 64, 66–8, 78n, 186–217
Australia, Muslims in, 188
Ayatollah Khomeini, 45, 48, 57n
Azeem, Fouzia, 176
al-Azhar, Sheikh Ahmed al-Tayeb, 10, 18, 20, 21, 25–32, 33n

Index

Bakhtiar, Nilofer, 168
Baloch, Qandeel, 176–7, 179
Banuazizi, Ali, 41–2
Barzani, Massoud, 151
Ba'th Party, 146–8
Ba'th regime, 151, 152, 154
Bayraktar, Sümeyye Erdoğan, 91
al-Baz, Rania, 66
Behind the Veil, 170
Beijing Platform for Action, 128, 130, 140n
Bekir, Latife, 80
Benazir Income Support Programme (BISP), 172, 174
Bhutto, Benazir, 172
Birzeit University, 141n
al-Bishr, Badriyya, 68
Blair, Tony, 191
'blue bra woman', 23
Bosnia, 8
Bosnian War (1992–5), 194
Al Botmeh, Reem, 136–7
Brazani, Massod, 162n
Brexit, 199
British Muslim identification, 200
Bush, Laura, 101, 115
Bush administration, 197

Caeiro, Alexandre, 191
Çağlayan, Handan, 85
CAIR (Council of American/Islamic Relations), 204n
Çakir, Ruşen, 92
Canada, Muslims in, 188
Catholic Church, 190
ÇATOMs (Multi-Purpose Community Centres), 86
CEDAW
  Afghanistan, 106, 111, 116
  Palestine, 127, 129, 131, 133, 138
  'technocratisation' of gender issues, 5
  Turkey, 88, 91, 97n
Centre for Egyptian Women's Legal Assistance, 34n
Cesari, Joscelyne, 198
Charlie Hebdo shootings, 195, 204n
Chechnya, 8, 194
Chehabi, H. E., 42
child marriages, 174
Christianity, 7
citizenship tests, 198
Clarion Fund, 197, 204n
Clinton, Hillary, 112–13
Cologne, Germany, 186

Committee for Commanding Right and Prohibiting Vice see al-haya
Congress of the International Federation of Women, 12th, Istanbul, 80
Convention on the Elimination of All Forms of Discrimination Against Women see CEDAW
Cooke, Miriam, 204n
Council of Europe's Convention on Preventing and Combating Violence Against Women and Domestic Violence (CAHVIO), Istanbul Convention 2012, 89
Council of Islamic Ideology (CII), 174, 178, 182n
'culturalising' citizenship, 191–2
Culture and Free Thought Association, 133
'culture wars', 198–9

Dad, Nighat, 176
daesh see Islamic State (IS)
Danish cartoons, 195, 204n
Daoud Khan, 103
Dar al-Ifta, 26–7, 33n
Daring to Drive, 68
daughters of Egypt, 22–6
Democratic Regions Party (DBP), 92
divorce
  'No to Divorce' campaign, 32
  Turkey, 97n
  verbal (*talaq shafawi*), 18, 26–31, 33n, 34n
domestic abuse, 66, 90, 155–6
domestic workers, 78n
'donor-driven gender activism', 5, 6, 88, 136–8, 160, 173
'donor-driven Islam', 12–13, 169–70
al-Dosari, Hala, 76

East Jerusalem, 122
education, 69, 82, 87, 146, 191–2
Education and Training Organisation of Tehran (ETO), 50–1
Egypt
  2012 Constitution, 20
  2014 Constitution, 20, 29
  2014 Protest Law, 21
  Constitutional Committee, 20
  Constitutional Court, 20
  controlling women, controlling protests, 24–5
  Council of Senior Scholars of Al-Azhar, 27

INDEX

Egypt (cont.)
  Gaza, 122
  High Constitutional Court, 30
  homosexuality outlawed, 21
  Justice and Freedom Party, 20
  Ministry of Religious Endowment, 28
  al-Nahda, 21
  National Council for Women (NCW), 29, 30, 34n
  NGOs, 6
  'No to Divorce' campaign, 32
  al-Nour Party, 20, 21
  Organization for Divorced Men, 30
  People's Assemby, 30
  Personal Status Law 2000, 30
  'pious masculinity', 28
  pious women, 7
  popular uprisings, 2
  protests, 10, 18–39
  'red line', 18–39, 33n
  Religious Committee, 27
  'revolution' 2011, 19
  sexual harassment law, 26
  Shoura Council, 24
  Supreme Constitutional Court, 30
  Supreme Council of the Armed Forces (SCAF), 19–23
  threat to masculinity, 25–6
  vigilantes, 24–5
  'virginity test', 217
  women's demonstration against sexual violence, 22–6
'Egypt's Great Women', 23
Election Commission of Pakistan, 174
Elimination of Violence Against Women law (EVAW Law), 107–10, 111, 116
employment, women's, 71–2, 87, 136–7, 146
'enlightened moderation', 166–8
Ennahda, 8
'Enough Divorce in Egypt' campaign, 30
Erbakan, Necmettin, 96n
Erdoğan, Recep Tayyip, 83, 85, 89, 90, 193
Ettelaat (newspaper), 50–1
European Union (EU)
  Muslims in, 188, 203n
  Pakistan, 181n
  Quartet, 140n
  Turkey and, 86
  Turkey's accession, 11, 83, 88, 89, 93–4
Ewing, Katherine, 196
Ezzelarab, Bahaa, 25

Faisal, King, 72
Farkhunda, 115
al-Fassi, Hatoon, 72–3
Fatah, 122, 125–6, 128, 138
feminism, 3–5
feminism-as-imperialism, 7
'femocrats', 125
Fethullah Gülen community, 83
Flying Broom Association, 87
Foucault, Michel, 42–3
France
  banlieues, 192
  al-Baz, Rania, 66
  laïcité, 190–1
  Muslims in, 203n, 203–4n

Gabriel, Brigite, 197
Gaza
  donor community, 122–3
  funding, 140n
  governance, 12
  Great March of Return, 123
  Ministry of Women's Affairs (MOWA), 127–8, 131–8
  sovereignity, 120
  Supreme Council for Women, 133–4
  Women's Affairs Centre, 133
  Women's Affairs Ministry, 133–4
  Women's Affairs Technical Committee, 133
gender
  definitions, 3–7, 14n
  politics of, 1–17
'gender agenda', 4–5
'gender ideology', 7
gender segregation, 44–53, 56n
gender-segregated spaces, 40–1
General Federation of Iraqi Women (GFIW), 147–8
General Union of Palestinian Women (GUPW), 125–6, 127
Germany, Muslims in, 186, 196, 203n
Gezi protests 2013, 85, 94, 96–7n
Ghafourifard, Hassan, 45–6
Ghamdi, Javed, 170
Ghani, Ashraf, 11, 113, 114–15
Ghani, Rula, 112
The Girls of Riyadh, 72
'good Muslim'/'bad Muslim', 13, 190–1, 193–4, 198
'governance feminism', 5
guardianship (*wilaya* or *wisaya* system, 62–5, 68, 68–70, 131

Gül, Abdullah, 85
Gülenists, 94
Gulf War (1990–1), 148, 194

Habibi, Shahla, 45, 48–9
Hafez, Sherine, 25
al-Hais, Sheikh Hamid, 157
al-Hakim, Abdel Aziz, 152
Hamas
  funding, 140n
  gender equality and justice, 138
  Great March of Return, 123
  Islamist women, 126
  Ministry of Women's Affairs (MOWA), 128–9, 132, 136
  NGOs, 133
  PLC, 122
  sovereignity, 120
  Supreme Council for Women, 134
  women's rights instrumentalised, 12
Hammami, Rema, 137–8, 141n
haribat (runaway girls), 66–7
Haroun, Amira, 135–6
al-haya, 65, 75, 77–8n
headscarves
  and gender inequality, 204n
  'No Vote If There is No Candidate with a Headscarf!' campaign, 91–2
  Tavakoli, Majid, 216
  Turkey, 82–4, 92, 95n, 96n, 97n
  see also veiling
health, 54, 55
High Council of Iranian Youth, 50
'High Level Symposium of Afghan Women's Rights and Empowerment', 112
'Homo Islamicus', 170
honour-based crimes, 159, 168, 176, 179
House of Saud, 2
al-Howeider, Wajiha, 73, 73–4
Hudood Ordinances, 180n
Huma, Zille, 172
Hussein, Saddam, 147–8, 149, 158
al-Huthlul, Lujain, 73

Ibrahim, Samira, 22
Ifta Council, 131–2, 140n
immigrants, 186–217
Inge, Anabel, 194
institutalising 'Islam', 189–92
internally displaced people (IDPs), 154–5
International Criminal Court, 129

International Development Law Organization, 109
International Monetary Fund (IMF), 6
Iran
  'cultural invasion', 48, 50
  culture, 43
  funding, 140n
  gender segregation, 9
  Green Movement, 216
  (un)healthy citizens, 40–61
  identities, 161
  Islamic Republic of, 3, 10, 42–8, 50, 52–6
  manufacturing consent, 40–61
  Ministry of Interior, 51, 52, 57n
  Parks and Green Space Organisation of Tehran Municipality, 53
  Presidential Centre of Women's Affairs and Participation, 48, 51–2
  reform era (1996–2004), 50
  Revolutionary Council, 45
  Social and Cultural Commission of the City Council of Tehran, 53
  state power, 41–3
  Tehran Parks and Green Space Organisation, 51
  Women's Office of Tehran Municipality, 53
Iranian Revolution 1979, 192
Iran–Iraq war, 45, 46, 56–7n, 147
Iraq, 145–64
  anti trafficking law, 155
  Arab Sunni community, 149
  Arabs, 152
  Commission on Violence Against Women, 155
  conflict, 11–12, 187
  Constitution 1959, 152
  continuum of violence, 154–6
  Council of Ministers, 152–3, 155
  Council of Representatives, 156–7
  al-Fadhila party, 153
  Governing Council, 151–2
  High Committees of Combating Violence Against Women and Families, 155
  Ministry for Women's Affairs, 158
  Muslim solidarity, 194
  National Coalition, 145
  'National Strategy on Combating Violence Against Women', 155
  'new Iraq', 149–51
  NGOs, 6
  Organization for Women's Freedom in Iraq, 159

INDEX

Iraq (*cont.*)
   Personal Status Code, 159
   personal status code, 151–4
   Shia Islamic Supreme Council of Iraq, 152
   Women's Network, 158, 159
   women's political participation, 156–9
Islamophobia, 197, 200, 202
'Islamophobia industry', 199
Islamic dress, 193–4, 195
'Islamic feminism', 126
Islamic law, 106, 132, 140n, 152, 180n
Islamic morality, 44
Islamic Republic of Iran *see* Iran
Islamic Resistance Movement *see* Hamas
Islamic State (IS)
   Iraq, 150–1, 154
   Kurdistan, 92
   recruitment of women, 198
   Saudi Arabia, 63, 74–5
   security measures, 195
   violence against women, 201
Islamic transnational movements, 192–5
'Islamisation' of public space, 93–4
Islamisation policies, 12–13
Israel, 121–3, 129, 137, 194
Istanbul University, 82

Jad, Islah, 12
Jafari *fiqh*, 108
Ja'fari Personal Status Law, 152–3, 159
Jalal, Ayesha, 165, 167, 170–2
Jamia Hafsa women, 167, 180n
Al-Jawaheri, Yasmin, 148
Jelodarzadeh, Soheila, 53
Johnson, Penny, 141n
Jonssen, Stefan, 192
Jordan, 65
Joseph, Suad, 146, 147
Journal of Muslims in Europe,
   'Conceptualising Muslim Diaspora', 203n
Journal of Women's Studies, 97n
Justice and Development Party (AKP), 8, 81, 83–5, 89–94, 96n

KADER, 87
Kandiyoti, Deniz, 11, 14n, 25, 33n, 45, 49
Karaman, Hayrettin, 96n
Karbaschi, Gholamhossein, 47
Karzai, President Hamid, 11, 105, 109, 111, 113, 114–15

KDP *see* Kurdistan Democratic Party (KDP)
Kemalist regime, 80, 84, 86–9
Kerry, John, 112
Keshavarzian, Arang, 55
Khadem, Rasool, 53
Khalif, Fadhila Hanoosh, 157
Khan, Deeyah, 199–200
Khan, General Ayub, 165, 174–5
Khan, Meagan, 62–3
Khatam, Azam, 46
Khatami, Mohammad, 50
El Kholy, Heba, 10
khulu, 29–30, 34n
Khwajasara, 175
Khyber Pukhtunkhwa province, Pakistan, 174
Korkman, Zeynep Kurtuluş, 89
Korteweg, Anna, 204n
KRG *see* Kurdish Regional Government (KRG)
KRI *see* Kurdish Region of Iraq (KRI)
Küçükkırca, İclal Ayşe, 86
Kurd, Ahmed Al, 122–3
'Kurdish Opening', 85–6
Kurdish Region of Iraq (KRI), 150–1, 155–6, 157, 159–60, 161, 162n
Kurdish Regional Government (KRG), 146, 149, 150–1, 155, 155–6, 157, 160
Kurdish women
   'civil society women' activists, 11, 91
   Iraq, 147
   mobilisation of, 159–60
   Saturday Mothers (Cumartesi Anneleri), 82
   tokenism, 157
   Turkey, 84–6, 93
Kurdish-led People's Democratic Party (HDP), mobilisation of, 92
Kurdistan, 149
   Constitution, 159
Kurdistan Democratic Party (KDP), 151, 160
Kurdistan Workers Party (PKK), 93, 96n, 151
Kurds
   Iraq, 152
   Turkey, 2, 82, 84, 92, 96n
Kuwait, invasion of, 148, 158
Kyber Pukhtunkhwa province, 168

Lal Masjid uprising 2007, 167, 180n
LGBTQ, 4, 175, 194
London 2005 (7/7) bombings, 195

Index

Madrid Conference 1991, 140n
Madrid train bombings 2004, 195
Maghrebis, 192
Mahmood, Saba, 7, 168
Mahmud, Sabeen, 172
Mai, Mukhtaran, 168
al-Malaki, Prime Minister Nouri, 150, 156, 157
'Malala Day', 176
Manchester Arena bomb 2017, 195
Mandour, Sahar, 29
Mansour, Adly, 20, 21, 26
marriage, 108, 153
'masculinist restoration', 10, 11, 14n, 19, 31–2, 33n, 45, 217–18
masculinity, 4
   Egypt, 25–6
   'pious masculinity', 28
McKinsey Global Institute, 75
Meyer, John, 43
Millennium Development Goals (MDGs), 135, 178
Moaddel, Mansoor, 52
'moderate' Islam, 7–8, 31, 33n
Molyneux, Maxine, 91
'moral crimes', 154–5
'morality', 28
Morsi, Mohamed, 20, 21, 30
Moruzzi, Norma C., 54
Moshir, Zahra, 53
mosques, 195
Mothers of the Plaza de Mayo, Argentina, 82
Mothers' Paradise, 40–1, 43, 52, 53–5
Mubarak, Hosni, 2, 31, 33n
Mubarak, Suzanne, 34n
'mufti marriage' bill, 91
Muhammad ibn Salman, Prince, 75–6
mujahedin (Afghan Islamists), 102, 104–5, 109, 115, 193
Musharraf, General Pervez, 2, 12–13, 165–8, 170, 173–5, 180n
'Muslim awakening', 189, 192, 192–5
Muslim Brotherhood, 2, 8, 10, 19–21, 23–4, 28
'Muslim community', 190
'Muslim diaspora', 7–9, 13, 186–214
Muthahida Majlis Amal (MMA), 168

Naber, Nadine, 194, 196
Nasif, Sahar, 64
NATO, 108, 112, 114, 116
neo-liberalism, 189–92

Netherlands
   citizenship tests, 198
   terrorism, 195
NGOisation, 5–6, 88, 160
NGOs
   Afghanistan, 107, 111
   donor-funded women's, 5–6, 200
   Egypt, 26
   Iraq, 159
   Islamic women's, 11
   Pakistan, 166, 170–1, 173, 179
   Palestine, 123, 125, 130, 133–4, 141n
   Saudi Arabia, 71
   Turkey, 85–9, 91
9/11
   al-Qaida, 193, 194–5
   military interventions, 2
   'Muslim diaspora', 187
   Pakistan, 7, 166, 168, 169
   radical Islam, 12–13
   Taliban, 101
   US anti-Muslim hate crime, 204n
Norway, 112, 113
Nuri, Bayan, 158

Al-Obaidi, Jamila, 145
Occupied Palestinian Territories (OPT), 121, 126, 128, 135, 140, 141n
Occupied Territories, 120, 121
Oslo Accords (1993 and 1995), 121, 123
Oslo Agreement (1993), 121, 123, 124, 127, 138
al-Otaibi, Maryam, 63–4, 77n
'othering'
   Islamist women, 125, 202
   male dissenters, 25
   Muslim Brotherhood, 34n
   Muslims, 187, 194, 204n
   Orientalised, 195
   War on Terror, 197–8
al-Ouyouni, Fawziyya, 73–4

Pakistan
   Amendment to Offences in the Name/Pretext of Honour Act, 177
   'anti-obscenity' drive, 168
   Baluchistan province, 174
   Child Marriage Restraint Act 1929 Amendment 2013, 173, 178
   'civil society women' activists, 107
   Constitution, 172
   Domestic Violence Act, 178
   'donor-driven Islam', 6, 12–13

— 227 —

Pakistan (cont.)
  Federal Shariat Court, 180n
  gender-responsive governance, 177–9
  Generalised Scheme of Preference Plus (GSP Plus), 174, 181n
  Islam in gender-responsive governance, 169–71
  Islamic Republic of, 173, 175, 176
  Lawyers' Movement, 167
  'liberal' military rule, 167–9
  Muslim Family Law Ordinance 1961, 174–5
  National Commission for Human Rights (NCHR), 172
  National Commission for the Status of Women (NCSW), 172
  National Commission on the Status of Women, 182n
  'oppressed Muslim women', 168–9
  Religions and Development Research Programme, 170
  sexual impropriety, 174–7
  Sindh Provincial Assembly, 172–3
  support for *mujahedin*, 104
  Supreme Court, 168
  Valentine's Day, 179
  War on Terror, 2
  Women Living under Muslim Laws, 169
  Women's Action Forum (WAF), 167, 171
  women's movement, 165–85
  Women's Protection Act 2006, 167, 180n
  Zina (adultery) Laws 1979, 167, 173, 175, 177, 179
Palestine
  aid management structure, 139f
  Basic Law, 129
  British Mandate, 120
  Camp David peace negotiations, 121–2
  'communication' centres, 130
  conflict, 11
  Council of Ministers, 129–30
  Declaration of Independence 1988, 129
  fragmentation, 126–34
  imagined fragmented sovereignty, 120–44
  intifada, 121
  Islamist women, 12
  Israeli occupation, 9
  military interventions, 2
  Ministry of Women's Affairs (MOWA), 127–1, 134–7, 140n
  Muslim solidarity, 8, 194
  National Coalition for Combating Violence Against Women, 135
  National Strategy for the Advancement of Palestinian Women, 127
  national unity government, 134–6
  'revolutionary' era, 121
  Six-Day War 1967, 121
  Women's Affairs Ministry, 125, 126
  Women's Charter, 126, 129, 130, 130–4, 138
  women's movement, 123–6
Palestinian Authority (PA), 121–5, 128–9, 131, 133, 138, 141n
Palestinian Federation for Women's Action Committees (PFWAC), 124
Palestinian Initiative for the Promotion of Global Dialogue and Democracy (MIFTAH), 128
Palestinian Legislative Council (PLC), 122
Palestinian Liberation Organisation (PLO), 121, 123–5
Paris attacks 2015, 195
Park51 controversy, 204n
Patriotic Union of Kurdistan Party (PUK), 151, 160
Peoples Democratic Party of Afghanistan (PDPA), 103–4
'Peshawar generation', 114, 117n
Pew Research Center, 96n, 188
piety movement, 194
PNA, 128, 137
polygamy, 103, 108–9, 131, 133, 145
'protection', 6–7, 25–6, 29, 90
Purple Roof Women's Shelter Endowment, 87

Qalibaf, Mohammad Baqir, 52–3
Qassamiat, 134
Qatar, 140n, 161
Qom, clerics of, 53
Quartet, 122–3, 140n
Queer theory, 4
'quota politics', 114, 157

Rabaa al-Adawiya mosque, 21
Rafsanjani, Hashemi, 47–8
Al-Rasheed, Madawi, 10–11
Rehman, Parveen, 172
rescue narratives, 197
'running away from home' (*farar az manzel*), 110, 112
Rushdie Affair, 194, 204n
Russia, Quartet, 140n

Index

Al Sabti, Randa, 132
Sadat, President, 28, 33n
Sadeghi, Fatemeh, 54
al-Sadr, Muqtada, 150
Salafism
  Islam, 33n
  Islam and women's rights, 10
  'Muslim awakening', 192–4
  and Muslim Brotherhood, 20–1, 23
  and Shia Muslims, 200–1
  transnational Islam, 8
Saleh, Mariam, 140n
Salman, King, 69, 70, 74–6, 77–8n
al-Samaraie, Nawal, 157
al-Sani, Rajaa, 72
Saturday Mothers (Cumartesi Anneleri), 82
Saudi Arabia
  abused women, 73–4, 77n
  Baladi campaign, 72–3
  Campaign2Drive, 73
  Council of Ministers, 66
  discrimination and marginalisation, 65–6
  domestic workers, 66–7
  and Egypt, 28
  elections, 72–3
  family, religion and state, 62–79
  gender order and the state, 70–4
  guardianship (*wilaya* or *wisaya* system, 217
  and Iraq, 161
  Majlis al-Shura, 75
  media, 68
  'Muslim awakening', 192
  National Transformation Programme, 75–6, 77
  pilgrimage, 175
  politics of gender, 2–3, 10–11
  support for *mujahedin*, 104
  Vision 2030, 75–6, 77
  war on Yemen, 70
Saudi Association for Civil and Political Rights (ACPRA), 74
Sayyaf, Abdul Rasul, 105
sectarianism, 12, 151–4
'secularisation', 7–8
security measures and gender profiling, 195–6
Shahid, Zahra, 172
Shahrokni, Nazanin, 10
Shams, Alex, 47–8
sharia law, 27, 29, 199
al-Sharif, Manal, 68, 73, 77n

Sharon, Ariel, 140n
Shia Muslims
  Afghanistan, 108
  Dawa party, 156
  Iraq, 149–55, 161
  multinational, 200
  networks, 187
  Personal Status Law, 108–9
  Sadrist movement, 150
  Supreme Council of Iraq, 152
  Virtue Party, 152
  women, 145, 147, 200–1
al-Shimmari, Hassan, 152–3
Shojaee, Zahra, 51–2, 57n
Siam, Amal, 140n
Sindhiani Tehreeq, 169
Sinjar, Iraq, 154
el-Sisi, General Abdel Fattah, 2, 10
el-Sisi, Marshal Abdel Fattah, 20
el-Sisi, President Abel Fatah, 18, 21–2, 25–8, 34n
social media, 63, 64, 72, 97n, 176, 216
Southall Black Sisters, 191
Soviets, in Afghanistan, 2, 104, 193
Spellman Poots, Kathryn, 13
Steinmetz, George, 42, 43
Al-Sudairy, Hind, 71
Sufi Orders, 188, 194
Sunni Muslims, 2, 108, 145, 150–4, 201
Sustainable Development Goals (SDGs), 178
Swaine, Aisling, 117n
Syria, 63, 92, 92–3, 151, 187

Taghi, Masoomeh, 51
Tahrir Square, Cairo, 22
'Tahya Masr' ('long live Egypt'), 28–9, 34n
Tajer, Nadia, 10
Taleghani Park, Iran, 48–9
Taliban, 2, 101–2, 104–5, 107, 114, 116, 197
Tavakoli, Majid, 216
'technocratisation' of gender issues, 5
technology, 69
Tekeli, Şirin, 86–7, 95
terrorism, 21–2, 28, 195, 195–9
'Toghian al-sitat' ('tyranny of women'), 29–31
transgender, 175
transnational administrative law (TAL), 152
transnational feminism, 200

Index

Trump, Donald, 195, 199
Trump administration, 123
Turkey
  asylum seekers, 64
  authoritarianism, 2
  Civil Code 2001, 90
  diasporas, 193
  Directorate of Religious Affairs, 9, 90
  Directorate on the Status and Problems of Women, 88
  'Divorce Commission', 90
  EU accession, 11, 83, 88, 89, 93–4
  Family Academy Association, 97n
  'February 28 Process', 82
  funding, 140n
  General Directorate of Women's Status and Problems, 90
  hand-in-hand protest 1998, 82
  Higher Education Council, 82
  'Homo Islamicus', 170
  identities, 161
  instrumentalism and social engineering, 89–93
  MHP (National Movement Party), 93
  Ministry of Family and Social Policies, 90
  Muslim Initiative Against Violence Against Women, 96–7n
  'New Turkey', 2, 91
  'No Vote If There is No Candidate with a Headscarf!' campaign, 91–2
  Penal Code 2004, 90
  Platform for Labour and Justice, 96n
  The Platform for the Reform of the Turkish Penal Code, 87
  'project feminism', 88
  'Protecting the Integrity of Family', 90
  rights activism, 9
  'Solidarity Against Battering', 82
  Uludere incident 2011, 90
  uprisings, 217
  Welfare Party, 82, 96n
  Women and Democracy Association (KADEM), 91
  Women Jurists Association, 88
  Women's Federation, 80
  women's gender activism, 80–100
  Women's Initiative for Peace, 85–6
  Women's Library and Resource Centre, 87

Turkish Family Platform (TÜRAP), 91, 97n
'Turkish model', 94
Twelver Shia Muslims, 200

UN Convention on Refugees, 62
UN Security Council Resolutions, 117n, 129, 131, 135–6
UN World Conference on Women
  Beijing, 1995, 4–5, 127, 140n
  Mexico City, 1975, 4
  Nairobi, 1985, 4
UNDP, 129, 136, 148
UNIFEM, 107
United Kingdom (UK)
  Iraq, 150, 161
  'multi-culturalism', 191–2
  Muslim disapora, 187
  New Labour, 191–2
  Pakistan, 169, 170
  Prevent Programme, 196
  Salafism, 194
United Nations (UN)
  Afghanistan and, 106
  Beijing Platform for Action, 128
  Pakistan and, 172
  Palestine and, 135
  'protection of the family', 6–7
  Quartet, 140n
  Turkey and, 88
United States (US)
  Afghanistan, 101–2, 104–5, 112–13, 115
  anti-Muslim activism, 199
  Cold War policies, 193
  Iraq, 149–50, 151, 161
  'March Against Sharia', 199
  Muslims in, 188, 195, 204n
  Pakistan, 166, 169, 170
  Palestine, 122–3, 123
  Patriots Act, 195–6
  Quartet, 140n
  sanctions on Iraq, 194
Universal Declaration of Human Rights, 106
University of Tehran, 52
UNWomen, 129, 136
US–Afghan Women's Council, 113

van Gogh, Theo, 195
veiling
  Egypt, 31
  and gender inequality, 204n
  Iran, 40, 48, 51, 54–5, 56n

Index

Islamophobia, 196
Pakistan, 168–9
Turkey, 96n
see also headscarves
Velayat Park, Tehran, 54
verbal divorce (*talaq shafawi*), 31, 33n, 34n;
  see also divorce
violence against women (VAW), 107–8,
  128, 135, 136, 137, 141n, 173
'virginity test', 22, 113, 217

Wahba, Dina, 24
Wahhabi clergy, 2, 70–1
Wahhabi orthodoxy, 193
Wahhabiyya, 70
War on Terror
  Afghanistan, 105
  identities, 187
  'othering', 197–8
  Pakistan, 2, 166, 168, 172
  'protection', 186
We Look Out for Each Other, 97n
West Bank
  governance, 12, 122–3

Ministry of Women's Affairs (MOWA),
  126–8, 131–40
sovereignty, 120
Willen, Julia, 192
Wimpelmann, Torunn, 11
Women, Islam and the State, 1, 7, 80, 146,
  165, 186–7
women-only parks, 40–1, 43–56
Women's Paradise, Iran, 52
World Bank, 48, 88

Yazidi women and girls, 154
Yemen, 187
Yurdakul, Gökçe, 204n

Zaidi, Akbar, 169
al-Zaidi, Ibtihal, 157–8
Zaim, Sabahaddin, 170
Zakaria, Rafia, 197
Zan e Rooz magazine, 45, 49
Zia, Afiya Shehrbano, 12–13
Zia-ul-Haq, General Muhammed, 165, 167,
  175, 180n
Zubaida, Sami, 193

EU representative:
Easy Access System Europe
Mustamäe tee 50, 10621 Tallinn, Estonia
Gpsr.requests@easproject.com

www.ingramcontent.com/pod-product-compliance
Lightning Source LLC
Chambersburg PA
CBHW070348240426
43671CB00013BA/2437